THE LAST YEARS

SØREN KIERKEGAARD

THE LAST YEARS

JOURNALS 1853–1855

EDITED AND TRANSLATED BY
RONALD GREGOR SMITH

HARPER & ROW, PUBLISHERS
NEW YORK AND EVANSTON

Library of Congress catalog card number: 65–11561

© *Ronald Gregor Smith, 1965*

Printed in Great Britain for Harper & Row, Publishers, Incorporated,
49 East 33rd Street, New York 16, N.Y.
by Cox & Wyman Ltd, London, Fakenham and Reading

CONTENTS

CONTENTS

PREFACE

The scope of the present volume is indicated in the title. In particular, the period covered by the diary proper is from 1 March 1854, to its end some time early the next year with the entry numbered $XI^2 A 279$. The rest of the volume is selected from loose sheets deriving from 1853 to the last entry which is dated 25 September 1855, exactly one week before Kierkegaard collapsed in the street and was taken to hospital to die.

The justification for concentrating upon such a short span in Kierkegaard's life is twofold. In the first place, the material here presented has not, with rare exceptions, hitherto appeared in English. The exceptions are some twenty-five pages in Mr. Alec Dru's one-volume selection, *The Journals of Søren Kierkegaard*, which came out in 1938. At that time the final volume of the twenty-volume Danish edition of the *Papirer* had not been published. In the course of the last few decades there have also appeared a few quotations in various studies of Kierkegaard. In the second place, the last years of Kierkegaard's life saw a remarkable concentration of the motifs which controlled his whole authorship. This comes vividly to life in the present selection from the journals and papers of that time, and casts light on all that went before it.

The method of identifying the references follows the internationally accepted style of the Danish edition. The Roman numerals refer to the volume, with small Arabic numerals attached to indicate the part-volume, and the letter A to indicate diary material proper, while B indicates material connected in some way with the published works. The whole of the material presented here is derived from $XI^1 A$ and $XI^2 A$, with the exception of a few pages derived from $XI^3 B$. The final numerals for each entry follow the Danish sequence, and the gaps in this sequence will give the reader some idea of how much has been omitted.

I have used points ... to indicate omissions from Kierkegaard's text. On the rare occasions when Kierkegaard himself used points at the beginning of an entry, I have changed these into a dash —. Square brackets, usually round a biblical reference, indicate an addition by myself. The titles of the entries are Kierkegaard's own.

My thanks are due in the first place to the publisher of the Danish edition, *Søren Kierkegaards Papirer*, 1909–48, ed. P. A. Heiberg, V. Kuhr (with E. Torsten for the later volumes), the Gyldendalske Boghandel Nordisk Forlag, for their kind permission to use this truly model edition.

A number of people have been kind enough to help in sorting out difficulties in the text. In particular, I have pleasure in mentioning the help given by Miss Oddveig Røsegg, cand. phil., M.A., lecturer in Norwegian at Glasgow University, and by my own student, Mr. Eric Snider, B.A., B.D. The President and Secretary respectively of the Kierkegaard Society in Copenhagen, Professor N. S. Søe of Copenhagen, and Pastor Niels Thulstrup of Holbaek, were patient and helpful in answering my questions. But I cannot hope to have made a flawless translation, and I hereby absolve all my helpers from any share in my blunders. At least I can say that I have tried to be faithful to Kierkegaard's direct and even colloquial style. I have not tried to smooth out the roughnesses, sometimes even the breakdown in syntax, nor have I consciously tried to improve on Kierkegaard by saying what I think he *ought* to have said.

With one important word I have deliberately varied the translation. *Præst* is the normal Danish word for the Lutheran pastor of the Established Church. This I have translated variously as priest, parson, and minister, since I do not think that in Kierkegaard's view the word is limited to the Danish Lutheran *præst*.

It is a pleasure also to record the helpfulness of the staff of the Royal Library in Copenhagen, who permitted me to handle the original manuscript notebooks.

Lastly, I have to thank my publishers, Mr. Mel Arnold of Messrs. Harper and Row in New York, and in particular Mrs. W. A. R. Collins of Messrs. Collins in London. It was her persistent encouragement which brought me to the conclusion of this task, or to the conclusion of one volume of a task which I had fought shy of for many years – indeed since 1939, when under Professor Geismar's guidance in the University of Copenhagen I first became acquainted with the riches of Kierkegaard's journals.

University of Glasgow,   *RGS*
Whitsun, 1964

INTRODUCTION

This volume of selections from the journals and papers of the last two or three years of Kierkegaard's life offers rich material for many different kinds of readers. Someone coming to Kierkegaard for the first time will find the motifs of his entire life presented in sharp focus, and cannot fail to receive the impression of a passionate and unique person. Those who are already acquainted with his writings (which are now all available in English),[1] will find that much in them is illuminated by the journals. Those who know him only as the precursor of certain modern writers will certainly have to ask whether they have really penetrated to the depths of his enigmatic personality or of the many possibilities of his thought. And such writers are many and varied – direct interpreters, detractors, and borrowers of one kind or another: Martin Heidegger and Karl Jaspers among existentialist philosophers, Karl Barth the protagonist of Protestant neo-orthodoxy, Paul Tillich and Rudolf Bultmann among Christian radicalists, Gabriel Marcel, Theodor Haecker and Cornelio Fabro among the notable group of Roman Catholic scholars, Sartre and Camus among the existentialists of the left. All these writers are intimately related to Kierkegaard; yet with what different results for their thought!

But perhaps the best reader whom Kierkegaard himself might have wished for this volume is the one who comes to it with the chief desire to meet a man who is above all

[1] With the exception of his thesis for the master's degree, *The Concept of Irony*, which will, however, shortly appear in a translation by Mr. Lee Capell.

passionately concerned, in the utmost integrity of thought, with the question, 'What does it mean to become a Christian?'

Can the direction of Kierkegaard's thought, as indicated in this volume, open up a new way of answering this question? Or does his thought end in a *cul-de-sac*? Is he just to be written off as a sick man, a hypochondriac or a megalomaniac? Let such a reader judge for himself in the end.

Certainly, the present writer must confess to the same overwhelming impression as has been indicated by Karl Jaspers, when he writes, of Nietzsche as well as of Kierkegaard: 'They cannot be classified under any one type (poet, philosopher, prophet, saviour, genius). With them a new form of human reality appears in history . . . it is as if Truth itself spoke, bringing an unrest into the depths of our consciousness of being.'[1]

Of Kierkegaard it is certainly true that in his intense self-consciousness there are few like him. Perhaps St. Augustine in his *Confessions* is the nearest precedent. But Kierkegaard was more thoroughly aware of the ambiguity of his situation in Christendom. He recognized himself to be an exception, and called himself 'a mere interjection in a sentence . . . a sort of trial man'. But at the same time he becomes more and more clear, in these last years, that to become 'the single person',[2] singled out from the mass, the collective (Heidegger's *das Man*), the numerical or mere 'numbers', is the demand laid upon each man, and the possibility for everyone. The 'category' of the single person – 'my category', as he called it – finds expression again and again in these pages. He is thus by no means speaking of himself alone. As he puts it, he is 'calling attention to Christianity', for which the basic pre-requisite is willingness to be 'single'. How much richer and more complex this category is than mere solitariness or eccentricity becomes apparent from the journal entries on such detailed themes as the contrast between Christendom and Christianity, the

[1] *Reason and Existenz*, p. 38.

[2] I have preferred this translation of *hiin enkelte* to 'the individual' (Lowrie's translation), since, in spite of its slightly odd impression in English, it seems to convey the richness of the Danish word better than the rather flat word 'individual'. *Cf.* Buber's use of 'Einzelne', p. 12 below, which I translated as 'the Single One' many years ago.

meaning of witnessing to the truth and martyrdom, of dying to the world, of Luther's confusion, and from the crescendo of the challenge he throws out to the 'Establishment'. In fact, this category of the single person may be termed the chief clue to the labyrinth of these years – and indeed, of all Kierkegaard's authorship.

It was a category of which Kierkegaard became very early aware, and everything that happened to him served to deepen and strengthen his conviction of its importance. This is not the place to make a detailed study of his life, with the intricate reactions between external influences and his developing thought. But the main outlines may be briefly mentioned.

They are simple enough. They may be summarized in terms of four persons, whose importance increased rather than diminished even after their death or departure from the immediate scene. The first was his father, a pious, austere, passionate and melancholy man. Kierkegaard himself writes in his journal, in 1846: 'The terrible thing about the man who once, when he was a little boy tending his sheep on the Jutland heath, suffering greatly, hungry and in want, stood up on a hill and cursed God – and this man could not forget this, even when he was eighty-two years old.'[1] Kierkegaard himself could not forget this either, and it was his own melancholy which was the inwardness of his 'thorn in the flesh', and which determined his relationship to the second great influence on his life.

This was Regine Olsen, who when he first met her, when he was twenty-four, was a charming and gay-spirited girl of only fourteen. They became engaged in September of 1840, and in August of the following year he returned her ring. He never forgot her. Even though he once confessed, many years later in his journal, 'If I had had faith I should have remained with her,' the whole structure of his life and his writing was determined by the fact that he did not remain with her. The sympathetic and penetrating criticism of Kierkegaard's decision which is made by Martin Buber in his essay, *The Question*

[1] *VII A 5.*

to the Single One,[1] who says in effect that Kierkegaard here turns away from the world, when the right way to a relationship with God is in and through the things and persons of the world, does not, it seems to me, take sufficient account of the actual situation of Kierkegaard's life. At any rate, for Kierkegaard this renunciation deepened his sense of his exceptional relation to Providence. And even in the ordinary circumstances of his life in the 'market-town' of Copenhagen he did not thereby lose his relationship with people. But he could still be seen in the cafés, in the opera, or driving out to the forests around Copenhagen, or chatting with simple people in the streets.

But with the entry into his life of the third chief influence, that of Meir Goldschmidt, this too changed. Goldschmidt was the editor of the *Corsair*, a light-hearted weekly, witty, sometimes scabrous, but always a source of entertainment for the notabilities of Copenhagen, who shuddered and thrilled to see who was next to be pilloried in its pages. Kierkegaard knew Goldschmidt, and helped him in different ways. But in 1845 he challenged him to treat him as he treated all the other writers of the day – it was too much for Kierkegaard to be singled out for praise by such a paper. Goldschmidt obligingly obeyed, and for almost a year scarcely a week passed without something about Kierkegaard's ill-fitting trousers, or his spindly legs, or his crooked back. It might seem all rather childish, and it is not without a certain good-humoured scurrility. But the effect upon Kierkegaard was deep and permanent. He became a pariah whom the boys and the women of the streets ridiculed and despised. His old enjoyment of strolling the streets and chatting with the simple people was over. It is not too much to say that through this experience he deepened his understanding of Christianity as identical with suffering. And it was this experience which led him to a deeper view of the single person as contrasted with the mass, typified by the anonymous journalist, the 'hirer-out of opinions', the irresponsible promoter of the collective, that

[1] In the volume of collected pieces, *Between Man and Man*, Fontana Library.

arch-enemy of authentic spiritual existence. Kierkegaard's attitude is prophetic for our time, but it is prophetic also in the sense that he is a voice crying in the wilderness of our society.

It is only in the last years, as reflected in the present volume, that the fourth influence on his life reaches its immense – some would say its grotesque – final proportions. This was the person of Bishop Mynster, who is the object of the first entry which we reproduce in this volume. It is not necessary to detail the kind of man he was, in his immense and continued influence on the religious life of Denmark over many years, in his prudent, benevolent, shrewd and brilliant worldliness, in his promotion of what Kierkegaard called a 'Sunday-Christianity', or, even more sarcastically, a religion of 'quiet hours in holy places'. All this appears in the biting and brilliant language of Kierkegaard himself. Pre-eminently it may be read in the articles which Kierkegaard wrote for the newspaper *Fœdrelandet* and in his last pamphlets *The Instant*. But in the journal entries of these last years the intensity of the preparation for this challenge may be read, in a fascinating variety of forms.[1]

Superficially, what Kierkegaard attacks in the person of Bishop Mynster is Protestantism, 'especially in Denmark'. Basically, however, his challenge is to the whole of Christendom. In a narrow sense this challenge is founded upon the contrast between New Testament Christianity and the whole subsequent development of Christianity – to which Kierkegaard will not allow the name of Christianity. He is even suspicious of the earliest successes of the apostles in drawing in three thousand persons in one day into the church (*cf.* Acts 2. 41). And to this contrast Kierkegaard devotes some of the most scathing and most brilliant of his entries in these years. The contrast which he detects here is unambiguous. Though

[1] The newspaper articles and the ten pamphlets may be read in the volume translated and published by Walter Lowrie under the title *Attack upon Christendom*. But this would be more properly entitled *Challenge* to Christendom. *Cf.* the penetrating essay by Marie Thulstrup in the symposium *A Kierkegaard Critique*, Harper and Row, 1962, pp. 266 ff.

there are other extremely important entries where the weight of his criticism falls on Protestantism as he knew it in the Lutheran State Church of Denmark, with a corresponding sympathy for certain styles and forms characteristic of the modern Roman Catholic Church, it seems to me that the basic intention of Kierkegaard's critique does not permit us to say that if he had lived he would have become a Roman Catholic.[1] The critique is too thoroughgoing for any such comparatively facile solution.

If I may recall the words of Karl Jaspers about a 'new form of human reality', we face here a challenge to all the traditional forms of 'Christianity', Protestant and Catholic and even sectarian. For however strong the pietist influence upon Kierkegaard (and Fabro is right to emphasize this in his introduction to his edition), it is neither here nor in any other specific form of the Christian tradition that we can finally classify Kierkegaard. Rather, we have to regard his challenge as directed against *all* traditional forms. In the same sense in which a member of the present Vatican Council is reported to have said, 'The Counter-Reformation is over', Protestants in face of Kierkegaard's challenge must be ready to say that the old Reformation is over. We face now an unprecedented situation in Christendom.

Yet even the word 'Christendom' has lost its point. This is at least in part the effect of Kierkegaard's critique. On the other hand, it is not enough for us today to comfort ourselves with the thought that Kierkegaard was concerned with a certain hypocrisy in his time and place, which is no longer applicable to our time. It is true that those who attach themselves to the public life and worship of the churches today no longer do so out of a need to be socially acceptable. But do they do so with the passion of the single person, chosen for suffering, which Kierkegaard regarded as the basic movement in the life of the believer? And do they move on from this to the further

---

[1] This is the point where the deep insight and affection of Cornelio Fabro, the Italian editor of the journals, for his subject seem to me to falter. See his splendid edition of the *Diario*, 2nd ed., 2 vols., Morcelliana, 1962.

endless movement into a realm where the old forms, the old doctrines, and the old styles of living are set into an agonizing and fructifying ferment? The questions need no detailed answer. The forms of the church today still fall under Kierkegaard's judgement, and the people who in all sincerity today turn to Christianity for the meaning of their life are themselves well aware of the traps – pietism, individualism, religiosity, doctrinal anachronism, a religion of works – into which it is only too easy to fall.

From the theological standpoint the shift which Kierkegaard has brought about in the question about becoming a Christian is not to be located in a certain anachronistic, even romantic tendency which can be seen in the journal of those last years: I mean, the tendency he has to identify Christian existence with the 'imitation' of Jesus as the Model. This is undoubtedly an authentic motif for the Christian. But Kierkegaard, it seems to me, was at this point not as thoroughgoing in his dialectic as he was when at an earlier stage in his thought – especially in the *Philosophical Fragments* and the *Concluding Unscientific Postscript* – he rejected the 'objective certainties' of the expansion of Christianity, of the authority of the Bible, or the Church, or the Pope, as the basis of his faith. It is certainly impossible in our time, with the advance of biblical criticism, to accept the picture of Jesus in the Synoptic Gospels as an authoritative objective ground for faith. At this point, too, the Kierkegaardian critique of this kind of historical absolutism must be maintained and developed.

But all the same the direction of Kierkegaard's thought is of paramount importance. It has often been suggested that he was not in fact challenging the dogmatic basis of Christianity. There are many entries in his journals which seem to substantiate this suggestion. Thus, in 1850, he writes: '. . . The difficulty of my task is that I say that the doctrine which is presented is on the whole right. So I am not disputing about that. But what I am contending for is that something should be done about it.' And again, 'Communication of Christianity must in the end mean "witnessing", for on the Christian understanding the truth does not lie in the subject, but in a revelation which must be proclaimed.'[1] But there are other passages where the relation of his faith to dogmatic 'certainties' and 'objectivities' has a much more ambiguous ring. Thus we have his comment on the 'subjectivity' of the *Concluding Unscientific Postscript*, where he writes of its pseudonymous author, Johannes Climacus: 'In Johannes Climacus we have inwardness, subjectivity, at its maximum proving to be objectivity once more.'[2] But this must be understood in terms of a later entry, where he writes: 'God himself is *how* one relates oneself to him.'[3]

The direction of thought indicated in these last two illustrations is clearly away from every kind of objective certainty, of objectified metaphysics either of the spirit or of culture. Kierkegaard himself, in his faith, is his only foothold, his Archimedean point. But he is not an object to himself, rather he is a movement, he is in movement, an individual self transcending himself. And this self-transcendence he understands as being grasped by Transcendence, in the absolute relation with the Absolute.

But it would be wrong to see Kierkegaard at this point moving out into an unhistorical world. His absolute relation with the Absolute is strictly determined by the paradox of faith, by the entry into history of the God-Man. In this regard, at least, he holds by what traditional theologians like to call the objective truth. But the point of Kierkegaard's critique is that this objectivity is only possible as a venture, held and constantly renewed in faith, which in its movement into existence has shaken all the old doctrines out of their traditional fixity as external guarantors and substantial entities.

In brief, the movement of Kierkegaard's thought is so far away from the traditional ways of regarding the truth of Christianity that in comparison with the effect which this may still have on theology and through it on the future of Christianity, his attack on the current contradictions, hypocrisies, and worldliness of the 'priests' is a mere bagatelle. The

[1] *X A 221.*
[2] *X² A 199.*
[3] *X² A 644.*

real challenge is to the whole established form of society, and not just to the ostensibly Christian elements within that society.

This excursion into the theological significance of Kierkegaard's last journals may be useful as indicating how much work has still to be done with him, along the strict lines of Christian inquiry which he himself laid down. He is certainly much greater, much more many-sided, ambiguous and fruitful in his thought than any of the 'schools' of thought, whether philosophical or theological or even literary, which acknowledge his influence. It has also been necessary to make this analysis, in order to reach a position from which we may attempt an answer to the question whether Kierkegaard was in fact 'in character' when he entered upon this last bitter attack upon Christendom.

It was his complaint that Bishop Mynster and the rest of the Establishment were not 'in character', that is, that they did not practise what they preached. And it was his avowed purpose to 'call attention' to Christianity. Sometimes he admitted that this meant that he had to be extravagant, if he was to be a corrective to the faults of his time. But more generally, he found himself faced with the question of the relation of thought to being, or of faith to action – with the question of how to communicate existence.

Did he himself overcome the disjunction? Did he enter into Christian existence? What do these journals tell us of himself?

Now in a sense they tell us everything. We hear him as he speaks of the very depths of his consciousness, in relation to society, and to God. In another sense, they tell us nothing. And Kierkegaard himself deliberately veils the issue. He says, for instance, that he does not call himself a Christian. And he says that perhaps only Christ and the Apostles have really lived their faith in terms of authentic existence. What he therefore wants to do is to describe the ideal, he tells himself what Christianity ideally is, and what it ought really to be. He screws the price so high that scarcely anyone is able to claim that he is a Christian.

Perhaps at this point it is necessary to remember that there is a problem here which is inherent in the very nature of Christianity. Christianity in virtue of its ambiguous relation – on the one hand to its Lord, on the other hand to the world – is always both complete and incomplete. It is complete in relation to him who cried, 'It is finished.' And it is incomplete in relation to the evil world in which it finds itself and in whose evil it shares. It is therefore, in truth, impossible to enter completely into authentic existence. Perfectibility is an optical illusion, and progress is likewise a will o' the wisp. But in faith in the God-Man it is possible to live in and with the hope of completion. In a deep eschatological sense this hope is already realized, and this is the extreme possibility open to faith. But just because this is an eschatological hope, it remains paradoxical and ambiguous. It is this ambiguity which Kierkegaard illustrates in these last years. It is a tragic story, and the tone of the very last words he wrote, which may be read at the end of this volume, is profoundly disturbing. At this point I should venture to say that Kierkegaard, in the thick of the battle, saw only one aspect of the truth. But that these journals point all the same to the reality of Christian faith cannot be doubted.

RGS

1813	5 May	Born at 2 Nytorv, Copenhagen (now No. 27)
1819	14 Sept.	Death of his brother Michael, aged twelve
1822	15 March	Death of his sister Maren, aged twenty-four
1823	23 Jan.	Birth of Regine Olsen
1830	30 Oct.	Enters the university
	1 Nov.	Enrolled in the Royal Life Guards
	4 Nov.	Discharged as physically unfit
1832	10 Sept.	Death of his sister Nicoline, aged *c.* thirty-three
1833	21 Sept.	Death of his brother Niels Andreas in the U.S.A., aged twenty-four
1834	26 July	Visits fishing-village of Gilleleie
	31 July	Returns from Gilleleie. Death of his mother
	29 Dec.	Death of his sister Petrea Severine, aged thirty-three
1837	May (between 8 and 16) Meets Regine for the first time
1837–8		Teaches Latin at his old school
1837	1 Sept.	Receives from his father the first of an annual allowance of 500 *Daler*, and sets up on his own
1838	13 March	Death of the poet Poul Martin Møller
	19 May	Experience of 'indescribable joy', at 10.30 a.m. (*IIA 228*)
	9 Aug.	Death of his father in his eighty-third year
1839	29 Aug.	Inherits 31,000 *Rigsdaler*, enough to provide a comfortable income
1840	3 July	Passes his theological examination with *laudabilis*
	19 July–6 Aug. Visits Jutland
	10 Sept.	Becomes engaged to Regine
	17 Nov.	Enters the Royal Pastoral Seminary
1841	12 Jan.	Preaches his first sermon
	16 July	The Philosophical Faculty accepts his thesis on *The Concept of Irony* for the degree of Master of Arts
	11 Aug.	Returns Regine's ring
	11 Oct.	Final breach with Regine
	25 Oct.–6 March In Berlin
1843	16 April	Regine nods to him in the *Frue Kirke*
	8 May–June Visits Berlin
	July	Learns of Regine's engagement to Fritz Schlegel

| 1838 | 7 Sept. | *From the Papers of One Still Living* |

| 1841 | 16 Sept. | *The Concept of Irony* |
| 1842–3 | | *Johannes Climacus or De omnibus est dubitandum* (unfinished, and published posthumously) |

1843	20 Feb.	*Either-Or*
	16 May	*Two Edifying Discourses*
	16 Oct.	*Fear and Trembling; Repetition; Three Edifying Discourses*
	6 Dec.	*Four Edifying Discourses*

1844	16 Oct.	Move to his father's old house, 2 Nytorv, where he stays till 1848
1845	13–24 May	Visits Berlin
1846	2 Jan.	First attack on him in *The Corsair*
	2–16 May	Visit to Berlin
	2 Oct.	Goldschmidt gives up editorship of *The Corsair*
1847	27 Aug.	Preaches in the *Frue Kirke* on the Friday before Communion
	30 Aug.	Refuses permission for a second edition of *Either-Or*, as the publisher's offer is too low
	3 Nov.	Regine marries Fritz Schlegel
	24 Dec.	Sells 2 Nytorv
1848	26 Aug.	Meets Regine's father in Fredensborg
	March–April	Rebellion in Schleswig and Holstein, and constitutional revolution in Denmark
1849	4 June	Short visit to Bishop Mynster
	22 June	Calls on Bishop Mynster but is not received
	25 June	Calls again, but is told Bishop Mynster has no time
	1 July	High mass at *Helliggeistes Kirke*, Regine also present. But he 'keeps his eyes averted' (*X¹ A 570*)
	19 Nov.	Writes to Schlegel with a letter for Regine, which Schlegel returns unopened
1850	18 April	Moves to 43 Nørregade
1854	30 Jan.	Death of Bishop Mynster
1855	2 Oct.	Collapses in the street and is taken to Frederiks Hospital
	11 Nov.	Dies

1844	5 March	*Two Edifying Discourses*
	8 June	*Three Edifying Discourses*
	13 June	*Philosophical Fragments*
	17 June	*The Concept of Dread; Prefaces*
	31 Aug.	*Four Edifying Discourses*
1845	29 April	*Three Discourses on Imagined Occasions*
	30 April	*Stages on Life's Way*
1846	27 Feb.	*Concluding Unscientific Postscript*
	30 March	*A Literary Review*
1846–7		*The Book on Adler*, completed, but only published posthumously
1847	13 March	*Edifying Discourses in Different Veins*
	29 Sept	*Works of Love*

1848	26 April	*The Dialectic of Ethical and Ethico-Religious Communication; Christian Discourses*
	24–7 July	*The Crisis and a Crisis in the Life of an Actress* *The Point of View for my Work as an Author* (published posthumously)
1849	14 May	*The Lilies of the Field and the Birds of the Air;* second edition of *Either-Or*
	19 May	*Two Minor Ethico-Religious Essays*
	30 July	*Sickness unto Death*
	13 Nov.	*The High Priest – The Publican – The Woman who was a Sinner: Three Discourses at Communion on Friday*
1850	27 Sept.	*Training in Christianity*
	20 Dec.	*An Edifying Discourse*
1851	7 Aug.	*My Activity as a Writer; Two Discourses at Communion on Friday*
1851–2		*Judge for Yourself* (published posthumously)
1851	18 May	*God's Unchangeableness* (preached in *Citadelskirken*, but not published till 1 August 1855)
	10 Sept.	*For Self-Examination*
1854	18 Dec.–26 May, 1855 Articles in the newspaper *Fædrelandet*, 21 in all
	16 May	*This has to be said; so be it now said*
1855	24 May– 24 Sept.	*The Instant*, nine issues in all; the tenth was published posthumously
	16 June	*What Christ's Judgment is about Official Christianity*

THE JOURNALS

Bishop Mynster

Now he is dead.

It would have been most desirable if he could have been persuaded to end his life by confessing to Christianity that what he represented was not really Christianity, but a milder form of it; for he supported a whole generation.

The possibility of this confession had therefore to be held open to the end, to the very last moment. Perhaps he might have wished to make it on his death-bed. That is why he could never be attacked, and I had to stand everything, even when he did such monstrous things as in the Goldschmidt affair. For no one could be sure that it would not react upon him and move him to make the confession.

Now that he is dead without having made it, everything is changed; all that is left is that by his preaching he has hardened Christianity into a deception.

And everything is changed in my melancholy devotion to my dead father's pastor. For it would be too much if even after his death I could not speak more freely of him, even though I know well that my old devotion and my aesthetic admiration will always have a certain fascination for me.

At first I wanted to transform my whole work into a triumph for Mynster. Later, when I saw things more clearly, my wish was unchanged, but I had to ask for this little confession. I did not want it for my own sake, and so – this was my thought – it could be made in such a way that it was a triumph for Bishop Mynster.

From the time that a hidden misunderstanding came between us, it was my wish that I should at least succeed in avoiding any attack on him during his life-time. And I thought that I myself might die first.

And yet it almost came to the point where I believed I had to attack him. There was only a single sermon of his that I •

did not hear, and that was the last. I was not hindered by sickness, on the contrary I went to hear Kolthorf. For me the meaning of this was that now it must happen, you must break with your father's tradition. It was the last time Mynster preached. Praise God, is that not like a sign of Providence?[1]

If Bishop Mynster could have yielded (and it could have been concealed from everyone, and become for them his triumph), then my own outward circumstances would have been less troubled than they were. For though he certainly made concessions enough to me in his inmost heart, in matters of the spirit, he reckoned with worldly prudence that in the end I would yield to him in one way or the other, because I could not hold out against him financially. A phrase he often used in his conversations with me, without pointing it directly at me, was highly characteristic: it is not a question of who has most strength, but who can hold out longest.   *XI¹A 1*

An understanding that is too high for a man

How much easier it was in the times when some of the most difficult things in Christianity could be explained with the help of devils!

When a man really desires to serve God, and everything goes wrong; when a man denies himself in order to please God, and everything goes wrong; when it looks as though one would be much better off by having nothing at all to do with God – in former times this was explained with the help of devils. God was the giver of good gifts – the rest came from devils, who acted in defiance of God, so that God too almost suffered from it.

But this explanation will not do, for even if it comes from devils, still God is responsible for it.

The explanation lies elsewhere, in God's being, in his – if I may dare to say – infinite distinction as Spirit. Just when one does his will, and it looks (through misfortune) as though it

[1] Mynster preached for the last time in the *Slotskirke* on 26 December 1853, and died 30 January 1854. RGS

were displeasing to him, the meaning is, 'I am Spirit, infinite distance'. On the other hand the meaning is, 'I demand of you that you be spirit'. There is here an infinitely qualitative distance from a father's relation to his child. For when the child simply does what his father wishes, then the father dances with joy. But God, who is love, is also spirit, so that this infinite distance almost corresponds to the child having to say of his father, 'He is out of his senses. For if I simply have nothing to do with him, simply do not do what he wants, I can get along very well with him, so that he seems most gracious and mild. Only when I have to do with him, and really do his will, does he seem to be angry.'

No man can grasp this, and that is why the New Testament teaches that God's Spirit must help a man to grasp that he does it for love, and that Spirit cannot love in any other way . . .   *XI¹A 2*

Christ says to the man who wanted him to divide the inheritance between him and another: 'Who made me a judge or divider?' – and yet Christ came to the world precisely in order to judge and divide. Yes, he judged and divided between time and eternity: either-or. And on the contrary he did not wish to be a judge and divider within temporal things in all their twaddle and wretchedness.   *XI¹A 3*

The wine denied to laymen in Communion

Perhaps it was not just a desire to dominate which determined the clergy to deny the wine in Communion to lay people, but a certain – if one may put it so – feeling of decency. For the layman's life in general, his whole activity, his aims and achievements, seem to have no relation to the terrible duty of drinking the blood. But one must remember that it was not then in the church as it is now, especially in Protestantism, that everything that makes Christianity a duty has been stroked through, and Christianity is taken as a 'gift', indeed so thoughtlessly as a gift that one ends by giving our Lord the lot!

So it could be a feeling of decency. But then the question would arise whether the clergy too should not be denied the cup . . .

What a simple solution Cyprian had for the whole difficulty of refusing the wine to laymen, when he replied that if they are asked to pour out their blood for Christ's sake, can one deny them Christ's blood?   *XI¹ A 4*

God's majesty – the only thing which interests him is obedience

It is easy to see that for him to whom everything is equally important and equally nothing there is only one thing left which can interest him, namely, obedience. This is absolute majesty. It is not so with a relative majesty, there are always one or several points which interest him. There are differences. For him one thing is more important than another, one thing is significant and another is insignificant, and so on. But this is just what prevents him from reaching the infinite elevation, the real majesty which is interested only in obedience.

But this view of God's majesty and of obedience does not really please us men. So we have got rid of it, and let ourselves pretend we can fool God with differences, as though something were more important, one important point. This is a discovery which works to the advantage of the more favoured, who imagine that they are nearer to God in virtue of the difference between man and man. And at the same time we have made this discovery because we prefer to have to do with differences. Thus a man will happily govern perhaps a whole land, and would at the same time like it to be so important in God's eyes that God would not look too closely at details. And there's the rub! As I have said, it is a fearful burden for a man that the only thing which interests God is obedience, and that in this way something of the utmost insignificance can be transformed into something that is more important than the whole history of the world – that is to say, from the moment it pleases God to lay stress upon it as a task for our obedience.

It is so easy to have to do with God if we think that he is

concerned only with the most important things; and such a terrible burden to have to do with him when only obedience interests him, and when something of the utmost insignificance can interest him. Yet the first way reduces his majesty, and it is only in the second way that the majesty is expressed.

XI¹A 5

According to the New Testament to be a Christian is to be sacrificed

. . . for Christianity is the absolute, and to relate oneself absolutely to the absolute is *eo ipso* (for what is not absolute) to be sacrificed.

I am thinking of the passage in Mark 9. 42–50, which presents the absolute demand in the sense of *absolutely* avoiding offence. And here is what is said (that is, of those who absolutely avoid offence): 'For every one will be salted with fire, and every sacrifice will be salted with salt.' So the absolute means to be sacrificed, to become a sacrifice. Further, we read: 'Have salt in yourselves', so that even without becoming a sacrifice for others the Christian is sacrificed because of the absolute relation to the absolute.

That the Christian is sacrificed is also expressed in the image which Christ constantly uses, and which is repeated here: to be salt. For to be salt means not to be for oneself, but to be for others, that is, to be sacrificed. 'Salt' has no being for itself, but is purely teleological, and to be determined purely teleologically means to be sacrificed . . .

Understood in this way, there can be no objection to the absolute renunciation practised in the middle ages. The error, as I have shown elsewhere in the Journals, lay in a compromise with the world, by which the prestige of the extraordinary was desired, instead of a simple expression that this was the simple demand. Once again the absolute relation to the absolute was hindered through the interposition of an intermediate category of this finite kind.

XI¹A 7

Alas!

I read in a work of edification (Arndt) that in all our occupations we should have God in mind: alas, how often does it happen that even in an hour of devotion, when we should have God in mind, we think of other things!   *XI¹A 11*

Therefore!

Good Friday (14 April) 1854

'I find no guilt in this man, *therefore* I will chastise him.' How strange is the *therefore*!

'Pilate said three times, I find no guilt in this man, *therefore* I will chastise him.' [*cf.* Luke 23. 13–22]

The wretched religiosity of our time

Nowadays there is not so much as a heresy, there is not enough character for that. For a heresy presupposes (a) enough integrity to let Christianity really be what it is and (b) enough passion to be of a different opinion.

No, now we have falsifiers, and this miserable falsification of playing at Christianity, of pretending that it is Christianity which is taught and which we have, whereas it is really a diluted and effeminate sentimentality and refined epicurism.

Oh how much better were the times when one let Christianity be what it is, and so either accepted it seriously, or broke with it seriously.

But now the only Christianity we have is a falsity – and here is the greatest danger. So there is no philosophy so harmful to Christianity as the Hegelian. For earlier philosophies were honest enough to let Christianity be what it is – but Hegel had both the stupidity and the effrontery to solve the problem of speculation and Christianity by altering Christianity – and then everything was splendid.   *XI¹A 14*

Socratic ignorance

means also primitiveness, inwardness; it means away with all the twaddle of historical knowledge of how these thousands and thousands behaved, how they lived, and so on – I want to be alone with the idea.

And what 'Christendom' needs in the largest possible measure is just a man (not an aping of what it is to be a man, an aping of 'the others', the historical, and so on), just one man, and the New Testament, one man alone with God's Word, safeguarded by Socratic ignorance. *XI¹A 15*

'Beware of men' – the monastery – to suffer persecution

Man is by nature one of the animal creation. Therefore all human effort tends towards herding together: 'let us unite,' etc. Naturally this happens under all sorts of high-sounding names, love and sympathy and enthusiasm, and the carrying out of some grand plan, and the like; this is the usual hypocrisy of the scoundrels we are. The truth is that in a herd we are free from the standard of the individual and the ideal.

From the Christian point of view the law is then either out into solitude, away from men, that you may have the standard of the ideal undisturbed by the chatter and haggling of the number (for to count here means to haggle); or you remain among men, and then you must see that you suffer persecution – in order to preserve your heterogeneity, which in turn assures the standard of the individual and the ideal. But in direct continuity with the herd Christianity is impossible.

Here again we may see what a lie it is to claim that our present life (direct continuity and conformity with 'the others') is superior to the monastery. *XI¹A 16*

To found a party, form a school, and the like

Why do I do nothing of this kind? It is clear that Socrates did it, and Christ even more.

To this the answer must be that it is precisely the error of our time to found parties, form schools, maintain solidarity and the like: consequently for the sake of the truth one must emphasize the opposite as strongly as possible.

However, this answer is not decisive. For to found a party or form a school can be something inferior to what I am doing (like the whole political activity of our time), as it can also be superior as with Socrates and Christ.

What matters is the state of affairs in which one does it, or the stage of development. It is easy to see that founding a party or forming a school means to acquire more or less material power; so one can want to form a party or a school for purely egotistical reasons. In that sense my position is higher.

But if suffering belongs to the truth, if it is only in suffering that a man is initiated into the true forms of the truth, then it is surely important, both for truth's sake and, I think, for our own sake, that we do not unseasonably become such a material power that we escape suffering.

As for Christ, he knew well that he would be the sacrifice, he was divinely sure about himself: consequently he could form a school with the greatest equanimity. As for Socrates, he began to form a school only when he was so strongly developed, and his life was so far given up for others, that in reality he was sacrificed.

He who has not reached this maturity, who has not progressed so far, whose life is not so well-marked, can easily deceive himself by forming a school: is it not egoism that determines him rather than interest in the truth? $XI^1 A 18$

Clerical jargon

Christianity uses the same expressions and words, the same language, as the rest of us, but it understands by each individual word precisely the opposite of what the rest of us understand by it.

For example, Christianity says 'Come to me, I will take

away your burdens [Matthew 11. 28], make things easy for you,' and so on. By 'burdens' Christianity means riches, might, power, earthly goods. Aha! This is divine language – and yet the same word 'burden' is used as in human language.

We humans understand the matter differently. By 'burdens' we mean poverty, want, obscurity, and so on. We run with our tongues hanging out to collect wealth, to become something, to avoid the perils of time. So we are bound to find it very ironical if someone should say to a millionaire, 'My friend, come to me, I shall take your burden from you, the burden under which you sigh, give me your million and you will see how easily' – and so on . . .   *XI¹ A 19*

Christianity

This is the true state of affairs.

The God-Man is the model, who of course does not live more than once, any more than as Reconciler he dies more than once.

The God-Man is the model. So Christianity is the examination of existence, which asks whether you will be a disciple or at least be in a true relation to it.

This is begun afresh with each generation – all that about the history of Christianity is nonsense and trickery. First, it is nonsense to change the question about relating yourself absolutely to the absolute into a matter of striving from generation to generation in a continual approximation. For where the demand is either-or it is nonsense to speak of a fraction of a generation's striving. And again it is nonsense to want to strive in an association, perhaps of millions; for where the demand is either-or, statistics are sheer galimatias.

Christianity is to be proclaimed for all, absolutely all – it does not want anyone to excuse himself through ignorance; but the result of the examination is another matter.

It is begun afresh with each generation. Herein lies the possibility of terrible, truly Christian conflicts arising even in 'Christendom', hating one's father and mother, and so on.

For since the new generation must on its own responsibility look into the New Testament to see what Christianity is, its view can perhaps be so different that a Christian conflict is possible. For from a Christian standpoint it is again nonsense and trickery to speak of direct continuity with the preceding generation, of holding fast to the faith of one's fathers, and so on. No, we have only the New Testament, and every generation has to begin afresh, and so far as it has to do with what has preceded it, this must be by way of a revision of its immediate predecessors.

If things are really as we men have changed them around, that Christianity is perfectible, has a history, and so on, then it is simply irresponsible of the God-Man to leave the earth without having said that in the course of several centuries everything will be so changed that his description of what Christianity is simply no longer fits. *XI¹A 22*

The way is narrow

[Matthew 7. 14]

These words indicate the nature of the 'voluntary' (+). For if Christ were not thinking here of voluntariness (which is related to 'following' him), then he should have said something like 'The way is sometimes narrow and sometimes easy, for some it is narrow and for others easy,' and so on. But he says, 'The way is narrow.' If one will not admit that this contains a reference to the voluntary, in any case something different is being said from the general statement that this earthly life can have afflictions. There is a special emphasis on the way being narrow, in such a way that it must either come from the voluntary or from God, who in particular sends suffering to the Christian. So he who wants to be a Christian is not free from suffering, but quite the contrary. *XI¹A 23*

[*In the margin*] (+) In any case free, voluntary, self-determination, etc., are implied in the words, 'Enter by the narrow gate' [Matthew 7. 13], for it is left to oneself whether one will or not, whether one wills to expose oneself to sufferings and troubles and afflictions. *XI¹A 24*

The daily press

is properly calculated to make personality impossible. For it has the effect of an immense abstraction, the generation, which has infinite power over the single person. It is a means which was unknown in former times. For in former times the battle between a personality and the abstract was not so immensely disproportionate as now, when an individual who is impersonal and scoundrelly can use this fearful weapon against the single person. *XI¹A 25*

Either-or

Either Christianity is saying that to be a Christian is to be related to God, in which case the model and imitation are characteristic, and the words 'Blessed is he who takes no offence' mean that being a Christian is, humanly speaking, to become unhappy in this life and to wish it.

Or Christianity is saying that the pagan dream of man's kinship with God is much too high – Christ is the mediator – and so for the rest you men can rejoice in life in your own way, but you are degraded. In that case 'imitation' completely disappears, and the words 'Blessed is he who takes no offence' must be understood to mean 'Take no offence that no more can be granted you, that you are not related to God, but degraded.'

The first view is clearly that of the New Testament and the early church, the second is that of Protestantism in particular. *XI¹A 27*

Peter went out and wept bitterly
[Matthew 26. 75]

That was fine of Peter! And it is a measure of the distance from normal human conduct. If there is a man against whom one acts in an inexcusable fashion, leaving him in the lurch, betrayed, etc. – and if the man is so noble that he utters no reproaches, does not hold it against you, then you take advantage of it, treat the matter as though it were nothing, as though everything were fine: this is normal human conduct.

XI¹A 31

A personal God

As everything that one hears is hypocrisy, so too with the talk about how blessed it is to have a personal God.

Certainly, in one sense! But in another sense it is in truth easier to have to do with blind destiny. For in a 'destiny' which is blind there is nothing exciting, one would have to be as mad as Xerxes to be able to be excited by the sea and the powers of nature.

But a personal power – when it begins to 'tempt' you; a personal power where something of the greatest insignificance can be commensurable with the most terrible decision – oh, in one sense what a torture, what a torture!

But this is what is left out, only the other side is taken, and that means lies and hypocrisy and twaddle, here as everywhere.

I doubt very much whether there is a single one of us capable of having to do personally with a personal God in the old Christian or Jewish sense. In comparison with those heroes we are mere rags and tatters, one of a series, we come in dozens, like shoals of herring.

XI¹A 35

Hypocrisy

. . . And therefore one speaks so much of God's majesty because one means by it that he is so immensely high – that he willingly submits to being mocked.

Indeed in this view – but in another sense – there is something very true. God can be much more easily mocked than my neighbour – but why? Because my neighbour is insignificant enough to take careful notice of me. But then, that God is easiest to fool means that God punishes – in a truly majestic way – by ignoring me.

And this is the point. In past times God has punished terribly – which meant that he found something which pleased him, that he did not give men up. Now the most fearful punishment has drawn near, the truly majestic punishment of 'Christendom', whose crime is *lèse-majesté*, that God ignores us entirely. That is why – terrible punishment! – in a worldly way everything goes splendidly, mankind advances by leaps and bounds in physical discoveries, etc. – but God ignores us.   *XI¹A 37*

The basic confusion – our time

The basic confusion consists in having reduced Christianity to the historical, to having a history and to saying – oh blasphemy! – that it is perfectible.

Even in one generation it can be confusing enough with these many millions (for what matters is that the 'single person' should be realized); but now to drag along these millions from many centuries – how on earth can it be possible to gain an absolute impression of the absolute?

No; a new beginning has to be made with every generation – and with the New Testament.   *XI¹A 38*

'I have come to save the lost' [Luke 19. 10] – to bring up a child in Christianity to become a Christian when he is still an infant.

What nonsense Christianity becomes, when one removes its foreground or its background. Christ says, 'I have come to save the lost' – and that is the background against which one can build Christianity.

Now everything is turned into twaddle by passing off an infant as a Christian.

And yet twaddle is what man feels the deepest need for, and as the one thing necessary, only in twaddle is he happy and at ease.   *XI¹A 39*

The Virgin Mary

Yes, all honour to her! O God, when the message comes to her, 'You shall live a life scorned by other girls, you will be treated as a giddy and conceited hussy, or a poor half-mad wretch, or a wanton woman, etc., and you will also be exposed to every other possible kind of suffering, and at the end a sword will pierce through your soul [Luke 2. 35] when you see that God himself will seem to have abandoned you' – and this is the glad news! Yes, all honour to her, that without hesitating a moment she could say 'Behold the handmaid of the Lord', and could raise the song of praise, 'Henceforth all nations will call me blessed.' O God, this is certainly something different from being able to speak to perfection every living and dead language (like our Danish girls): this is truly to speak in tongues.   *XI¹A 40*

The idea – the individual – the copy
also a word about myself

As nature formed the more delicate organs in such a fashion that they do not come into direct contact with objects, but are covered, for otherwise the organs would be destroyed, so ordinarily men cannot endure being related direct to the idea. [*In the margin:* But we must remember that from a Christian standpoint everyone can be the single person.]

So they are related only indirectly to the idea, by means of a tradition, through others, two, ten, or a million. So their life is not related to the idea; but, imagining that it is, they waste no time in this respect, and have all the more opportunity to fill up their time with finite things. And it is understandable that he whose life is directly related to the idea has enough to do, and willingly does without finite things.

This is what being a copy is; and being a copy is the easiest mode of existence, shielded from a direct relation to the idea, which would certainly be as fatal as a sunstroke.

The individual is related to the idea.

In the New Testament being a Christian is represented as not being a copy but having to be an individual. 'Christendom' has only copies. [*In the margin:* But according to the New Testament everyone can be a single person, therefore Christianity must be proclaimed to 'all', 'come unto me all' [Matthew 11. 28], go and proclaim to 'all nations' [Matthew 28, 19].]

As for myself, it is my contemporaries who have drawn my attention to this, and educated me. I have not really been in conflict with the generation; for the *Corsair* was certainly not the public opinion of the country. Yet the land is so characterless that I have really been treated as though I had tried to be more than a man by being the single person in opposition to the generation. This is not my fault, but on the other hand it has been an education to me . . .   *XI¹A 42*

'And a sword will pierce through your own soul also'

Luke 2. 34, 35

These words are a parenthesis in the prophecy of Christ becoming a sign, which shall reveal the thoughts of many hearts. So they must not merely be taken to refer to the pain at the sight of the Son's death; no, they must be understood to mean that the moment of pain, of agony, will come to her when – at the sight of the Son's suffering – she will *doubt* whether the whole thing was not imagination, a deceit, that

Gabriel was sent by God to announce to her that she was the chosen one, and so on.

As Christ cries, 'My God, my God, why hast thou forsaken me?' [Matthew 27. 46], so the Virgin Mary had to suffer something that corresponded in a human way to his suffering.

A sword will pierce through your soul – and reveal the thoughts of the heart, yours also, whether you dare still believe, are still humble enough to believe that you are in truth the chosen among women, who has found grace before God.   *XI¹A 45*

To have a cause – objectivity – hypocrisy

I wonder whether there is not something hypocritical in the talk about having a cause, being a serious man who stands for something, etc.

Indeed, yes: the fact is that in our time no one dares to be a person. For each man is so afraid of 'the others' that he, that is, nobody, dares to be an I. Fear of men is what dominates, and as was already said in classical times (by Aristotle somewhere in the *Politics* or the *Ethics*),[1] 'Tyranny and democracy hate one another as one potter hates another'; that is, they are the same form of government, only in a tyranny it is one man, in a democracy it is the crowd which is the tyrant.

But to return to 'standing for a cause'. For fear of the others one does not dare to be an I, and so one strives to become impersonal, a cause, the cause, a principle, etc.

This has in turn led to anonymity. In such a small place as Denmark anonymity is almost necessary to prevent envy and the tyranny of the many from being set too powerfully in motion.

Everything tends to abolish personality; but of course this takes place under the hypocritical protest that of course this means great progress, that this is a seriousness of a quite different kind from the days of the I and of personality.

What hypocrisy! No, it is cowardice, and at the same time a

[1] *Pol.* **V** 10, 1312b, 4 *ff*. RGS.

40

whining desire always to be the many – and never daring to be alone, to be an I. But when there is a 'cause', straightway there are many, so that one is above all safeguarded from the danger one fears most in our wretched demoralized times – the danger of being alone, a solitary I.   *XI¹A 51*

Culture

It is not difficult to see that culture makes men insignificant, perfects them as copies, but abolishes individuality. Here is just one example which occurs to me.

According to the book of Genesis it is a distinguishing sign of man that he gives the animals their names [Genesis 2. 20]. Now is it not quite characteristic that the common man, the man of the people, still has this power? When the simple man has seen a bird for some years in succession, which he has not seen before, he immediately has a name for it, and a characteristic name. But take ten professors, and how hopeless they are at finding a name! What a satire to read scientific works about animals and plants and the like, and contrast the names that come from the common people with the wretched and silly names that are given when now and again a professor has to provide one. Generally they cannot think of anything else but to call the animal or the plant by their own name.   *XI¹A 55*

Two things I have heeded

. . . What is basically wrong with our time is partly that it reduces every higher effort to worldly and finite terms; that is, it denies that there is in truth a striving for something higher. That is why it is so important that I should preserve my heterogeneity, that I should not found a party, collect followers, and become a material power, so that it would almost be as profitable for people to cling to me as to the establishment. No, no; no thank you. You may keep your profits, your

41

sleekness and your velvet – I have to take heed that to cling to me brings not the least profit; I have to take heed that from a divine point of view I do not weaken my cause by strengthening it from a worldly point of view.

The other thing that is basically wrong in our time is that it is demoralized by intellectuality and has become character-less. That is why I must take heed that my cause, for God's sake, does not become – quite seriously! – an academic dis-cussion, in which a mob of professors and dons could take delight in joining in. No, either indirect communication, or in all seriousness, if it were to come about, a matter of life and death. But above all no academic discussion.   *XI¹A 56*

Contemporaries

The God-Man lives on earth – among his contemporaries there is not a single one, literally not one, who remains faithful to him: the thousands scorn and mock and spit on him, they curse him, the educated set traps for him, the crowd helps them to overthrow him as the greatest curse, and his few disciples flee, even the most faithful forsake him. – So he dies.

And then centuries later – when Christianity, note well, has become a habit and custom – millions of pilgrims go on their knees to see the places where he lived – and among all these millions there was of course not a single one, literally not one who would not at that time have turned tail, and then would have joined in the scorn, the mockery, the spitting and the ridicule.

How nauseating!

But the really nauseating thing are those false teachers, the priests and the professors, who confirm the really more innocent generality of men in their pious fancy that to be a Christian means to follow after, to play after, without any danger.   *XI¹A 59*

The economy of existence

Think of a clever mother. She has a child, and that child, like all children, likes to hear stories. Now the mother only knows a dozen or so.

Now suppose that the child were heroically determined, for just one day, to do nothing but hear stories, this would be enough to embarrass the mother, her fund of stories would dry up completely.

Her art then consists in distracting the child. For example, she has just told a story. The child wants to 'hear another'. But instead the mother, for example, says, 'Look, Johnnie, look at the fly buzzing past.' That changes the situation. Now Johnnie has to get going. Perhaps he falls, or hurts himself, and so on and so on. In this way the mother has a thousand distractions, and Johnnie is convinced that his mother has an inexhaustible fund of stories.

So it is with Providence, or with existence in relation to the idea.

For the whole of existence – and this is the divine art, even though at the same time we are to understand how Providence treats us like children – is contrived with the utmost economy. It is so contrived that there is just as much idea as will suffice an individual for his whole life, even if he were concerned only with the idea on the largest possible scale. But if a new individual could begin in the following generation where the other left off, and be just as exclusively concerned with the idea, then existence would go bankrupt.

The art of existence thus consists in – fooling little Johnnie. For example, a dozen years are filled up with a European war, there are dispatches every day, and so on and so on. From the standpoint of the idea all this is a matter of complete indifference, not a single idea enters the world in this way – but little Johnnie is given something to think about. So far as a relation to the idea is concerned, God's relation to man and man's relation to God, a European war has absolutely nothing to teach.

But how seldom is there even one man who is so developed

that numbers do not exert their sway over him. So millions of men live and die, they are just numbers, and the numerical is their horizon, their all, that is to say, they are just copies.

And Christianity which – in the divine love – wants to make every man an individual, has been transformed by human bungling into precisely the opposite.

Yet no wonder; for becoming an individual is bound up with such terrible torments that men much prefer to have nothing to do with it. I know this very well from my own experience. In part it is profound inner torments, but chiefly it is the miserable and bestial conduct of my contemporaries towards me, which have compelled me to be on the alert. My contemporaries have been like Joseph's brethren: they meant evil, but God turned it to good [Genesis 50. 20].   *XI¹A 60*

The state church

Here is the whole secret!

There must once have been a band of robbers, as Holberg says, who made the state believe that the suffering and death of Jesus Christ, and eternal blessedness, were things that money could be raised on.

Splendid! So the state – in *Christian* terms! – took over the whole business of Christianity.

In Denmark, for example, there are one and a half million inhabitants. About 600 to 700,000 talers a year are raised from them, and this is used to pay the clergy and so on.

But the point is that no man, and just as little no community, has from a Christian point of view the slightest right to interpose itself between Christ's suffering and death and another man with financial claims.

In both forms the state is equally in the wrong, in both forms from a Christian point of view this is the crime of *lèse-majesté*.

If a man feels the need and the desire to hear about Christ's suffering and death, the state has no right to push itself in and say, 'Good, that will cost you ten talers, and we shall fix it for you.'

And just as little in the other form. If a man feels the desire to hear about Christ's suffering and death, the state has no right to say, 'Yes, whether you wish to hear it or not, you are quite free, you shall not be compelled to hear it, but all the same, devil take it, you must pay me the ten talers, for we have taken over the business of Christianity.' Things ought not to be and cannot be like this. It ought not to be as at present, that when a man is unwilling to pay the police are called in to collect the ten talers. On the contrary, when someone comes and demands the ten talers of a man, then it is he who should be able to send for the police and ask for protection from this as from every other assault or swindle.

Christianity is the most serious matter in the world. Therefore (as always with the most serious things) it is recognized by means of a negative criterion, something that seems to be lower. In this life, from the Christian point of view, men should be allowed to behave entirely as they wish. The state, which is much inferior, cannot for its part concede this kind of freedom in civil affairs – but (and this is the serious point), you single person, every single person, you are going to face the reckoning of eternity.

But the truth is that judgement and being called to account and the seriousness of eternity have entirely gone out, and then in order to get a little seriousness into life people make use of the police. What a bottomless depth of nonsense! All the same we are on our way to face an account in eternity.

This is the truth: the utmost seriousness and severity (the judgement of eternity) are known in the utmost freedom. In this life you are allowed to act in this matter entirely as you wish.

This is Christianity. The other thing is a human invention, which abolishes eternity and replaces it with a bit of seriousness about the police.

This seems to me to be as easy and clear as possible. And surely my proposal is the mildest possible, that we should at least be so honest towards Christianity as to admit openly what the state of affairs is.   *XI'A 63*

Misunderstanding

This is how we men understand it (I know it from my own experience).

Even if a man knows that he is a great sinner, they say, 'Only believe that you are forgiven, be quite sure, so loving is God, this is just what Christianity is. Yes, that is just what will please him, that you seek quite care-free to rejoice in life; for everything, everything is forgotten, and the more you can give expression to this, the more God is pleased.'

And when someone is fortunate, and when everything he does prospers, then everyone is completely certain both that this is Christianity and that it is pleasing to God – this is Christian openness.

Oh, and in Holy Scripture it is constantly demonstrated that those whom God has loved are always unhappy, must suffer, and that everything goes wrong for them, etc.

XI¹A 66

Beware of those who go about in long clothes

[Mark 12. 38 and Luke 20. 46]

As soon as the preacher is one who goes about in long clothes, then *eo ipso* in one way or the other Christianity is on the way to becoming official.

But there is nothing more opposed to Christianity than all that even just smacks of 'official Christianity'. Even the most extravagant heresy is less opposed to Christianity than official Christianity.

For Christianity is heterogeneity with this world. The moment it makes even the least beginning with official Christianity it begins to be homogeneous with this world.

Official Christianity is diametrically opposed to true Christianity, it turns everything round, even the smallest proportions . . .
XI¹A 68

A modern parson

When I think what was meant by a grocer's boy in my father's childhood – a helpless and handless lad from Jutland – and what is now meant by it, a skilful and active gentleman, then we certainly have a kind of progress.

Much the same is true of the modern parson. He is a skilful, active and quick man, who finds it perfectly easy, with the aid of attractive conversation and bearing, to introduce a little Christianity – but as little as possible. In the New Testament, Christianity is the deepest wound which can be inflicted on a man, calculated by the most terrible standard to bring him into conflict with everything. And now the parson is perfected in the skill of introducing Christianity in such a way that it means nothing. And when he can do it perfectly, he is a model. It is disgusting. Oh, it is all very well for a barber to be able to shave off a beard without a man feeling it, but when it is a matter of something that is intended to inflict a wound, it is indeed abominable that a skill should be perfected to make it quite innocuous.   *XI¹A 69*

A fearful discovery – the orthodox church – playing at Christianity

From the earliest days of the church there has been opposition between the orthodox church on the one hand and heretics and schismatics on the other.

But note well, the orthodox church was really a believing church, it was a community of men who more or less did possess the character of faith, indeed even their outward circumstances forced this upon them.

Let us see whether in our time – terrible thought! – everything is not quite confused. The same opposition between the orthodox church and heretics and schismatics is maintained in our time, and people boast that they belong to the orthodox church. They speak as though everything were fine, if only there were not these heretics and schismatics, who however, God knows, are neither so many nor so significant.

Let us see whether the true state of affairs is not a horrible discovery, whether what is understood by the true believing church, the orthodox church, is not a community of people who certainly are not guilty of any heresy or schism – oh no! – but who *play at Christianity*. Is the official orthodoxy of our time not a playing at Christianity? The people do not possess the character of Christianity, but they pass it off on to the clergy. The clergy possess the character of Christianity just as little as the people, but they preach the doctrine *objectively*.

In this way the orthodox church is much more dangerous for Christianity than any heresy or schism.

People play at Christianity; they use all the terminology of orthodox Christianity – but all without character. They are not even fit to form a heresy or a schism, for some character is always necessary for that.

No, the whole thing is intact: the Christian sacraments and customs, Christian terminology – but it is all decoration, a manner of speaking, the parson is the actor, the artist.

But in that case Christianity is mythology and poetry – and the difference between the orthodox pastor and a freethinker is that the freethinker says it, but the pastor says, 'For God's sake let us not speak about it, but just put a bold face on it – otherwise everything will come to a bad end.'

Is it not a fearful thing that the list of heresies and schisms never contains the most dangerous thing of all – playing at Christianity? Yet it is understandable, for it would be too terrible for such a thing to be listed along with other heresies. No, this fearful thing must have a rubric for itself. And the question is whether this is not just what the New Testament calls 'apostasy from Christianity'. *XI¹ A 70*

The true state of affairs

. . . My proposal is therefore surely the mildest possible – oh, it is so weak! – my proposal is that at least we should make the true state of affairs known.

How fundamentally disgusting it is that we have all these

millions playing at Christianity, celebrating Whitsun – and now we are to have a bishop ordained on Whit Monday,[1] and what declamations there will be about the 'Spirit'; how disgusting, how odious it is, when the true state of affairs is that there is not a single one among us who dares to pray seriously for the Holy Spirit.

What terrible satire: it is believed that with the help of the Spirit Christianity has so spread that now we are all Christians – good heavens, the truth is that it has happened through the departure of the Spirit, and so the phenomenon of expansion is easily explained, for expansion and absence of spirit are exactly matched. And the true state of affairs is that the moment the Spirit comes again the whole thing will collapse, or it will be clear that there is not a single Christian.

XI¹A 72

Crime story

Not only does Christianity not exist, but it does not exist in the sense that New Testament Christianity is precisely that which we guard against as an abominable and ungodly thing. Certainly this is an astute and comforting stroke; but it is also very criminal. In truth there are thousands who take part in this thoughtlessly, and many who do so *bona fide*; there must also be, and have been, some proper rogues among them, for otherwise how could the thing have been started, far less continued?

. . . Oh, it is the most revolting of all crime stories!

XI¹A 73

Protestantism

If Protestantism is to be anything but a necessary corrective at a given moment, is it not really man's revolt against Christianity?

[1] Martensen was nominated as bishop on 15 April 1854 and consecrated on 15 June, Whit Monday. RGS

If Christianity is to be proclaimed as it essentially is in the Gospels, proclaimed as, and actually being, imitation or following, sheer suffering, groaning and lamentation, heightened by a background of judgement in which every word must be accounted for, then it is a terrible series of suffering, *angst*, and trembling. Indeed, yes. But where do we read in the Gospels that God wishes this earthly existence to be otherwise?

What human nature constantly aims at, on the other hand, is peace, *nil beatum nisi quietum*, peace to carry on with finite things, to enjoy life here.

Is then Protestantism not really man's revolt against Christianity? We will and we must have peace – peace for Christianity! So we turn the whole of Christianity around, and out of the terrible pessimism which Christianity is in the New Testament we obtain an insipid optimism. We want peace – so be as peaceful as possible, with the help of baptism, and infant baptism, and grace, a man is saved by grace alone – it is even presumptuous to try to help in the least towards one's own salvation – and so by these means we get rid of Christianity, and we can devote ourselves to earning a living, and getting children, and all the finite busyness and enjoyments of life, etc., etc.   *XI¹A 76*

What a satire!

In contrast to Catholicism Luther emphasizes the gospel – and even in his life-time he experienced how people (quite rightly!) took this high spirituality so literally that he was not in a position to get the pastors a little to live on. Poor Luther; in one way you have deserved this satire; and just think, dear Luther, many centuries later, to what trickery this high spirituality must lead.

That Luther complains about the turn of the matter can be seen in many of his sermons; at the moment I recall, for example, the one on the Gospel for the 26th Sunday after Trinity.   *XI¹A 77*

The single person – the many – God's sovereignty

No one wants to be a single person, everyone shrinks from the strain.

But not merely for this reason does no one want to be a single person, but also from fear of the envy and opposition of the surrounding world. As soon as ten people are united, you have an abstraction; and no envy is directed against an abstraction. 'Numbers' make us all alike. For names that are united work anonymously, and envy does not hate the anonymous.

But God is also a sovereign, and when he wishes to express his sovereignty he humbles human sovereignty – and so he uses only the single person.

To be such a person is therefore in one sense inevitably the most eminent distinction for a man; but since he has this distinction in the highest sphere, where everything is paradox, he is also distinguished by the negative that he is sacrificed.

XI¹A 82

To live peacefully and get happily through the world

Perhaps, you say, it is true that the world is in the power of evil, but so far I have succeeded in living quietly and getting along happily.

The answer to this must be, take good care whether this is really possible. It does not help for you to say with your lips that the world is in the power of evil, for by getting through it well your life expresses that the world is really quite a good place. No, if the world is in the power of evil, if it is a demoralized generation you live in, then you are not permitted to get through well, that is to say you are not permitted unless in one way or the other you are an accomplice.

And on the other hand, when God's judgement falls upon a generation, it spares no one who has not suffered evil in the evil world. That is to say, it treats the others as accomplices, and their guilt is not that they have done something, but that they have not done anything. Or do you think that when Sodom and Gomorrah were destroyed everyone was literally a fornicator, etc.? Do you not think that there was a whole crowd of decent people? But none was saved except him who had suffered evil. For to be an honest man in an evil world in such a way that the evil world regards him as an honest man is *eo ipso* to be in one way or the other a dishonest man. And to conceal oneself as much as possible in order to be allowed to live well in an evil world means to be an accomplice and to shirk the service of the good. *XI¹A 84*

The monastery

It is commonly thought that it is cowardice to flee from the world and enter a monastery.

Now perhaps it is sometimes indeed the case that such a man doubts whether he can endure the bestial laughter and ridicule, the persecution and maltreatment which may result from his having to express the 'spirit' in the midst of animal creatures.

But the matter can be regarded from another side. Such a man flees because he does not have the heart to upset the others, of whom he knows very well that he will never entirely win them to his view, and so he will only be a torment to them. Or if you should be quite sincere, you who prefer to enjoy this life, and have children who in their turn enjoy it – would you not much prefer to be rid of a man who speaks only of one thing, of dying, of dying to the world? And would it not then be a kind of delicacy on his part to conceal himself, since the consequence of his remaining among you would be that you became much more guilty than you ever thought possible? For the consequence would be that, in order to defend yourself against such a man, you would have to persecute him with the utmost ferocity, and so sink to the depths of brutality. For when the idyllic enjoyment of life is not related to 'spirit' it certainly has some beauty, but alas, in relation to spirit, it either becomes spirit itself or bestiality. *XI¹A 85*

Life – death

To live is naturally pleasurable, to die is terrible.

Oh, but when the demand is to live like a dead man, then living in this life is the most terrible, terrible of torments. But then again, to die is blessed, ineffably, indescribably blessed, for it means to come into one's element.

And if a Protestant parson were to read this, he would perhaps think it fine, splendid – and it would be used as a purple passage in his next sermon.

What an abomination are these Protestant pastors, who at most read what has cost others mortal struggles, and then use it as purple passages in their sermons. *XI¹A 86*

The seriousness of Bishop Mynster

As when a child plays, the parents or someone else in authority is there to see that things should not become serious, so Mynster sat there, with his immense sagacity, governing and carefully watching – and it must have been quite a strain – that for God's sake this matter of Christianity should not become serious. And when he was assured that everything in the land was as he desired, then he felt well disposed and in the mood to take part in the game himself; and he knew in himself (and it was also true) that he was the man who could play the game most artistically: he put on his velvet, he made his appearances with admirable dignity, he depicted things with great talent, as a speaker he was consummate – he wept, he beat his breast, the very glance of his eyes seemed to come from heaven, and so on and so on. *XI¹A 90*

Seriousness

Christianity is the utmost seriousness: in this life your eternity is decided.

That which has been called Christianity in Protestantism

for many generations by millions is a game which makes game of the fact that men have lived for whom this life was decisive for their eternity: and that is their Christianity.

These millions keep out – not of the game but – of the seriousness of the game; they keep out, for as far as they are concerned it was decided almost before they were born that they are Christians, and certain of eternal blessedness. Even if one could cut out a three-months' foetus from a dead mother, I believe that the 'priest' would happily baptize it too and declare it to be a true Christian: the more the merrier, and the sooner the better – and in both ways we make sure that Christianity is turned into a farce. *XI^{1}A 91*

The natural sciences

The enormous development of the natural sciences in our time shows that humanity despairs of becoming spirit; science is a distraction.

The analogies in individual life can be easily indicated.

XI^{1}A 94

Christianity does not unite men, on the contrary, it separates them – in order to unite each single person with God. And when a man has reached the point of belonging only to God, then he is dead to what unites men. *XI^{1}A 96*

Society does not merely accept (as I see the Chinese do) five cardinal virtues (politeness is the fifth); no, society accepts and establishes only one – politeness. *XI^{1}A 99*

Cannibals

We certainly live in civilized states, and think that we are infinitely superior to cannibals – and yet it is easy to see that we are guilty of a cannibalism which is more gruesome and revolting than any cannibal's.

The 'priest' (the Protestant priest, the pastor) and the professor are cannibals; yes, that is the right word: they are cannibals.

And they are more abominable and gruesome than the cannibals.

It is easy to see that they are cannibals: for they live on the fact that others have been killed, persecuted, maltreated for the sake of the truth.

And this is more gruesome than the cannibals. For evil is always more horrible the longer it lasts. Cannibals kill a man and eat him – and that is that. It lasts only a short time, and when it is over, there is as it were a hope – till the next time – that the cannibal become a different man, might become better. But the priest and the professor make their preparations (with cold calculation) once for all to live on the sufferings of those saints. They get married on the strength of them, they beget children, they organize an idyllic and thoroughly enjoyable life. They live on the torments of the saints. Then they calculate how to augment their income – so with revolting coolness they arrange to live as cannibals: but no cannibal was ever so disgusting. In vain those saints cry to us, 'Follow me, follow me!' The priest and the professor stifle those voices, so that we do not hear them. And so they live, having taken possession of their prey – the saints on whose sufferings they live.

And that is not all. The cannibal does not pretend to be the best and true friend of the man he kills and eats. But the priest and the professor at the same time enjoy the honour and the prestige of being the true friends and followers of the saints.

Truly, as the New Testament says [Matthew 21. 31] that harlots and tax-gatherers shall enter the kingdom of heaven before you (you Pharisees), so I believe that cannibals shall enter the kingdom of God before priests and professors!

XI¹A 100

In vain does Christ (the Humiliated, the Poor, the Persecuted, the Crucified One) cry to men, 'Follow me'. In vain the apostles cry, in vain the martyrs. Between the Saviour of the

world and men, between the apostles and men, and so on,
there presses in a class of men, who live with their families on
depicting those sufferings – and thus preventing true following.
It is therefore of the utmost importance that absolutely nothing should be heard of following.

Truly, if these despicable creatures do not devour widows
and orphans, they do devour the martyrs (and this is equally
horrible): they eat them.   *XI¹A 104*

A Protestant discovery

The parson is very easily embarrassed when there is not a
single contemporary Christian who can be pointed to as a
model; this can easily rouse suspicion.

Catholicism always has some who are Christians in character.

Then the Protestant ministers made the discovery that up
and down the land there are true Christians living, who are
true Christians in all secrecy – and indeed, in the end we are
all true Christians in hidden inwardness, we are all models.
How charming! If the New Testament is to decide what is
meant by a true Christian, then to be a true Christian in all
secrecy, comfortably and enjoyably, is as impossible as firing
a cannon in all secrecy.   *XI¹A 106*

*A difficulty with the New Testament, that in one
sense it is unusable in real life*

In the New Testament all the proportions are large; hence the
proportions of error and corruption and so on are also large,
they are set forth in ideal proportions.

But it is unfortunate that precisely the greatest and most
widely spread and most successful error and misunderstanding
of any time is scarcely warned against in the New Testament:
it is as though the New Testament were so ideal that it
was not able to think, or did not wish to imagine, that

men could sink so low or find themselves in such a wretched situation.

The New Testament denounces false doctrine, hypocrisy, arrogance in works, and so on. But against the orthodoxy which is twaddle and mediocrity and frivolous nonsense, against the orthodoxy which is mere playing at Christianity and living with clichés and the like, the New Testament provides no texts at all. It is almost as though it were beneath the dignity of the New Testament to think of such things.

But alas, this is just the true Christianity and orthodoxy of millions and billions and of the official ministers. And so they make use of the fact that the New Testament is silent about such things to make themselves into the true church.

The New Testament contains the divine truth. As high as this is over all errors and extravagances, so low does mediocrity and frivolity, childishness and twaddle lie beneath all one-sidedness. But since nonsense of this kind has the quality of not being one-sided, it makes use of this to pass itself off as the divine truth, which in fact stands high above all one-sidedness.

And so we have the course of history, with millions and millions of Christians. The New Testament is indeed a strange book. It is always right, even if the opposite appears to be the case. When one considers 'Christendom' and these millions of Christians, and then reads in the New Testament, 'The way is narrow and only few find it', 'You shall be hated by all', 'He who slays you will think he serves God' [Matthew 7. 14; 10. 22; John 16. 2] and so on, then it does really seem as though the New Testament were wrong, and shown to be untrue. Oh, my friend, be at peace, the New Testament is only too right . . .   *XI¹A 107*

Our rebellion against the Christianity of the New Testament

. . . The minister preaches so objectively. And when he has filled up his time with the business of preaching, where on earth shall he find time to do something of what he is speaking?

The congregation excuse themselves by saying that no one can demand of them the kind of religiosity which can be demanded of the minister.

But in that case Christianity is just mythology and poetry – and it is not the free-thinker who says this, but the orthodox church which itself expresses it, when you look closer.

XI¹A 110

Docendo discimus

It is an excellent saying of Schopenhauer's that this proverb is not unconditionally true, because there are many professors who by their perpetual teaching *ex cathedra* are themselves prevented from learning anything. *XI¹A 111*

Is moral philosophy not, like astrology and alchemy, a science which has to do with something which does not exist?

Schopenhauer inveighs against Kant's way of treating morality by presenting the ideal 'Thou ought', ideal virtues and duties, without considering whether anyone actually performs them.

No, says Schopenhauer, moral philosophy like every other science must cling to real life, describe real life. But – he goes on – one could object that in that case moral philosophy becomes a science like astrology and alchemy, a science which has to do with something which does not exist.

Schopenhauer himself does not seem to notice how infinitely witty he is at this point; he makes this objection with all seriousness, demonstrates it with all seriousness – and then proceeds to write his own moral philosophy. *XI¹A 112*

Progress with the years

There are men for whom life's progress seems to mean, or whose progress in life means, that they become stupider and stupider.

Of those who knew them from their earlier days, even from their childhood, no one had an inkling (so people are accustomed to speak of distinction), no one could imagine that in that child, who was just like the rest, there could reside such a stock of stupidity as was now seen unfolding more and more richly in the course of the years. *XI¹A 113*

My God, my God, why hast thou forsaken me?

[Matthew 27. 46]

It is perhaps not true (as I said in *For self-examination*, turning it all too hastily into a theory) that every martyr must have this experience, though in a feebler form.

The difference between the God-Man and the witness to the truth is that the God-Man took suffering upon himself absolutely freely – hence this ultimate and most fearful suffering.

The witness to the truth is qualitatively lower; even if he is willing God has still to compel him in many ways – so perhaps he is spared this suffering. *XI¹A 115*

The end of Luke 14

The end of this chapter has always impressed me strangely, as though Christ were dissuading one from becoming his disciple and encouraging prudence.

But that is not the meaning. The meaning is that if you will not renounce everything you cannot be my disciple – for the world's resistance will be so great for you that you will be better to make a pact in time with him 'who comes against you with twenty thousand men'. The world will cast down your tower, or laugh at you for having begun at all.

So it is not Christ who casts you off; no, Christ simply fore-
tells the consequences if a man does not forsake everything
and yet wishes to be a disciple of Christ.   *XI¹A 116*

Little children

We must note that it is not Christ who turns to the little
children or bids men bring them to him. No, the disciples want
to drive them away, along with their mothers – and then he
says, 'Let them come to me.'

Christ does not deny that the disciples are right in thinking
that Christianity is not really for infants – but at the same
time he admonishes the disciples to become like children.

XI¹A 123

The Christianity of most people

consists approximately of these two lessons, which could
actually be called the two most ambiguous extremes of
Christianity (or as the minister says, the solid ground one
must cling to in life and death): first the saying about little
children, that one becomes a Christian as a little child, that of
such is the kingdom of God; and second the thief on the cross.

Men live their life in the strength of the first, and in death
they look for consolation to the image of the thief.

That is the whole of their Christianity; and, characteristically enough, it is a mixture of childishness and crime.

XI¹A 124

The conflict in my public life

The conflict in my public life is certainly a rare thing; and I
dare not expect to be understood by my contemporaries – my
life has far too high an aim for this (+). Yes, much too high.
This reminds me of the late Bishop Mynster. What he paraded

throughout his life as profound Christian seriousness was abominable, and the objection he openly levelled against me was that my life was too high – and then he himself took part in the mean opposition to me.

My conflict arises from the fact that in a little land and in restricted surroundings there lives a man who is equipped with extraordinary powers, favoured with independent means, and possessed of the rare gift to win individual men to himself.

So he sets to work. His first achievement is in principle enough, everything is won, everything is opened up before him or has to yield to him.

But now comes the conflict: this man is both too melancholy and too religious to want to be a success in this world. Further, he is too much in love with ideals and with the true saints of the past to accept the idolatry of a market-town. So after the most calm and consecrated reflection he rejects it, and goes on rejecting it. And the market-town becomes more and more furious at – his pride, his arrogance, etc.

The very few who possess the presuppositions to be able to see what was noble in his conduct are envious of him, and therefore make use of the fact that he makes difficulties for himself in this way, that he incites the mediocre against him, who naturally can only understand it as madness or as arrogance that a man should defend himself not against being brought low but against being put high, with acclamation, something that surely, devil take it, everyone should be pleased as Punch about!

This is the conflict. Mynster's shabby and paltry proclamation of Christianity over many years has put a premium on mediocrity, and has naturally contributed to the fact that in Denmark there is probably not a single man who is not in the thrall of mediocrity.

This is the conflict. My reward in this world is suffering. In another world I expect the reward that when I see the saints they will agree that I have been honourable towards them, and that I have not made use of the market-town to ascribe falsely to myself what belongs to them.

That is why I think that perhaps I will not come to lie in

my grave as an honourable man, as Bishop Mynster wishes for himself – for I do not expect to be acknowledged by my contemporaries (++). But I expect that that will be the judgement about me among the saints.

And since I have happened to think of that wish of Bishop Mynster's, let me add a remark about it. His 'Recollections' end with this wish. That is like him. In a certain sense he was a deceiver in a big way. Thus we have this last effrontery in his words as well. It seems to me that when one has defrauded the saints in his style by falsely enjoying for his whole life such esteem as though he were one of them – then, it seems to me, one should not be so immodest as to wish to lie in one's grave as an honourable man: one should be thankful if things held out just as long as one lived. *XI¹A 125*

[*In the margin*] (+) That posterity will pretend to understand me is of course nonsense, since such a posterity will then be the contemporary world, and will act as contemporaries.

(++) That is to say, I do not expect that the contemporary world will understand the extent to which I have been honourable and upright towards the saints – for is the charge of dishonourableness not just what they bring against me *qua* writer?

For present, Protestant orthodoxy, Christianity is mythology and poetry

Let us imagine for a moment that in a certain sense Christianity exists objectively, even though this is certainly not true, for even its objective existence is far from being precisely Christianity.

Well then, objectively it exists. But what does not exist is that kind of passion which is the formal requisite for being able to accept the content of Christianity – unconditioned passion, the passion of the unconditioned.

This kind of passion has quite literally ceased to exist in the world. Indeed, it is so long since it has been present, that even the novelists and poets in our time do not dare – for fear of being regarded as mad, or liars, or fools – to depict a passion which is so profound.

But when the formal requisite for being able to accept the content of Christianity does not exist, then Christianity's objective existence, so-called, is an existence which in another sense is not an existence: this is the state of so-called orthodoxy.

. . . Oh, as in a confused and slack time some man in authority might well say, Nothing will be any good, till we reintroduce the death-penalty – so some man in authority in religious matters in our time might well say, Nothing will be any good, till we seriously reintroduce the punishments of hell. Oh, but I tremble when I think of the torments with which the man would be martyred and hardened who introduced them. War and pestilence no longer have an effect on men, against such things they are armed by their spiritual insensibility. *XI¹A 126*

The true state of affairs

Christianity in the New Testament, merely from the human standpoint, is the most terrible of all things; there is nothing like it in Judaism or paganism – and it is also a judgement upon Judaism and paganism.

Under the momentum it received from the founder and the apostles, it ran a short time – but soon the story began which is really the history of Christendom, the history of the subtle discarding of Christianity. Note that men did not dare to revolt, but they hypocritically changed things, putting a spell on them to make it seem that they still had Christianity, when in fact they had the very opposite. All the lies and crime stories among Jews and pagans alike are child's play compared with this history of lies in Christendom.

Christianity is the religion, adherence to which means that you are a priest (and so there is no layman): to be a Christian is to be a priest.

Further, Christianity is the religion in which being the priest means at the same time being oneself the sacrifice (and so not a priest who brings a sacrifice – far less who lives off it).

So since being a Christian is being a priest, being a Christian means being sacrificed.

This kind of worship of God does not please us men at all.

And so through the long long story of what is called Christendom the cowardly and hypocritical effort has succeeded, step by step, in turning the whole religion round, so that in Protestantism it has ended up as sophisticated enjoyment of life . . .   *XI¹A 128*

The standard for being a man

. . . In the New Testament the standard for being a man is eternity: not a people, or an epoch, or a land, or what is distinguished in a time, or a time itself as a whole, a miserable time, and so on. And now think of those horrible falsifications in the direction of what I should describe in one word as Goethian, or Hegelian, which aim at indulging the time.

Above all in the New Testament the standard for being a man is being a single person – and now everything is 'association'.   *XI¹A 130*

Wretched times

I have made various sacrifices; and if I now press on to real self-denial, would there not be someone in our time whom that would encourage to follow me? No, no. On the contrary something else would happen. A few professors would take possession of the intellectual booty of my life – to lecture about it. And since they are clever enough to look to the profit, they would profit by it and so they would be understood by our contemporaries. And a few poets would take possession of my life's exertions, and find motifs for their poetic descriptions; and since the poets in our time know how to look to the

profit, they too would profit by this, and so be understood by
our contemporaries, who would perhaps also be remotely
affected by the impression of my life. And so during my very
life-time I would be turned to profit.

The poets of our time have themselves long felt that it
would be most desirable that there should appear some day
an extraordinary phenomenon which would help people to
believe a little more in their fiction. It is so long since the
extraordinary has been seen that novels themselves begin to
suffer. And as one longs for fresh meat after having had a long
diet of salt meat, so one desires to have the impression of
something extraordinary – not in order to follow it, oh no, but
in order to make literary use of it, and that the public might
be more receptive to one's inventions . . .   *XI¹A 131*

Jesus and Judas

If I dare to speak for a moment quite humanly about this,
then I should say that Christ had the advantage that Judas,
quite simply, and known by all, was the traitor, and that is
why Christ could be magnanimous towards him.

But as the world becomes more and more clever, it also
becomes nastier, and its nastiness becomes more cunning.
In the modern style the traitor would be so artful that at the
end of the day Christ himself would be the only one to see
that he was the traitor, whereas the others, the apostles,
would suppose that Judas was his true friend.

And so he, the magnanimous one, would find himself in the
difficult position of himself having to denounce the traitor –
and perhaps be neither understood nor believed. And so the
impression of his magnanimity would be a little weakened.

XI¹A 132

The retreat

The retreat we have to make is of a peculiar kind.

Back to the monastery, from which Luther (this is the simple truth) broke out: we must go back to this. This does not mean that the Pope must triumph, nor that the papal police are to lead us back.

The fault with the monastery was not asceticism, celibacy, and so on. No, the fault was that the demands of Christianity were reduced, in that the monastery was allowed to regard itself as containing extraordinary Christians – while the sheer nonsense of the world was regarded as ordinary Christianity.

No, asceticism, and all that belongs to it, is merely a first thing: it is the condition for being able to be a witness to the truth.

So the turn which Luther brought about was a mistake: it was not a reduction but a raising which was required.

That is why the question has always struck me whether it is really possible that God could be with Lutheranism. For wherever God is present the progress which is made can be recognized through the demand becoming greater, and the difficulties growing. Whereas a purely human matter is always recognizable through its being done more and more easily, and the progress consists precisely in this.

So the fault with the middle ages was not the monastery and asceticism, but that basically the world had won because the monk paraded as the extraordinary Christian.

No, first of all asceticism, which is gymnastics, and then the witness to the truth: this is, quite simply, what makes a Christian – and good night to all you millions and trillions and quadrillions.

Luther should therefore either have put the matter in this way, or he should have made it clear that he was making an additional reduction on account of the increasing wretchedness of the human race.   *XI¹A 134*

My task

is so new that in Christianity's eighteen hundred years there is literally not one from whom I can learn how to behave.

For all extraordinary men who have hitherto lived have

aimed at spreading Christianity. My task is to put a halt to a lying diffusion of Christianity, and to help it to shake off a mass of nominal Christians.

So none of the extraordinary men of the past were so literally alone as I am, far less did they see their task to consist in defending their loneliness; for if this halt is to be made it is easy to see that the less the personal element enters in the more nearly the task may be accomplished.

Yes thank you! When I die, there will be something for professors! These wretched rascals! And it does not help, it does not help in the least, even if it is printed and read over and over again. The professors will still make a profit of me, they will lecture away, perhaps with the additional remark that the peculiarity of this man is that he cannot be lectured about. *XI¹A 136*

Christianity – Judaism

Judaism is really of all religions outspoken optimism. Certainly Greek paganism was also an enjoyment of life, but it was uncertain and filled with melancholy, and above all it had not divine authority. But Judaism is divinely sanctioned optimism, sheer promise for this life.

And just because Christianity is renunciation, Judaism is its presupposition. *Opposita juxta se posita*. Renunciation can never be more radical than when it has a background of divinely authorized optimism.

But instead of seeing this, in the whole history of Christendom there is a constant tendency to resuscitate Judaism as being on a level with Christianity, instead of Christianity making use of it as a repelling force, or as something to be forsaken, since Christianity preaches renunciation, absolute renunciation. *XI¹A 139*

The Christianity of our time

In the New Testament the matter is put thus: 'Let all these trifles, these little egoisms with which men fill up their lives, buying and selling, getting married, having children, becoming something in the world – let them all go, break with them, and then let your life be devoted to loving God, to being sacrificed for mankind: be salt!' This is what our Lord Jesus Christ calls Christianity. When a man plans to get married, the invitation comes to him (*cf.* the Gospel): leave it, and become a Christian. When a man has bought six yoke of oxen and wants to go out and try them, the invitation comes, Leave it and become a Christian, and so on.

Now Christianity has become the very opposite: the divine blessing has descended on all the trifles and philistinism of finitude and life's temporal enjoyment. Lovers send for the minister, and he blesses them . . .

Of course it is Protestantism in particular which is a complete absurdity.

Therefore Protestantism has also put women so much into the foreground, or rather, has put them first. Everything turns on women. Charming! So one can be sure that everything turns on idle chatter, on bagatelles, and (in a refined manner) on sexual relations. So far women can be said to have ennobled social life, that we no longer murder and drink and carouse like those old heroes, but refined voluptuousness and carefully concealed fine innuendoes about sexual relations – these are what (in a Christian sense!) ennoble social life.

This is how various of my pseudonyms have presented the matter, and what, as I now see, Schopenhauer in his way is inveighing against: women are not to blame, but they are destined to humiliate men, and reduce them to insignificance. Existence is also a sovereign, and like all sovereigns it understands to perfection how best to keep its power – namely, by humiliating and breaking the one it rules over.

This is where women excel, when men enter into a serious relation with them. First and foremost men are humiliated by women. One may generally assume that every married man is in his inner heart crestfallen, for he feels that he has been made a fool of, when all that high-flown stuff of the days of falling in love, all that about Juliana being the very incarnation of beauty and grace, and the possession of her being the summit of blessedness, ends in a false alarm. That is the first blow the man receives. And this is no insignificant matter, for a man cannot easily endure having to confess to himself that he has been fooled, and that both he and Juliana have been mad. The other blow is that the man and Juliana (who for her part has had the same experience) agree to keep a stiff upper lip and to conceal the truth from the rest of the world; they agree to lie, that marriage is true happiness and they in particular are happy.

When all this is in order, then Providence knows that this fellow is easy to govern: he is one of those who makes no conquests in the world of ideas. For such continued lying brings the man into the utmost degradation. It is another matter with the woman, for she is a born liar, a virtuoso who is never really happy unless there is a little lying; one can be *a priori* sure that wherever a woman is concerned, there will also be a little lying. In a sense she is innocent in the matter, she can do nothing about it. One can never think of being angry about it; on the contrary one can regard it as in the highest degree an amiable quality, she is in the power of a natural destiny, which with the utmost cunning makes use of her in order to weaken the man.

So as the story progresses (I mean the story of marriage) there enter in, with the woman, all the follies of finitude, the philistinism, and an egoism such as only the woman has. For as wife and mother – oh, here is an egoism of which the man has no conception at all. Society has accorded it privileges by calling it love; but no, in reality it is the most powerful egoism, in which, it is true, at first she does not love herself, but through egoistically loving her own and all that belongs to her she ends by loving herself. From this moment ideas, and likewise every higher, infinite aspiration, can whistle for a man; indeed, even if our Lord and his angels were to try to move him, it would be of no avail. Mother's egoism is such an immense power that she can hold him fast.

The woman, quite differently from the man, has the most dangerous relation to finitude; she is, as the Seducer says, a mystification.[1] There is a moment in her life when she makes the deceptive impression of being infinity – and that is when the man is caught. And as wife she is quite simply finitude.

That is why the church has laid more emphasis on the preservation of the woman's virginity than on the man's, and has honoured the nun more than the monk. For the woman, when she renounces this life, and marriage, gives up more than the man.

XI¹ A 141

Hypocrisy

. . . I should like to put forward a quite different objection that can be made against the Christian infinite demand upon the single person. Does not Christianity make me into the most immense egoist, or does it not develop my egoism to a quite abnormal degree, since by terrifying a man with the greatest horror it leads him to be concerned about his own salvation alone, without regard to the possible weakness or imperfection of all others? It is easy to see that if a man aspires seriously to the absolute, and is no more than a little serious about it, then he will soon find himself surrounded by men who are by comparison far behind. Then does this not mean that Christianity is making him into an immense egoist, when it forbids him to delay by helping them, but on the contrary continually commands him to go farther and farther out, by which he will so confuse his contemporaries that perhaps they will slay him, and thus through him acquire the greatest guilt?

To this one may answer that truth cannot comport itself otherwise. If there is some arrogance or pride in presuming to carry on this game with weaker men, then certainly that is one's responsibility. But if what determines a man in this is

[1] See *Samlede Værker².* VI, 87 RGS

concern with his soul's salvation, then he has no responsibility, the responsibility rests with Christianity, with Providence, which also will do all things for the best.   *XI¹ A 148*

Protestantism, especially à la Grundtvig

In every way it has come to this, that what one now calls Christianity is precisely what Christ came to abolish. This has happened especially in Protestantism, and especially among the Grundtvigians.

The Grundtvigians are in fact in the strictest sense Jews. I undertake to prove that they have such a Jewish conception of marriage that they do not merely, as in Christianity, regard it as permissible (in contrast to celibacy), nor as a *diaphoron*: no, they believe that one cannot be a proper Christian without being married, that a flock of children and a numerous posterity are a blessing of God and a sign that God is well pleased – an entirely Jewish conception.

Further, in place of circumcision they have baptism (again an objective matter) to which they appeal just as the Jews do to circumcision.

Further, a right Jewish superstition about descent.

Further, the illusion that they are God's chosen people, either simply that the Christians (the baptized) are God's chosen people, or that the Danes are.

This is Jewish optimism, the most dangerous sort of epicurism, that, namely, which turns enjoyment of this life into religion.

And this is supposed to be New Testament Christianity!
    XI¹ A 149

Marriage

It is decisive for every religious view of life, for every religion, how marriage is regarded, which I understand as the ethical expression for the propagation of the species.

Besides the instinct and all that belongs to it, which can determine a man to marry, there is another consideration which I would emphasize. I find it expressed both in Plato and in Aristotle, as well as in the Fathers (in Böhringer occasionally, and I have marked the passages in my copy), that to leave offspring behind is a consolation for not being immortal, that the propagation of the species is a substitute for individual immortality, and therefore that man, who clings so hard to life, when he does not believe in his immortality seeks to prolong his life by leaving offspring behind.

Now this has never been so strongly emphasized as in Judaism, where everything circles round this notion of increasing and being fruitful, of succession and genealogy – all with the divine sanction. That is why the Jews did not have the idea of immortality.

Then came Christianity with the notion of virginity, which means the religion of the spirit.

There will always be this oscillation between the immortal individual on the one hand and on the other hand the individual, not immortal, but consoling himself with his posterity: between these two, or rather, in them, is to be found the clear differentiation for all religions.   *XI¹A 150*

The New Testament

What makes it so difficult for us men to have the right impression of the New Testament is that the reduplication which is the divine majesty is so totally foreign to us that we have no criterion for the 'egoity', which is always as great in the thesis as in the antithesis, in the divine prodigality and no less in the divine parsimony, as great in giving as in withholding.

When one says, 'Come unto me' [Matthew 11. 28], and then, 'I have come to the world not to judge it but to make it blessed' [John 12. 47], immediately we men get it all wrong, we at once imagine millions and millions of saved, the whole world, and so on. It escapes us that, at the same time as the Saviour of this world holds fast to what he has said, divinity is this immense egoity, and that *summa summarum* only very few will be saved, yet, even if not a single man were saved, without his wishing to change what he first said, Come hither all, I have come to the world not to judge but to make the world blessed.

In 'Christendom' Christianity has therefore become what we could call barber's chatter: isolated theses have been taken, without their antitheses, especially sayings which seemed suited to take people in, and so this infinite nonsense of 'Christendom' has come into being. Truly an injustice was done to Columbus when America was not called after him: in a quite different way an injustice was done to Jesus Christ when Christendom was called after him.

But as I have said the New Testament is the divine majesty, and that why there is always a thesis and an antithesis; which also means that what is demanded is faith, and what is prevented is any kind of direct familiarity and *camaraderie.*

XI¹A 154

Christianity

... Take some examples from our life today. No honest man, with the New Testament in his hand (and the minister is bound by oath to it), can conduct a wedding as it is now done. No, remember that the New Testament is intended, with divine sharp-sightedness, to wound the natural man in the severest possible way. The pagan praised it as the greatest happiness to be in love, and to be happily in love; humanly speaking a pair of happy lovers is the most beautiful spectacle. But from the Christian point of view it is a funeral ceremony. If it must be a festival, then it should be like our present funerals. How sad, says Christianity, here are two people who want to unite in this way in order to belong more firmly to this sinful world, and to propagate this sinful race further with their offspring!

So we have the kind of festivity in use today – and when the minister takes part we have, from the Christian standpoint, a lie, the most impudent lie. No honest man can take this from the New Testament – and the minister is bound by oath to the New Testament.

With the New Testament as his teacher the minister should behave as follows. He should first call the lovers before him, and warn them that the solitary life pleases God more, is truer for the Christian, whose life is and ought to be a crucifixion. Then he can read Paul's words to them, that nevertheless it is better – that is, better-pleasing to God – to marry than to burn [I Corinthians 7. 9].

Let this be the text for the marriage ceremony – and a quiet sadness should be from the Christian point of view the ground tone of this sad occasion.

On the other hand, no honest man, with the New Testament in his hand (and the minister is bound by oath to it), can take part in the kind of ceremony that a funeral is today. From the Christian point of view it should be bright and gay, we should be dressed in white (as in the early church, instead of which we now put on white at weddings), here sounds of joy should be heard, blessed, blessed, blessed, as nowadays at a birthday celebration (the day of a man's death was regarded by the early church as his birthday) or at a wedding (and again, the early church regarded the day of death as the wedding-day, for the soul was then united with the beloved).

And so on every possible point modern Christianity is a wretched lie, so far as it pretends to be the Christianity of the New Testament. *XI¹A 157*

Discipleship

Christ comes to the world as the model, with the constant words of injunction, Follow me.

Soon the relationship was turned about, men preferred to *worship* the model, and at last reached the presumptuous stage in Protestantism of wishing to be like the model. But the model is the Reconciler only.

The apostle then follows Christ, and admonishes his hearers, Follow me.

Soon men turned it round, and worshipped the apostle.

And so things begin to slide . . .

There is one thing which is the divine discovery, the only kind of worship God demands, discipleship. Man is only willing to respond in one way, by worshipping the models.

XI¹A 158

False interest

. . . Presumably we shall now experience the same with Christianity. In no time novelists and poets will probably be hurling themselves on early Christianity, presenting it and depicting it, everything in an aesthetic manner – the best proof that for them and their readers Christianity has ceased to be a religion. And the asinine clergy are probably capable of singing their praises as being a sign of awakening Christian interest. *XI¹A 160*

The enemies of Christianity

It is to this extent a good thing that Christianity still has enemies, that these have for a long time been the only people from whom one can obtain some reliable account of what Christianity is. (+) The Christians naturally reserve the right to adapt it to their taste.

Yet soon Christianity, represented by what are now called Christians, will be so insignificant that it will not even be able to acquire any enemies. The reason why it still has enemies is doubtless mainly its past history, its historical significance.

XI¹A 161

[*In the margin*] (+) This is because the enemies hate the Chris tians, and so they can describe what Christianity is, their hate helps them to see what Christianity in the New Testament is.

Hatred, of course, of being a man; but nowadays the Christian does not truly hate himself, therefore he does not know, and does not want to know, what Christianity is.   *XI¹A 162*

'Christendom' – the Saviour of the world

. . . In the New Testament Christ appears as addressing himself to men, inviting all, and saying to each single person, 'Do you wish to be saved?' But now the nonsensical dogma has been fabricated that Christ saves the human race. This is sheer blether. I should say that even if Christ had wished this, he could not have done it. For the 'race' is in fact the category of destruction, and to be saved means precisely to be saved from the 'race'. By means of the human race I can belong to the ruined race, but I cannot be saved by means of it, any more than when I am saved, am I saved *into* the human race.

But being a Christian has become almost synonymous with being a man; we are not far from thinking that Christians beget Christians. And so the category of the race has been introduced everywhere, and individuals have been degraded to being copies. So the way has been opened for a happy and enjoyable earthly life, such as can be led by mere copies.

Presumably this theory of Christ as the Saviour of the human race is the reason why the pathos of gratitude for one's salvation has been quite abolished. Originally the individual, the single person, understood that his salvation had cost the life and death of Jesus. Here was true pathos. So the Christian's gratitude knew no rest until he had given his life as a thank-offering. But when the turn-over of salvation takes place in such enormous lots, the whole human race, these millions and millions, then presumably this point falls away, and it is a great deal if each single person says thanks merely *en passant* . . .   *XI¹A 168*

The infinite richness of existence

Most men would despair if they were told how infinitely rich existence is, and that one man, just a single man, is enough, is all, and that with him the greatest happenings are possible.

The many think – and it is logical of the many – that a European war is an event, and that 100,000 millions are something – but a single person is nothing.   *XI¹A 175*

Greek

Even before Hegel there lived philosophers who undertook to explain existence and history. And it is doubtless true of all such attempts that Providence must really smile at them. He has not perhaps exactly laughed at them, for they had a certain human and honest seriousness about them.

But Hegel – oh, let me think in the Greek manner! – how the gods must have guffawed! Such a miserable professor, who penetrated the necessity of all things, and then got it all off by heart: ye gods! . . .   *XI¹A 180*

Schopenhauer and Christianity

Schopenhauer makes light of Christianity, he ridicules it in comparison with the wisdom of India.

That is his affair. I regard Schopenhauer as a most significant author, who will also be significant for Christianity.

Yet there is something not quite true in his Indian melancholy that to live is to suffer. All the same it can be very good for our time to be given such a dose of melancholy, to make it attentive to Christianity. This is what Johannes Climacus expresses in the proposition that to be a Christian is to suffer, which is indeed the teaching of the New Testament as well.[1]

I have nothing against Schopenhauer's furious and powerful attack on the 'wretched optimism' which Protestantism in

---

[1] See *Samlede Værker*² VII, 391, 420*ff*, 572*ff*. RGS

particular excels in; I am very glad that he shows that it is not Christianity. But the proposition that to exist is to suffer I must protest against, for then Christianity vanishes in a way that perhaps Schopenhauer never imagined. For Christianity preaches that it itself is suffering, and that to be a Christian is to suffer. But if simply to exist, to be a man, is to suffer, then Christianity is deprived of its dialectic, its necessary preliminary, that which helps to make it negatively knowable. Then Christianity becomes a pleonasm, a superfluous observation, sheer galimatias; for if to be a man is to suffer, then it is ridiculous that there should be a doctrine which proposes the definition that to be a Christian is to suffer.

No, Christianity does not say that to exist is to suffer. On the contrary, it applies itself to Jewish optimism, and uses as background the most highly potentiated enjoyment of life which has ever got attached to life, in order to present Christianity as renunciation, and to show that to be a Christian is to suffer, including suffering for the doctrine.

There is another difficulty in Schopenhauer's position, which could easily be a kind of self-contradiction. Let me take another situation. Slander, calumny, base attacks, and so on, are well versed in the worldly prudence which does not suddenly reduce a man to a mere cipher and then go on year after year attacking him in the most vigorous possible manner. For this is a self-contradiction: if he really is a mere cipher it is ridiculous to see this immense operation set going in order to destroy a cipher. But this is just what is happening with Schopenhauer's asceticism. Christian asceticism rests in the thought that to exist is not identical with suffering – and then there is meaning in the asceticism. If to exist were to suffer, then asceticism would easily become eudaimonism, which is precisely what Schopenhauer urges against the Stoics (+). Take another situation. Christianity does not maintain that riches cannot in a certain sense be called a good, and that is precisely why it can say, Give all to the poor. But if someone were to say that riches are an evil, now show your asceticism by giving your riches away, this would be a self-contradiction, for if this were the true state of affairs it would not be asceticism to give away your riches.

In how many situations, wherever there is a dialectic, there is a zeal which is so zealous to enjoin the second point that in its zeal it gets rid of the first point, and therefore basically makes the second point impossible. *XI¹A 181*

[*In the margin*] (+) Asceticism on Schopenhauer's view aims (by mortifying the desire to live) at reaching non-existence, even though one exists: pushed to this point, asceticism is to die to all things. But if to exist is to suffer, then to exist as though one did not exist, as though one scarcely knew whether or not one existed, is obviously eudaimonism – of course, as far as our feeble capacities reach. That is to say, it is the utmost eudaimonism when one believes, with Schopenhauer, that to exist is to suffer. If to exist is to suffer, eudaimonism cannot be sought in the direction of existence,+ it must be sought in the direction of non-existence,§ and the utmost eudaimonism becomes the highest approximation to non-existence.

+ or in the direction of intensifying existence.

§ or in the direction of de-potentiating existence.

XI¹A 182

Christianity and Judaism

. . . That Christ was born of a Virgin would not have scandalized the pagans, but for Judaism it was bound to be a scandal. For Judaism culminates in regarding marriage as so divine that it is God himself who has instituted it. Judaism has ideas of the propagation of the species as a kind of religion. And then, to be born of a Virgin! Basically this is a denial of the whole of the Old Testament, a removal of its essential powers.

For the rest, there have been so many concessions in this case too to the traditional idea, that the contemporaries could not quite escape from the phenomenon of the birth by documenting that this Messiah was not the Messiah. If Christ, for example, had not been of the stock of David, that would have been decisive. But he is of David's stock, and yet he is not for he was born of a Virgin, and therefore outside the stock. And as I have said, in view of the Jews' exalted idea of race and belonging to the race, being born of a Virgin can never be presented as something higher, but only as something inferior. *XI¹A 184*

Miracle

In the New Testament miracle is presented as inseparable from being a Christian (Mark 16. 17), and this is also the view of Christianity, so that instead of the nonsense about miracles being no longer necessary we can without any ado make the assertion that where there are no more miracles there is simply no Christianity.

But miracles have a quite special function. One does not have them in order with their help to obtain money or profit, or to escape dangers and suffering. On the contrary, in this respect God always leaves the 'apostle' or the 'disciple' completely in the lurch, he brings him into all kinds of torments, and demands that he freely expose himself to them – and then he has the gift of miracles. From the purely human standpoint it is another immense torment to have the gift of miracles on this condition: to starve – and then to have the gift of miracle. Further, the gift of miracle is calculated to excite man's opposition to him who has it.

And that is why miracles are no longer required today. We prefer to be the teachers of Christianity on condition of proper assurance of a sleek livelihood with regular promotion for a well-educated man with a family . . . *XI¹A 187*

Important note

Those three thousand who were added *en masse* at Pentecost to the community – is there not something wrong here, that is, in the very earliest days of Christianity? Should the apostles not have asked themselves whether it was right that thousands of people should thus become Christians in one fell swoop? Has not something very human overtaken the apostles, that having an all too vivid recollection of their despair at Christ's death, when everything seemed to be lost, and now being overwhelmed with joy at the effect they produced, they should forget what Christianity really is, forget that if true following is what constitutes Christianity, then such an immense conquest as three thousand at one time will simply not do?

The matter is so immensely difficult, because there is a strange meeting between two thoughts, almost as when two meet one another in a narrow passage and cannot get past one another. In Christ Christianity moves in the direction of intensity. That is, it is pure intensity. The task of the apostles seems to move in the direction of expansion, the more expansion the better. But in the same degree as I emphasize the intensity I bring the expansion to a halt – yet surely it was true Christianity which the apostles had to spread.

In Christ Christianity is the single person, the unique single person. In the apostle it suddenly becomes the community (+). But this transfers Christianity to an entirely different sphere of ideas. And it is this idea which has been the ruin of Christianity. To this idea is due the confusion with the state, the country, the people, and kingdoms which are Christian.

XI¹A 189

[*In the margin*] (+) And it is a question whether the principle of having to hate oneself, which is a principle of Christianity, is not so a-social that it prevents the formation of a community. In any case it is from this point of view that one can see the absurdity in state churches and national churches and Christian countries.

XI¹A 190

Being a Christian in the New Testament – unrest – the martyr – Luther

In the New Testament being a Christian is expressed by the apostles: it is like spirit, spirit's utmost unrest, the impatience of eternity, sheer fear and trembling, all heightened by being in this evil world, which crucified love, heightened again by fear of the last reckoning, when the Lord and Master will come again and judge whether they have been faithful.

If this is so, then having to be a martyr, which Christ prophesied for Christians, far from being an aggravation is rather an alleviation. For one could say that only such external sufferings, and at the end a martyr's death, are able to alleviate and assuage the torments of soul which accompany the effort to be a Christian in the New Testament sense. So martyrdom is not a cruelty, but on the contrary it is what bodily sufferings so often are in relation to torments of soul. On the other hand it would have been cruel if Christ had said to the disciples, 'After my time you have nothing more to do; see that you get married, and especially let each of you see that you get a nice little livelihood, and scrape some money together, and be a good fellow who goes to church once a week and to Communion thrice a year.'

In the New Testament, then, the two things correspond: unrest in the Christian demands martyrdom as a kind of alleviation – and martyrdom is what is demanded. But soon the unrest slackens in 'Christendom', that dead spiritless mass.

Then in the Middle Ages asceticism was emphasized (it was thought that there was no longer either occasion or opportunity for martyrdom). And as I have often observed, the error was not here, but in the fact that there was such a compromise with the spiritless mass of Christendom's millions of Christians that the ascetic was honoured as the extraordinary Christian, instead of the confession being made that Christianity had gone back, and had been reduced.

So it became more and more clear that Christianity just caused one trouble, if one wanted to live quietly and enjoy life. So this at last finds expression in Luther (who for the rest was right in opposition to Catholic abuse).

Luther discovered that Christianity is there in order to tranquillize.

I have often observed that Luther has altered Christianity.

As I now see, Schopenhauer maintains that Luther by altering the concept of virginity has altered Christianity. This view I have shared so far as I have thought that Luther should have made it quite clear that his marriage was an exception, a corrective. But what I have particularly pointed out is that Luther has altered Christianity by altering the concept of martyrdom.

So Luther turns Christianity upside down. Christianity is intended to calm; Christ, he adds, came into the world in order to calm anxious consciences.

This is the very opposite of the New Testament. Christ comes to the world to save a sinful world, a world lying in the power of evil. But a sinful world does not in fact suffer from an anxious conscience. The point is that unrest must be awakened.

But the unfortunate thing with Luther is that a particular state of Christendom, at a special time and place, is transformed into the norm. Luther suffered extremely from an anxious conscience, he needed treatment. Very well: but is that a reason for completely transforming Christianity into a matter of calming anxious consciences?

The more I consider Luther, the clearer it seems to me to be that he confuses being the patient with being the physician. He is an extremely important patient for Christendom, but he is not the physician. He has the patient's passion for expressing and describing his suffering and what he feels he needs in order to relieve it. But he does not have the doctor's over-all view. And if Christianity is to be reformed there must be first and foremost an over-all view of the whole of Christianity.   *XI¹A 193*

Hypocritical falsification

The law of existence is, the more insignificant, the easier (a plant's life is easier than an animal's, an animal's than a man's, a child's than a man's, the simple man's than the wise man's, and so on).

Worldly wisdom therefore constantly tends to make life insignificant (to get rid of ideals, higher aspirations, and so on), for this makes life easy.

Now Christianity has made man as significant as possible, as being kin to God and striving to be like him, by imitation. Christianity, which has given as much significance as possible to being a man, has of course also made it as difficult and painful as possible.

And it is this which men cannot tolerate. But they will not honourably confess the true state of affairs. So they hypocritically get rid of Christianity by saying that they are far too humble to desire anything so lofty.

'Significant' and 'difficult', 'insignificant' and 'easy' are correlative, if you take the one away you also take the other away. So men say hypocritically, I do not desire the 'significant', I am far too humble for that – and this means, I want to get rid of the 'difficult'. And this is indeed what happens when I get rid of the significant.   *XI¹ A 194*

The wild goose – an image

Everyone who knows even just a little about the life of birds knows that between the wild goose and domestic geese, however different they are, there is a kind of understanding. When the passage of the wild goose is heard in the air, and the domestic geese are down on the earth, they straightway hear it, and to a certain extent understand what it means: they too raise themselves a little from the ground, they beat their wings, they cry and fly in disorderly and unlovely confusion for a little while, close to the ground – and then it is over.

Once upon a time there was a wild goose. In autumn, about the migrating time, it noticed some domestic geese. It fell in love with them, it seemed a sin to fly away from them, it hoped to win them for its life, so that they would resolve to accompany it when the migration began.

To this end it took up with them in every possible way, it tried to attract them to rise a little higher, always a little higher in their flight, that they might if at all possible take part in the migration, released from the miserable and mediocre life of waddling around on the earth as respectable domestic geese.

At first the domestic geese thought it was quite amusing, and they developed an affection for the wild goose. But soon they got tired of it, they rebuffed it with rough words, chiding it for a fantastic fool without experience or wisdom. But alas, the wild goose had become so familiar with the domestic geese that they had gradually acquired power over it, their words impressed it – and the end of the story is that the wild goose became a domestic goose.

In a certain sense the wild goose's plan was a good one, and yet it was a misunderstanding. For this is the law, that a domestic goose can never be a wild goose, whereas a wild goose can certainly become a domestic goose.

If the wild goose's plan is to be approved in any way, then it must above all watch out for one thing – that it keeps itself intact. As soon as it notices that the domestic geese are getting some power over it – then away, away with the migrating flock!

For the genius the law is that a domestic goose can never be a wild goose, while on the other hand a wild goose can certainly become a domestic goose – so watch out!

But in the Christian life it is different. Certainly the true Christian, with the Spirit over him, is as different from the ordinary man as the wild goose from the domestic ones. But Christianity teaches just what a man can become in life $(+)$. So here there is hope that the domestic goose can become a wild goose. Therefore stay with them, with these domestic geese, stay with them and be intent on one thing, to try and win them for the change – but for God's sake take care of one thing: as soon as you notice that the domestic geese begin to get power over you, then away, away with the flock, lest the story should end with your becoming a domestic goose, happy in misery. *XI¹A 195*

[*In the margin*] $(+)$ Being a Christian is decidedly not man's original state in the sense that a genius is original, but it is what a man becomes; so here we do not have the arrogance of the exclusive, but the equality of the humble.   *XI¹A 196*

To become a Christian

Jesus Christ the Saviour of the world lives in poverty and humility, then is persecuted and hated, finally is tortured in every way and crucified.

His teaching is essentially his life. So what he says is essentially, Follow me; hate yourself; forsake everything; crucify the flesh; take up your cross; hate your father and mother, and so on. Further, You shall be hated by all men for my name's sake and so on. And lastly, There is a reckoning hereafter, where I am the judge.

But alas! when one is born within Christendom, especially in Protestantism, especially in Denmark, when one is in every way bewitched from the days of childhood that one is a Christian, when from one's earliest days one is crammed full of all the trickery which turns Christianity into optimism; when one lives in a so-called Christian state, that is, in a community which by every possible means takes care to strengthen one in the illusion that one is a Christian, and which even uses civil punishment to compel you to be a Christian: indeed, in all these circumstances it is immensely difficult to become a Christian.   *XI¹A 199*

Sympathy

I keep coming back to this point, whether by God's help I could so conquer myself as really to follow Christ . . .

I know well that I have been demoralized through being brought up from my childhood's days in Christianity. But this is how I see things: I do not understand how a man is able to endure life when he believes that he will be blessed and the others are going to hell, lost for ever. This is because, as

I say, I am demoralized. Through the accursed twaddle that I heard as a child I have really lost respect for the divine majesty.

Only when a man fights for his soul's eternal blessedness can he manage to endure the afflictions of the first Christians – but this means *eo ipso* that the others are lost. If a man says, I for my part will endure it, provided that it does not mean that the others are going to hell, then the reply must be, In this way you will not manage to endure everything. You shall see that when things go badly for you, and you do not have a greater conviction that you are fighting for your soul's eternal blessedness (but if you are convinced then *eo ipso* you believe that the rest are going to hell) – you shall see that in this way you cannot hold out, but you fall away. For only in this tension of fighting for his eternal blessedness can a man really succeed in enduring all things.   *XI¹A 200*

A happy coincidence with Christianity – in a special sense

Christ says, Judge not, that you be not judged [Matthew 7. 1]. It is in the sermon on the mount. When the demand for being a Christian is put so high as it is by Christ, when the Christian is understood to strive to the utmost of his capacity, then the danger is only too near that he judges others. It is so human, when one has to strive to the utmost of one's capacity, even so far as to hate one's own life, to want to judge others severely as well.

In our time, and especially among us, it is part of our very deceits that we are not at all disposed or willing to judge. It is regarded as much cleverer to abstain from judging, for we ourselves know best how we are placed. And so, especially among us, there prevails a rare Christian sentiment in this regard, we completely abstain from judging one another. Of course we do. For the Christian life has almost died out – so let us at all costs not give it life and movement again by judging others. For it could not be done without a certain amount of disturbance – and one can never tell how far that will lead.

Therefore see to it that we follow Christ's command, Judge not – what frauds we are!

No, in our time and especially among us it is to Christianity's interest that we get men to judge – in order to expose their false pretexts, and get a little personality into this objective trickery or this trickery with objectivity. *XI¹A 201*

Optimism – pessimism

If the world, as Christianity teaches, is a sinful world, is in the grip of evil, then *eo ipso* the good citizen, from the Christian standpoint, if I may dare to say, is he who does not propagate this sinful species . . .

Optimism exacts a fine from celibacy; pessimism exacts a fine from marriage. *XI¹A 204*

Consolation with others

The Christian can naturally not find true consolation except with one who has suffered as much, or even more.

The matter is quite simple. If suffering stood in a casual relation to the higher life, so that one who was leading such a life was preserved from sufferings, while another was tempted by it – so the sophists speak, as, for example, that liar of blessed memory, Bishop Mynster – then there would certainly be sense in a Christian's finding consolation with a happy man who is prosperous and contented with life.

But the situation is that to be prosperous in this world, to be without suffering and therefore happy and contented, quite simply verges on insignificance, through every relation to the spirit having been avoided.

But to be consoled by such a man is from the Christian point of view sheer nonsense. The Christian could as well be consoled by a cow, which also is well off. To be consoled in this way would lead to the extinction of the higher life – and that would be the most grievous thing of all.

So the Christian can find consolation only in one of two ways. Either he himself comforts other sufferers, or if there should be another who lives in the same or even greater suffering, in whom the spiritual is so much stronger that he can bring comfort, of course not through tending to be like a cow, but becoming spirit. *XI¹A 208*

This sinful world

This is the meaning of Christianity. Man is a fallen spirit. And as, for example, in Russia a nobleman who has done wrong is punished by being put into the army as a simple soldier, so the fallen spirit is punished by being put into a slave's dress, which is the body, and sent to this penitentiary, which is the world, because of his sins.

But as those simple soldiers among whom the nobleman is put do not notice that it is a punishment, but are perfectly happy, so with these countless battalions of animal creatures devoid of spirit, among whom the Christian is put: they are perfectly happy and contented, they think it is a wonderful world, they regard the slave's uniform as a gala costume, they think it splendid to eat and drink and have their bowels moving and beget children – and just think! mother has had triplets, which wins a state premium – which is just as indecent as to award a prize for other bodily functions.

What I write is from a Christian standpoint so true, so true, and from a Christian standpoint this is how I must write . . . And yet I can say that what I write here tortures me to produce, I do not do it with good will, but it is repugnant to me (+). Oh I have loved men with true sympathy . . .

Oh, it is so sad, yet this is how it is. Behind everything there is a Providence which says, This land is morally decayed, and as surely as I live they shall not escape punishment. For this he must be used (that 'he' is I). But he too will not get off scot-free, even if for him there is always the comfort that it is my love which chooses him. But he shall not escape. His

contemporaries, as reward for his sympathy, will embitter
his life . . .   *XI¹A 209*

[*In the margin*] (+) Alas, in earlier times I suffered great pain
because it was impossible for me to enjoy life, this beautiful
human life. On a Richard III this has the effect of deciding
him to embitter life for others. But not on me: I meant to keep
my suffering hidden, and then to beautify life for others – who
has depicted marriage and all this kind of human existence
more beautifully and attractively than I? And there are men
who thank me by embittering my life – though in this way
again they lead me more and more into Christianity. And so
at last there comes a moment when Christianity seems to say
to me, My little friend, it was out of love to you that it became
impossible for you to enjoy life. But that had to be concealed
from your eyes, until you could endure Christianity, which has
a totally different view of this life.   *XI¹A 210*

Infinite aspiration supported by finite aspiration

To support an infinite aspiration by a finite aspiration is like
swimming with a swimming belt. This has the advantage that
one does not go out too far, for on the one hand earthly goods
are always to be found among the crowd, so that one cannot
strive for them by leaving the crowd, and remaining with the
crowd gives you security; and on the other hand the safety-
belt is always there to haul you back to land.

But from the standpoint of eternity there is no doubt that
this is the stupidest thing one can do: how awkward all these
clever people will feel, when their cleverness is wrecked on
eternity!   *XI¹A 212*

Style

. . . So I have sometimes sat for hours, in love with the sound
of words. That is to say, when the pregnancy of the thought

is echoed I have been able to sit for hours on end, like a flute-player entertaining himself with his flute. Most of what I have written has been said over many many times, often perhaps a dozen, before it was written down (+). The structure of my sentences could be called a world of memories, so much have I lived in and enjoyed and experienced the life of these thoughts and their search for form – even if in a certain sense they most often had found their form straightaway – until every point, down to the least significant (this was the later work, the stylistic business – everyone who really has thoughts has also immediate form) had its proper place, so that the thought could feel, as one says, that it was well organized in the form . . .   *XI¹A 214*

[*In the margin*] (+) In another sense most of what I have written has been written *currente calamo*, as one says; but that is because I get everything ready in the course of a walk.

XI¹A 216

A Christian NB

Everyone whose life, whose existence, is not marked by the form of existence which is established by the New Testament expresses thereby (whatever chatter or declamation or assurance he may utter with his lips) that for him Christianity is mythology, poetry.

The existential is the characteristic which differentiates poetry and mythology from Christianity. That is why Christ proclaimed Christianity as following, discipleship, in order to prevent a relation to Christianity merely through the fancy.

Only in relation to poetry and mythology can the individual reasonably have the freedom to organize his life in accordance with it or not. This in turn means that that in relation to which the individual assumes this freedom is for him only mythology, poetry.

But if Christianity is only mythology, poetry, then it is undeniable that the individual is exempted from the strain of having to do with a judgement and a reckoning, but has at the same time exempted himself from Christianity's promises concerning an eternal blessedness.

The one thing the individual cannot win exemption from is the punishment which eternity may exact. For however much the individual exempts himself from, Christianity reserves the freedom to itself to let him understand that Christianity is not poetry or mythology.   *XI¹A 217*

Woman – man

Woman is egoism personified.

Her glowing, burning devotion to man is neither more nor less than her egoism.

But his lordship the man has no idea of this. He regards himself as supremely happy, he feels himself flattered to the highest degree at being the object of such an ardent devotion, which is perhaps always expressed in the form of subjection because she has a bad conscience about it: that is, she is moved by egoism which as I say the man does not see, but he feels his powers multiplied by the devotion of this other I.

The woman herself does not know that this is egoism, she is always an enigma to herself, and by the cunning of nature this whole mystification is concealed from her, since the egoism takes the form of devotion. If the woman could understand what an immense egoist she was, then she would not be it, for in another sense she is too good to be an egoist.

The whole story of man and woman is an immensely subtly constructed intrigue, or it is a trick calculated to destroy man as spirit.

Man is not originally an egoist, but he becomes one, and with a vengeance, when he has the good fortune to be united to a woman. This union, generally known as marriage, could really be termed, in contrast to an egoism of light, half-timbered construction, a solid brick-built egoism, the real firm.

Once this firm is entered, egoism really gets going. And that is why there are two in the firm, in order (just as in the practical world one takes care to have an associate whom one can blame for everything) to have someone to blame, and to have a companion in lying.

And of course the man, once he has entered this firm, is essentially lost for everything higher.

And that is why Christianity and all deeper views of life cast a suspicious eye on the relation to the other sex, for they assume that to have dealings with the other sex spells man's degradation.

And that is why we hear, in the thieves' slang of men, that it is every man's duty to marry and that marriage is the truly ennobling life.

In this view of things it saddens me that a man of Luther's calibre went so far astray. He should have understood that his marriage was an exceptional action, a corrective, he should therefore, as I have said somewhere in my journal, have married, say, an ironing-board. I mean that he should simply have taken care to make the fact clear that though he was a monk nevertheless he married. The important thing is not the woman, but that an awakening was necessary. And the awakening would have been just as effective if he had married an ironing-board, which of course would have had to be kept secret. That would really have meant being salt! But instead Luther became the head of all that throng of philoprogenitive men, who trust him and believe that it is a part of true Christianity to get married.

As for myself, I cannot boast that I at once understood everything as I did later; if I had not once for all been wrecked on something special, I too should have been married.

Something quite special held me back, and now after a long time I see that what was special to me is what Christianity calls the general, the normal: I see that Christianity holds by man's single state and rather makes marriage the special case.

So here again a Providence has been with me. And in truth this was necessary. For how should a man, born and brought up in this Danish-Protestant eudaimonism, have any eye for what is Christian, unless a Providence helped him by first letting him experience constantly, in special conflicts, what Christianity is in a formal sense? And such a man still does not see that this really is Christianity, but on the contrary he thinks that this is something quite unusual – and then he is brought to see that it is indeed Christianity, true Christianity. And of course it is true that this has become something quite unusual, especially in Protestantism, especially in Denmark.

XI¹A 226

As wrong as possible

. . . But the natural man, animal man, shudders at the thought of becoming a single person even more, if possible, than at death (especially if there might be a hope – how ironical! – of dying *en masse*). But Christianity stands immovable, more immovable than the pole star, on its principle that the first condition of salvation is to become a single person.

To that extent one would be justified, from a Christian standpoint, in rejecting or scrapping practically the entire eighteen hundred years of Christendom as tending towards illusion rather than Christianity.

The mass will regard this as terrible arrogance; this helps neither me nor the mass, for Christianity does not change. God's sovereignty rests with eternally immovable firmness on this point, that everything that has to do with the mass is *eo ipso* perdition. And he maintains this immovably just because all human power lies in the mass. The mass can destroy every human sovereignty – but not God's sovereignty. The mass – and it has constantly happened – can persecute, maltreat and slay the instruments God uses to express his sovereignty – but his sovereignty remains eternally unchanged, resting upon this point, that everything that has to do with the mass is *eo ipso* perdition. And while no human power has been able to hold off cholera, eternity is able, and with infinite ease, to hold off the mass, eternity by merely being itself *eo ipso* holds off all that is called the mass.

This is the natural law of eternity, which no more permits

itself to be changed than does the natural law of time: if you want to prosper in this world, have profit and good days and earthly rewards, then you must work with the mass, for here the good things are to be found. So it is true, as the animals also believe, that to be in a herd is good. And because those who preach Christianity want to have earthly advantages, they have falsely worked with the mass.

But if anyone supposes that in the end there will be such an immense mass, of trillions and billions and millions, that eternity will tire of resistance, so that the mass will push through – my friend, you are mistaken. For eternity numbers are infinitely unimportant, or rather, numbers simply do not exist for eternity. With eternity everything is reversed: the greater the number the easier, if I may say so, it is to scrap them. It is very hard for eternity to scrap a single person. The very fact that he is a single person (alas, outside the mass, as would be said) makes him the object of the eternal solicitude, which has such an infinite longing to save him and such an infinite reluctance to rebuff him. But as soon as it is a question of 10,000 trillions and billions eternity blows them away more easily than the wind blows the pollen.

. . . When the people rise *en masse* against the sovereign, then the bodyguard cannot help, the sovereign is in the power of the mass. God is better guarded, he cannot be seized in this way. As soon as the mass appears, God is invisible: the mass – the omnipotent mass – can, if it pleases, batter its nose against the entrance door. But it will get no farther, for God only exists for the single person – this is his sovereignty. It is not as with human majesty, whom the adjutant approaches with the words, Your Majesty must really show himself on the balcony, there must now be 20,000 people in the street. No, when there is a crowd of 20,000 *en masse*, God does not show himself at all. When there is only the single person, yes, then the divine majesty, divine also in this, is so lifted up above all forms that there is no need even for an angel to announce this single person; no, the majesty – infinite love! – appears straightaway: for he exists for the single person . . .

XI¹ A 227

The 'priest'

It is not without its deeper significance that the 'priest' or minister goes about in women's clothes (+).

For the minister's characteristic fault tends in general to that of the woman, namely, cunning, subtlety and lies. Yes, just as one may say that a woman's element – though of her it has a more innocent meaning – is lies, and wherever a woman is concerned there is also a little lying, so also with the official clergy.

Further, characteristic of the clergy are a fainting and swooning, a coquettish element which does not want and yet wants infinitely. This is specially true of high-ranking prelates. Not long ago I read of one who had become an archbishop somewhere in Germany. In his inaugural speech of course he had to say that he had prayed God that this cup (namely to be archbishop) might be taken from him, but alas! in vain. That is just like a woman, who can be eager enough for the bridal bed and yet she swoons and will not – which the bridegroom would certainly misunderstand if he took it seriously. Only one must remember that the woman is innocent, it lies in her natural disposition, and therefore it would be a mean trick to be ironical with her. With the prelate it is another matter. But the reason for the analogy between him and the feminine is that there is an analogy with the synthesis, which is to be found in the sexual relation, of sin and desire. For the prelate is very well aware that from one side all this business of high-ranking worldly clergy is from the Christian standpoint sin – and yet he desires it. This is expressed in his official swooning. By swooning he satisfies in a way the Christian indignation at this worldly grandeur, just as the woman's moral sense, her modesty, is satisfied by her resistance. But as I say, with the woman the matter is always somewhat different from the coquettishness of the prelate. *XI¹ A 228*

[*In the margin*] (+) When I speak in this way of the priest or minister, it is of course with the reservation that there can always be as many upright men in this profession as in any

other. The fact is that they enter it *bona fide* and continue in
it *bona fide*. But the fault is that taking such a step should not
enter the mind *bona fide* in this way.

If the business of long clothes did not at once awaken the
idea of the Pharisee, the official clergy and all the ambiguity
(and it is precisely this ambiguity which produces the analogy
with women) which is attached to them, one would be disposed to see in the long clothes a symbol of a neuter sex,
tending, that is, to the androgynous.   *XI¹A 229*

A public personality

In other places in this journal I have shown that the general
view of the daily press is by no means to the point. The
general view is as follows: Title: the Daily Press is a Good
Thing; Sub-title: Sometimes harm is done when it is abused
and publishes lies, evil reports, and so on. But my point is
that the daily press especially in small matters is an evil
simply because of the power of diffusion, which is a quite
disproportionate means of communication for small matters.
It is thus a kind of madness which tends to turn the whole
community into a madhouse, just as laying a railway-line
criss-cross over a piece of land a mile wide would be a kind of
madness, and so far from benefitting would in fact confuse
everything. No, diffusion in and for itself is an evil. An example
I took was that if the daily newspapers were used to say of a
certain girl by name that she had got a new light-blue dress
(which was quite true) then this would be an attack on the
girl which would perhaps cost her life or her understanding.
Only few people are able to bear the immense celebrity which
follows such a broadcasting as the newspapers can ensure,
least of all when used in this way. Such a spreading of the
news would kill the girl. And even the most hardened man will
need almost gigantic powers to be able to hold out for long
when the newspapers are used against him in this way in
regard to small-scale matters. So diffusion is in and for itself
the evil . . .   *XI¹A 232*

The weaker sex

makes use of lamentations and cries and the like, and by their help the woman suffers perhaps much less than the silent and reserved man.

To this extent one might be tempted to say that woman is the stronger sex; for if it is strength to defend oneself against suffering, then the woman defends herself much better than the man.

But the truth is that strength lies in the power to accept, assume, and bear suffering; and weakness lies in defending oneself by every possible means against suffering. A woman's weakness is that she immediately has prayers and tears and sighs to defend herself against suffering, her weakness is precisely that by means of lamentations and cries she alleviates the suffering. A man's strength is that he does not possess any means for warding off or alleviating suffering, so that in virtue of his strength – and this is a paradox – he comes to suffer more than the weaker sex. This is paradoxical, but no more paradoxical than the equally true fact that health is a pre-requisite of falling sick; there are sickly people who are not healthy enough to be able to fall sick. *XI¹A 233*

. . . If I were a father and had a daughter who was seduced, I should by no means give her up; but if I had a son who became a journalist I should regard him as lost. *XI¹A 235*

Grandiose retaliation

The words, 'See, what a man' [John 19. 5],[1] are really mankind's judgement upon itself, by which it expresses the fact that it is prostituted.

And remarkably enough, as in the Passion story there are several expressions, with different nuances, for the abominable, revolting, cruel and inhuman thing which was here perpe-

---

[1] I give a literal version of the Danish, as the usual English, 'Behold the man', cannot support Kierkegaard's interpretation. RGS

trated, if these words, 'See what, a man', were not there, then there would be lacking the expression of the fact that mankind, besides everything else, was also guilty of prostituting itself.

The God-Man never lost patience, he never reversed the relation by saying, 'I am in no way related to you'; no, he persisted in affirming that he was related to them.

But mankind could not control itself, and declared, 'You are not related to us, see, what a man.' The God-Man wants to show what it means to be a man, he wants to educate man to a relationship with God. But mankind thinks it knows better, and declared that it is not related to him.

This is mankind's prostitution: this is the moment when it sinks below the human level and is nothing but an animal. A humorist would say that poetic justice demanded that in memory of this event man should be decorated with a tail, and that this tail should stand out perpendicularly from the body so that no tailor's art could conceal it, and be of such a kind that it could not be cut off, having the natural peculiarity that if it were cut, it would immediately grow again.

XI¹A 236

Augustine

Augustine has done incalculable harm. The whole of Christian doctrine through the centuries really rests upon him – and he has confused the concept of faith.

Quite simply, Augustine resuscitated the platonic-aristotelian definition, the whole Greek philosophical pagan definition of faith . . .

For the Greeks faith is a concept which belongs to the sphere of the intellect (especially in Plato's *Republic*, where the whole thing is magnificently done; Aristotle's *Rhetoric* also deserves attention). So faith is related to the probable, and we have the ascending scale of faith and knowledge.

From the Christian point of view faith belongs to the existential: God did not appear in the character of a professor who has some doctrines which must first be believed and then understood.

No, faith belongs to and has its home in the existential, and in all eternity it has nothing to do with knowledge as a comparative or a superlative.

Faith expresses a relation from personality to personality.

Personality is not a sum of doctrines, nor is it something directly accessible. Personality is bent in on itself, it is a *clausum* [something closed], an *aduton* [innermost shrine], a *musterion* [mystery]. Personality is that which is within, hence the word *persona* (*personare*) is significant, it is that which is within to which a man, himself in turn a personality, may be related in faith. Between person and person no other relation is possible. Take the two most passionate lovers who have ever lived, and even if they are, as is said, one soul in two bodies, this can never come to anything more than that the one believes that the other loves him or her.

In this purely personal relation between God as personal being and the believer as personal being, in *existence*, is to be found the concept of faith.

[*In the margin*: Hence the apostolic formula, 'the *obedience* of faith' (e.g. Romans 1. 5), so that faith tends to the will and personality, not to intellectuality.]

But even in Augustine's time Christianity enjoyed far too much tranquillity, it had time for theological learning to present its presumptuous and self-important misunderstandings – and so we have pagan philosophy, and that is supposed to be Christian progress!

Nor is it true, as is often said, that Augustine was a thinker 'who shirked no logical conclusion'.

As an example we are told that as a consequence of accepting the necessity of baptism for eternal salvation he accepted the eternal damnation of infants.

But wait a moment, look more closely. Augustine says, they go to hell, but to the mildest hell. Good God, and this is supposed to be a thinker, a logical thinker in the eminent sense, who uses such nonsensical categories as the *mildest* hell! This is sheer rubbish, and rather is the proof that Augustine was no thinker at all, at least not in the Greek or Socratic sense.

It is just this nonsensical category that has infatuated the mediocre, and which is expressly made for them, to be admired by them. *XI¹A 237*

The best of worlds

Everyone who has a little experience knows at heart that this is a rotten world. But just as it is the done thing in a prison to keep a stiff upper lip, as it is also regarded as the cleverest thing to do, and to pretend that one is having a good time, and as it is in consequence the custom in prisons to tease and torment the man who lets it be seen that he is suffering, so with the whole world or with mankind in the world. In general, anyone who wants to understand human life as a whole would do best to study the criminal world – this is the really reliable analogy. *XI¹A 243*

Christianity

Do a thousand women disguised as men make a thousand men? So the whole of Christendom is a disguise – but Christianity simply does not exist. *XI¹A 245*

Man's religion

The New Testament consists of the demand to dare as a single person to have to do with God. We men reply, Let us unite to worship God; the more we are the happier, the truer, and the more we shall please God.

O fools and knaves – for you are both!

For as Christianity puts it – as a single person to have to do with God – that is indeed a venture, which needs the courage of despair, and the greatest of all efforts.

But if we hold together (let us hold together) and unite to worship God, note well how every one of these united thousands constantly interposes between God and himself the intermediary categories of the others, the people, mankind – aha! in this way both the venture and the effort have been avoided . . .

But God's self-assertion, if I may dare to call it this, demands that he keep an eye on every human effort towards becoming the mass, the many, and the like. For God is the being for whom to be is to be the idea. Man is the being for whom numbers are the way to become a power. And that is why God set Babel in confusion, and why he is always suspicious of associations.

When men say, Let us hold together in order to unite in worshipping God, then the cunning content of this (perhaps not conscious but natural and instinctive) is, Let us rebel against God, let us see that we are strong in the face of God. Oh, man is instinctively a cunning knave – and he has an *angst* before God which results in a proper display of human virtuosity.

In Christianity God has entered into a relation with men of the highest possible standard: it has been made possible for the single person to be related to God.

Precisely in this immense concession is to be found God's self-assertion, in that he says, I will only have to do with the single person.

He wishes to have to do with the single person, with each one. This is immensely more than all paganism and judaism, where God always permits the single person to have to do with him only by means of an abstraction.

And so we live (with the help of deep, unfathomably deep thinkers like Hegel and not less unfathomably deep seers like Grundtvig) in Christendom (for example, also here in Denmark) in such a way that nationality and state and the single person's relation through them to the idea or to God is supposed to be higher than New Testament Christianity. You asses! *XI¹A 248*

That this world is a vale of tears, a prison, a penitentiary

There are certain kinds of indirect proofs which I value almost higher than the direct proofs.

For instance, how does it come about that suicide is always described in such terms as 'breaking out' – an expression that is used of breaking out of a prison or a penitentiary?

Or in the 6,000 years of the world has there ever been, among all the happy people, a single one so happy that in face of a suicide he has found it natural to say, The man must have been mad to kill himself and so make it impossible for him to enjoy any longer the indescribable joy of living in this splendid world? *XI¹ A 254*

My relation to our women

As I am regarded as a kind of religious functionary, I cannot avoid having some relation to women, who themselves have such an essential relation to religion.

In this respect I consider my situation from a religious point of view to be eminently desirable, in that I am preserved, as perhaps a man seldom has been, from the fatal misunderstandings that come from being in love.

The general impression women have of me is that he knows us, he knows all, he is very clever, he cannot be fooled, yet in a certain sense he is very devoted and well-meaning towards us – and so we take him in this way.

On the other hand I doubt very much whether it could occur to a single woman to set her cap at me, to set a trap for me. And why not? Is it because she regards me as such a model of virtue? No; but note well that to be regarded as a model of virtue is by no means a safeguard against feminine pursuit. And even if the persecuted model of virtue really was the virtuous man on whom all feminine seduction was wrecked, a woman is not so much afraid of being humiliated by virtue, humiliated by having tried to tempt; no: however humiliated she may be, she does not really feel that her being has been annihilated, for she, her power, are acknowledged to be something, perhaps a great deal, since the virtuous man's virtue shows its greatness by its resistance to the temptation.

On the contrary, what a woman is most afraid of, where she feels that her being and her power are annihilated, is when she has risked the utmost in seduction, and it ends with the laughter of her opponent.

And strangely enough, wherever they get it from – presumably from instinct – women seem to suspect that so far as I am concerned, just when they make the greatest efforts I would burst out laughing – and no woman will risk this at any price.

Alas, there is some truth in this, that it could end with my bursting out laughing. But the reason is neither my great virtue nor my great spirituality but – my melancholy.

XI¹ A 256

That Christianity does not exist, since there are no Christians –
this is how Christianity has been abolished

To have to hold fast to the fact that one is saved as a single person, in opposition to a whole world which is eternally lost, in opposition to one's own people, in opposition to all – this is such an immense tension that only the most terrible fear and trembling and the most frightful shocks of passion can keep a man at this point. – From another angle there is at the same time something immensely aristocratic in being the single person to this degree.

In Christendom there soon follows a slackening of the tension. The individual cannot hold out at this pitch. He wants a certainty which is without this frightful tension – and here is the source of the mistaken faith in an election of grace, that is, an election by grace which saves you, the single person, without any talk of tension or effort.

Further, the individual cannot hold fast to his aristocratic view in face of the others, it would also be dangerous – and here again we have the mistaken use of grace, by which the accusation of being aristocratic is avoided. For it is said that it is of grace, I cannot do a thing about it myself (for if he could do something about it, if it depended on his own effort, mediocrity would not put up with this aristocratic claim).

Finally, the individual feels to some extent the need to be free of this tension which arises from being the only one who is saved, the single person who is saved. It is much more pleasant and much more reassuring to the senses when there are many who are saved, it is much more reassuring to see oneself surrounded by one's companions in salvation, than to endure this tension and contrast with the others who are lost. And so the contrast gradually disappears, and pretty well all of us are saved.

So in the end mediocrity rises up as one man: it is of grace, solely of grace – and so we are all saved. And now life is pleasant and worth living.

So Christianity begins with one being saved, perhaps only one among millions, one in the whole world. And now we are all saved, all of us, perhaps including our cats and dogs – and this is the same teaching as you find in the New Testament, this is Christianity!   *XI¹ A 260*

The monastery

therefore went; instead of the monastery's unreasonable religion there came the true Christian religion, for we Protestants do not flee from life like cowards, any more than Christ did: no, we remain – just like Christ! – in the world – lost in a completely profane worldliness, worse than paganism.

Great, truly Christian progress! The truth is that worldliness won such a complete victory that it could no longer endure that the life of the monastery should recall the heterogeneity of Christianity.

We remain – like Christ! – in the world. Oh what a superb theme for lying and hypocritical rhetoricians! If great exploits

are themes for speakers in general, this ambiguity and falsehood is for hypocritical rhetoricians.   *XI¹A 263*

More knavery

. . . The idea of a *providentia specialissima* is Christian, but by
means of this idea subtleties enter in.

In the New Testament the situation is different. It is the
Christian who is accepted as the object of this *providentia
specialissima*. But the New Testament understands by a
Christian someone who has freely broken with all that is
called happiness in this world, who has thrown himself into
all sufferings both as victim and as sacrifice – and so he receives
the promise that he is the object of a particular care, so that
not a hair of his head is hurt without God's will.

But here as everywhere Christianity is handled with the
utmost arbitrariness. That which seems able to appeal to our
self-indulgence is selected, what does not please is discarded,
and so we concoct a knavish religiosity which purports to be
Christianity.   *XI¹A 267*

God's instruments

Just because it is, if I may dare to say, God's passionate
desire to show men their nothingness, he always deliberately
chooses his instruments with that in view. But that again is
precisely why it is such an immense strain for the – in one
sense poor – man who is to be the instrument.

To put an end to a world culture culminating in the utmost
refinement a simple man of the people is used; this, if I may
dare to say, satisfies God's passionate desire to make omnipotent use of a grain of sand in order to overturn the world.
Here we see the divine passion, in the most decided hatred of
all that in the least resembles human probability and calculation. Oh, and that is why it is also such a fearful strain to be
his instrument.

God's passion is to be found in the absurd; where this sign is to be seen, there God is present; it is as though one heard his voice there, in a sense more terrible than in the thunder, for the distance of the absurd is greater. It is as though one heard his voice there, saying to men, See, you scoundrels, see, I am here, see, the absurd! A simple man of the people, who has learned nothing, nothing at all, to overturn the culture of a world. Do you not notice, you scoundrels, that I am present, I the almighty, do you not see the absurd? A thin-legged, slender, sickly poor man, almost as frail in body as a child, such a figure as every animal man finds almost ridiculous as a man – he is used for efforts which giants would sink under. Notice this, you scoundrels, that I am present, I the almighty; do you not see the absurd? A single man, good God, what is a single man over against the many? And yet a single man is used, only a single man is used to break the many, the millions. Mark that, you scoundrels, that I am present, I the almighty: do you not see the absurd?

But as I say, that is why it is such a fearful strain for the in a sense poor man who is to be the instrument. *XI¹A 268*

The apostle Peter

Men speak disparagingly of his denial and then they exalt his later life.

But there is one point to which not enough attention is paid, that one look was enough for him to repent [Luke 22. 61]. Among the millions of men scarcely one could be found for whom under these circumstances one look would be enough. As men are now, each one would presumably have considered himself specially fortunate and would have been well satisfied to have left the Master in the lurch, and so far as he received a look would have felt quite self-satisfied, and thought, I am so clever that I pretended I noticed nothing.

XI¹A 274

To love God

No one has loved God in the Christian sense who has not sufficiently experienced both pain and repugnance at the bestial nature of men. To love God in the Christian sense is not on the same level as loving men: but the two relations are opposed.

But care is needed to understand this. In every generation there appear, if I may put it thus, a perhaps not negligible number of men who in their pride and arrogance despise men and love God; but no, this is not how the matter is to be understood.

It is to be understood quite differently. The beginning is, simply that you have loved men with profound sympathy disinterestedly, with true love.

Ah, if it were not true, as it only too surely is, that men are asses, so that love is rewarded by bestial treatment – if it were not so, then I should be tempted to suppose that the situation would be quite different. God in heaven would take note of such a man just because of his love to men, and as with the rich young man in the Gospel, he would love him [Mark 10. 21]. And then God would say to himself, 'I could wish that this man would love me, he pleases me. So there is nothing to be done but to let his relation to men be embittered, through their rewarding him with bestial treatment. For I cannot be loved in straightforward harmony with human love.'

This is how we are to understand pain and repugnance at the bestial nature of men. But this does not at all mean that we cease to love them. No, but the opposition is there in order to make the relation to God recognizable negatively.

So it is not possible to love God in the Christian sense, and be happy in this world. No, the God of Christianity is in opposition to this world, so that he who loves God in the Christian sense cannot be happy in this world.   *XI¹A 279*

The idea

In this world of time and sense and also (as Christianity teaches) of sin the idea can only exist in suffering.

Only once has the idea existed absolutely, in Christ: therefore his life was unconditioned and absolute suffering.

XI¹ A 280

Woman

In the Bible it is the woman (Eve) who seduces the man [Genesis 3. 6].

In return, or in compensation, there is the fact that a woman's love is by no means partial to the idea that the man she loves should be a paragon of virtue and perfection. On the contrary, there is not a single young woman whose love does not desire that her beloved should have gone a bit astray, and that the meaning of his relation to her should be that she saves him (in contrast to the Bible, where she seduces him). (+) Indeed woman is a loving egoist, but innocent: she knows nothing of this herself. Nevertheless it is egoistic to wish that the beloved should have gone astray in order that by her love she should save him.

For the rest, it cannot be denied that things are often as she wishes, that a man is saved from earlier dissipation by a woman's love, and by loving a woman.

Nevertheless, in a different and higher sense the Bible is right, in a Christian sense. Perhaps she does save a man here and there from excesses, and make a decent man of him, but she corrupts all men who marry by reducing them to finitude and mediocrity.

When the passions of a lad or a young man run wild, there are two powers attentive to save him: a loving woman, and God in heaven. If he is saved by the woman he is reduced to finitude. But if he is not saved by a woman's love, if he does not come to port here, but if he is nevertheless saved, then it is by God, and his existence will have significance. *XI¹ A 291*

[*In the margin*] (+) It is a similar bouleversement of the Bible when it is said in ordinary life that the man seduces the woman. This is not true either, but it is rather an expression of the woman's cunning: her seduction is so cunning that a decent chap always seems to be the seducer. *XI'A 282*

Existence without predications

Jehovah says, 'I am that I am.' [Exodus 3. 14] I am: this is the highest existence.

But to be in this way is much too high for us men, much too serious. So we have to try to become something: to be something is easier.

Full of tricks as everything human is, we express the matter thus: seriousness means to be something.

Most men, indeed almost every man, would die of fear of themselves if their existence were a tautology. They are more afraid of being in this way, and by themselves, than of seeing themselves. So the matter is softened, and made easier, for example, when a man can say of himself, 'I am a privy councillor, a knight, a member of a military commission, a town councillor, chairman of the club committee.' In a deeper sense all this is nothing but distraction. And yet, as I say, perhaps men are not in a position to endure true seriousness. What I am against is the deceit involved in making this distraction into something serious. Yet perhaps I am wrong here too, for in general men could probably not endure life if they were not allowed to imagine that this is the serious side of it. They would probably die of fear of life and of themselves if they should once grasp that their seriousness is mere distraction, even if no one wanted to deprive them of their distraction.

But it is certain that all these many predicates really are distractions, which prevent a man from having the deepest impression of what it means to be. And how infinitely far men are from being able to endure the real impression of seriousness can be best seen from the fact this life of predicates has been turned into Christianity. The men of our time are so little able to endure the seriousness of life that they must even get permission to imagine that distraction is Christianity.

XI¹A 284

My God, my God, why hast thou forsaken me?

[Matthew 27. 46]

These words indicate that the Model is not Stoicism, stoic self-satisfaction, but that he must and will hold out longer, to the point where the Stoic gives up (in suicide) because he merely wants to have an idea of himself, and when he can no longer have this he prefers to kill himself, if possible to annihilate his life.

These words are a consolation to disciples. For was there ever a martyr who in the moments of greatest torment, or in a weak moment, was not on the verge of losing his idea of himself, as though he were forsaken by God? Then his life seems to him to be infinite despair: he is lost for this life, he has himself turned it into a torment – and as for a better world, this must seem an even greater torment to him, to have to live a whole eternity and have the feeling, be persecuted by the memory, that he has lost his idea of himself.

This then is how the Model consoles us, by showing that this suffering is part of the following.

In a certain sense we may say that to feel oneself forsaken by God is part of the complete emptying of the human element in face of God, and that being a martyr is not a matter of human self-satisfaction.

But if this is so, then there is nothing depressing in being reminded that one has endured this human suffering of feeling oneself forsaken by God, of losing one's idea of oneself. For precisely this ultimate suffering restores in an eminent degree the idea of oneself.

XI¹A 285

111

This is a fine world!

Imagine a prison, with all the prisoners gathered together –
and a man steps forward and addresses them thus: 'My right
honourable gentlemen, I request the favour of this respectable
assembly's attention and lenient judgement' and so on, then
is it not true that all the prisoners would burst out laughing
and regard the man as mad for calling them a respectable
assembly?

The ludicrous element lies in the contradiction between
prisoners and 'this respectable assembly'.

So they laugh at the ludicrous side of it, and they will have
their fun with this speaker; but they will not think of anything
else.

And why not? Because as prisoners they are surrounded
by a much more numerous world which possesses the power to
tell them, You are thieves, etc.

But now imagine this gathering of prisoners as a world for
itself, where there was therefore no world round about it
which enforced upon them the truth that they were thieves –
imagine this gathering of prisoners as a world for itself: do
you believe that they would still burst out laughing if someone
stepped forward and addressed them and used the words 'this
honourable assembly'? No, not in the least. On the contrary,
they would understand it thus: it is quite true, we are the
world, so we have power to impose the idea that we are fine,
respectable, virtuous men. How should it occur to us to
laugh when we are called honourable? No, this is just what we
want: to describe us in this way shows that the speaker himself
is a serious and honourable man, and to speak in any other way
would be ridiculous and foolish.

So also with the world: if this world were surrounded by
another world, if it were a little world within a world which
compelled us by overwhelming power to see the truth about
what we are, namely, rogues, then we would all laugh every
time a man stepped forward and addressed us as this honourable assembly and so on. But this world is itself the overwhelming power, and that is why we are not mad enough

to laugh; no, we have it in our power to impose the view that we are a fine world. *XI¹A 286*

Criterion of distance

This may pretty well be regarded as a Christian reflection without any addition of human folly, nonsense or knavery:

A man is born in sin, he enters this world by means of a crime, his existence is a crime – and procreation is the fall.

When this comes by way of a crime, a sin, then it is not difficult to guess where one arrives when one is born – one enters a prison, this world is a prison.

And the punishment – and as always the punishment fits the sin – the punishment is to exist. Since to exist by way of procreation is what is displeasing to God, the punishment is just this: all right, you will get tired of this enjoyment; you will become so sick and weary of this life, that you will thank your God that some time through death you may get out of it.

To this extent from a Christian standpoint death is not a punishment, on the contrary it is God's pity for these unhappy creatures that leads him to put an end to their existence. On another level death can be regarded as a painful catastrophe, as belonging to punishment, the punishment which the child suffers on account of his parents' guilt.

Make use of this to measure the distance it is from what we call Christianity, this sheer pagan sensuality, where the reproduction of the race poses as life's seriousness, where it is the supreme benefaction to endow a child with life, and so on and so on. *XI¹A 289*

Suicide

Just because, from a Christian standpoint, this life is a suffering of punishment, and because Christianity in its turn promises (when the last suffering, death, has been endured)

H   113

a blessed, eternally blessed life, it is displeasing to God when someone wilfully breaks out of this life.

It is of course lies and nonsense, mere trickery invented by the prison to encourage one another in the idea that this is a fine world, to assert that this life is a great good, and that suicide is therefore to be censured as ingratitude.

No, but just because this life is suffering, and just because it expects an eternal blessedness, if one patiently endures, Providence is against suicide.

It is as when children on Christmas Eve have to wait in the dark room – just because their parents know how much effort and trouble have been taken to make the joy great, and that time is required for this end: that is why impatience is displeasing in this situation.   *XI¹A 292*

The future

It will cost fearful struggles if Christianity is to be reintroduced.

For Christianity is not merely related to the human in such a way that it is that which does not issue from the heart of any man [I Corinthians 2. 9], in other words, that which is strange. But its terrible divine sharp-sightedness is as though intended to exasperate and embitter man in the most frightful manner – unless he can humble himself. For Christianity is the sovereignty of God.

Oh, and Christendom is pampered with the nonsense that the Christian God is a decent and harmless chap, a good fellow, and especially a friend of female busyness and of the begetting of children!   *XI¹A 293*

Christianity – celibacy

According to Christianity the world is a world of sin, the consequence of a fall.

Christianity is salvation but at the same time it is a stopping, it aims at stopping the whole continuation which leads to the permanence of this world.

And that is why Christianity holds by celibacy. By this the Christian gives characteristic expression to his relationship to this world, which is one of stopping. And that is why the New Testament too continually uses such words concerning the Christian as indicate this putting a stop to things: for example, to be salt, to be sacrificed, etc.

Yet it was not long before marriage was in full swing among the Christians – and this is where the confusing element enters in, that what is being fought against in the van is being encouraged in the rear. With marriage the Christian immediately has a different relation to the world than that of being a stranger and outcast, or salt, or being sacrificed, or putting a stop to things.

If anyone says that he is getting married in order to have children who may be brought up from their childhood in Christianity, in order to make true Christians for God, then I will answer, Nonsense! The fact is you feel the desire to beget children. But as for this method of creating true Christians, it is certain that if there is any man for whom it is almost impossible to become a Christian, then it is that man who was brought up in Christianity from his childhood. There is nothing more opposed to Christianity than that it should be anticipated in this way and so become just nonsense. *XI¹A 295*

For orientation in Christian problems

So soon as the question is raised whether a man's eternal blessedness is commensurable with a decision in time in relation to a historical factor which has entered into time, there immediately arises the horror of the torments of sympathy: when one thinks, namely, of the countless millions who will not be eternally blessed.

If one thinks, concerning the countless millions who lived before the historical events, and again of the countless millions who have lived afterwards, but in complete ignorance of the existence of the historical events – if one supposes that they could not well be eternally lost for this reason, and so finds a sympathetic relief, yet the matter remains painful in relation to the millions who have lived afterwards, and it is painful for each single person in relation to the countless numbers who are contemporary with him, and for whom this historical event is proclaimed, but who are not decisively impressed by it.

The more precisely one defines the conditions of salvation, the fewer there are of whom one can believe that they will be saved. But for sympathy it is a torment to be saved in contrast to others.

So I have reached the following view: the conditions of salvation are different for every person, for every single man. There is a general proclamation of Christianity, but in regard to the conditions of salvation every single person must be related as a single person to God.

This view undoubtedly alleviates the sympathetic pain. What therefore is so infinitely decisive for me that it is connected for me with the conditions of salvation, I understand as being only for me. The conditions of salvation are different for every single person.

Yet this alleviation of sympathy (which enables me to make an effort without having to be anxious about the fate of others) has also something sad about it. It implies that one man simply cannot help another, he can neither reassure another, in the deeper sense, nor can he find reassurance with him.

I must accept this state of things. But how am I to understand it? I understand it both as progress and as punishment, a judgement on Christendom.

What did men want? They wanted to cast off all authority. Very well: then there is the punishment; and as always the punishment fits the sin. You shall be free! And then when you lie on your death-bed, perhaps in despair, and you would give everything for a man who had authority to reassure you – no, my friend, now it is too late, you did not want to have authority, and therefore there is none.

This then is the punishment; but at the same time one can easily see that it is a progress: mankind is henceforth established in its right, every single person is commensurable with the highest.

And this formula, if I may dare to say it, will stand henceforth as a judgement both of Christendom and of progress.

Note. Compare the conclusion of my *Literary Report* of *Two Epochs.*[1]   *XI¹A 296*

Judaism – Christianity

In Judaism God is in a certain sense not so severe as in Christianity, he is not defined as spirit – therefore it is no more than a 'trial', and after some years you get your desire, and more.

In Christianity God is spirit – and therefore so immensely severe, from love: for he longs for spirit from man.

For the rest there is here a paradox, just as when Pascal says that in revelation God has become more obscure than before, the revealed God has become more incomprehensible than the God who was not revealed: so here God's love is harder than God's law.

But the difference between Judaism and Christianity lies in the different relation to eternity. In Judaism temporality is really without eternity, in Christianity everything is aimed at eternity – hence all the suffering of this life, no help in this life, no victory in this life.

But he who has been brought up from childhood in Christianity finds it impossible to believe that God can be so hard as he is in Christianity, the 'God of love' whom one knows so well from childhood days. Therefore he who has been brought up from childhood in Christianity finds it impossible to be more than a Jew.

God is never so severe with those he loves in the Old Testament as he is with the apostles, for example, whose life was

[1] See *Samlede Værker*[2] VIII, 114*ff.* cf. E. trans. *The Present Age* by A. Dru, Fontana ed. 90*ff.* RGS

117

sheer suffering and then a martyr's death. In the Old Testament it lasts only some years, or else God helps them secretly in some other way. But in Christianity you have really to suffer hunger and thirst and all manner of evil, then persecution and finally execution as a criminal – and in all this God is the God of love. In the Old Testament, when Daniel out of piety does not want to eat the prohibited food [Daniel 1. 8 *ff*.], God takes care that he thrives equally well on a different diet. In the Old Testament, when the prophet is in need, God always finds a way out – but as for the apostle, we have simply the prophecy [Matthew 10. 41] that he who gives him a cup of water for my sake, shall receive a prophet's reward. So there is no talk of unexpected help which shall bring him his strictest necessities; no, God just leaves him in the lurch, leaves him to die of hunger and thirst – it can be as severe as that. And yet it is the God of love, and what is more, it is done out of love. For everything here is reflected on to eternity. And the more tormented the life in time, the more blessed the life in eternity.

Alas, I shudder at such thoughts! I know only too well how my life has been botched through my having been brought up from earliest days in Christianity. What a distance between our life and that of an apostle! God is love. Consider that this was proclaimed by him who suffered more than any other in the world, by the saviour of the world. God is love, this was proclaimed by the apostles whose life was suffering from beginning to end, as the life of the righteous under the law never was. And yet early and late the apostles spoke only of a gospel they had to proclaim, a gospel, not the law.

So deny if you can that Christianity is a paradox.

XI¹A 299

1,800 years of Christianity

What if Providence thought as follows: I have now introduced Christianity – henceforth it is left to men. I shall send no one to represent it in the divine interest. I will see how far men can

get, and what will come of it. And God, who is infinitely concerned in love with a single person, and with every single
person, in another sense is majestically lavish with millions
and with centuries.

This would be an explanation of the fact that in the course
of these 1,800 years, since the time of the apostles, there has
been none who has really represented Christianity in God's
interest, hating human nature, hating himself, and in this hate
loving God, serving the absolute absolutely; whereas men of
great integrity are certainly to be found, but always serving
the interests of men.

This could be related to the words of Christ, When I come
again, shall I find faith on earth? [Luke 18. 8].

What if this were the thought of Providence – to use 1,800
years to see – and once the maximum of confusion was reached,
to intervene by once more sending individuals who in the
power of God would express Christianity in God's interest?

XI¹A 309

Celibacy

When the Pope in his time ordained that the clergy should be
unmarried the Christian point of view had already been long
lost, and a confusing accommodation or compromise with the
world had been introduced. For it is not that the priest
should be unmarried, but that the Christian should be unmarried. The distinction between priest and laity is unchristian, but this does not lead to the conclusion that the
priest should also be married.

For Christianity this is a sinful world, a child is conceived
in transgression and born in sin. Christianity aims at calling a
halt, at making satisfaction for the past, but not by beginning
afresh. As when someone pays another man's debts, he makes
one stipulation: that you don't begin to incur more debts –
so with being unmarried in relation to being a Christian.

But in Christianity married people are consecrated, and the
ceremony sanctifies this relation. How charming! So bandits

in the south sanctify murder by kneeling down beforehand at the altar.

With the ceremony married people sanctify their decision: splendid. At the foot of the altar, where the Saviour of the world hangs on his cross, he who by his death made satisfaction for the sin of the race, for original sin, and taught, Follow me, to follow is to be a Christian – there the lovers kneel and decide – they decide to continue original sin. Or if there were truth in the sanctifying of the sexual relation by this ceremony, then it would have to apply to the child who is born, that it is not conceived in transgression and born in sin.

'But Christ himself was present at a wedding.' Inimitable! Then he who was so strict about what it meant to be a disciple that (in order to prevent him from having to do with the world) he would not even let a man bury his father – he is supposed to think that being a disciple can easily be united with marrying and having children, that is, with being as thoroughly immersed in this existence as possible: and all this is proved from the fact that he was present at a wedding. Presumably in this way you also prove that true Christianity is a banquet, and you prove this from the fact that Christ was present at a banquet; or you prove that being a Christian is the same as being a swindler, since Christ was surrounded by publicans and sinners.

'But the apostle permits marriage.' Yes, he permits it, and from this you see that he is infinitely distant from the view of marriage which flourishes especially in Protestantism, especially in Denmark. He permits it; and if you are honest you will not be able to deny that the apostle does so in a rather grudging spirit, he would prefer not to give way, he says, 'For it is better to marry than to be aflame with passion' [I Corinthians 7. 9]. That is, if the worst comes to the worst, then better marriage than being aflame with passion.

But we are happy with the religion which consists in having children. . . .

The only reliable views of what Christianity is are to be found partly (and chiefly) in what Christ and the apostles proclaim, and partly in the contemporary judgement of

Judaism and paganism. But this is unanimous in saying that Christianity is hatred of men. And it is the same in the New Testament. Christ expresses in his life that loving God means hating men. Hating men? He who was sheer love of men? Yes, certainly, from the beginning he understood, and held it fast to the end, that he was sacrificed for men, and so he was sheer love towards all that is suffering, forsaken, rejected, and so on; though not in the sense of helping them temporally with money, power, etc. The kind of love of men which we men describe as such, which consists in helping men to enjoy this life – this was quite alien to him. He knew only too well that Christianity makes men unhappy in this life, for to love God means to be willing to suffer.

So one can understand his troubled discourse to the apostles that they should not be offended with him. Likewise one can understand that what he prophesied to them was inevitable – that they should be maltreated, cursed, persecuted, slain. For in truth to have to say that loving God means hating men, or loving them in a way that human egoism never cares to be loved, and that it must be rewarded as it is rewarded, is easy to understand.

But we have this huge lie of Christendom, under the pretext of loving man, turning Christianity right round; and the truth of our way of living is that we love ourselves – and hate God. That is what is called Christianity nowadays. Naturally we take care not to say it, for we even reckon on making God think in the end that this is Christianity.   *XI¹A 313*

Socrates – Christianity

Socrates is right: when a man does not do the right, this is because he does not understand it. If he understood it, he would do it: ergo, sin is ignorance.

Christianity is right: sin is guilt. For when a man does not do the right, it is quite true it is because he does not understand it, for if he understood it, etc. But the reason why he does not understand the right is that he cannot understand it, and he cannot understand it because he does not wish to understand it. And this is the point.

And it is only by treating everything as criminal that Christianity has come to dominate the world and to maintain justice.   *XI¹A 318*

Homogeneity – heterogeneity

The contemporary world is continually trying to level everything down, to tyrannize over it and transform it into homogeneity, so that everyone may become just a number or a copy.

History on the other hand is interested only in what has maintained its heterogeneity in its own time, without of course simply regarding every heterogeneity as the truth.

The contemporary world presumably thinks that making everything homogeneous is to ennoble it and give it form. The truth is it uses individuals up, it wastes them. (+)
XI¹A 319

[*In the margin*] (+) When the individual has become entirely homogeneous with the contemporary world, and assimilated, as one says of digesting food, then his time has eaten him, he is as lost, wasted: the time, the contemporary world, tends to transform everything into waste (like hydrogen).   *XI¹A 320*

Christianity

Take one-tenth of Christian 'essence', and use it as an ingredient in man's own discovery, and you will learn (what thousands and thousands of lying professors and parsons already know) that this kind of 'Christianity' tastes so sweet, is so exquisitely, indescribably delicious that men do not know what to offer as recompense to the professor or the parson.

Take Christianity neat – and you will learn (what you, blessed martyrs and witnesses to the truth, already know) that even the most good-natured man seems to become mad, so madly embittered against this kind of Christianity that it is a matter of life and death.

Alas, God knows men! And since according to the New Testament to love God means to hate the world, God has carefully organized Christianity in such a way that it revolts equally the man who from the human standpoint may be called the most good-natured man, and the most defiant man. For God does not desire any direct transition from something human to being a Christian. According to Christianity man does not live in a splendid world which God loves – in this case there could be a direct transition from human good-naturedness and goodness to becoming Christian. No, according to Christianity every man is born in sin and lives in a sinful world which God hates, and to become a Christian is anything but a direct transition. From the Christian point of view so-called human good-naturedness and goodness are precisely as bad as defiance and the like. This is also to be seen as soon as Christianity is related in its truth to his human goodness and good-naturedness; for these are just as furious against Christianity as defiance and the like.   *XI¹A 324*

To be salt – to be the crowd – the judgement of eternity

As one lives in Protestantism one thinks that grace makes satisfaction; only one must live in such a way as to avoid civil punishment. So it is as though salvation was bound up with one condition, with circumstances connected with the existential. Perhaps it is admitted that public sinners are lost, in spite of their so-called faith and in spite of grace. But as soon as this is admitted, it is impossible to call a halt at civil justice, for if there is one set of circumstances, one condition connected with the existential, then civil righteousness is as little adequate as public sinners are. In this case we cannot call a halt before the circumstances and the condition demanded by the New Testament, namely, discipleship, asceticism leading to martyrdom. Either grace makes unconditioned satisfaction, saves us all, including public sinners as well as those who are not Christians at all – or we cannot halt till we reach what the New Testament defines as the condition, namely, renunciation and discipleship.

But it is easy to see that in this whole view of identifying being the crowd with being a Christian the judgement and accounting of eternity have been essentially abolished. It is supposed that we shall all be saved, that we are Christians from birth – and instead of the fearful effort of having to make use of this life for an eternal decision it is supposed that everything is already settled, and at most it is a question of whether out of gratitude we live a reasonably decent life, which in any case from the purely earthly and worldly point of view is the most prudent thing to do.

But as I say, as soon as there is one set of circumstances, one condition connected with the existential, which is decisive for our eternal salvation, then all talk about civil righteousness does not matter at all. Either grace is extended in a latitudinarian way *ad absurdum*, or one holds by the circumstances, the condition prescribed by the New Testament, namely, discipleship.

Here again we have the distinction between being salt and being the crowd. This is a qualitative difference: to confess a religion of which one desires both temporal and eternal profit, or to confess a religion for which one suffers.

But then there arises another difficulty: being in truth a Christian is so heterogeneous with being a man that in eternity they can never come to an understanding with one another. For there is an eternal qualitative difference between having been a man in this life in such a way as to let others be sacrificed for oneself, and having been a man in such a way as to be sacrificed for the others. It is therefore something that causes both laughter and tears, when one hears these purely worldly existences speaking of entering the blessedness promised to the Christian: they do not reflect that they will find themselves in the company of men whose life was and is qualitatively different from theirs. *XI¹A 325*

124

Human dishonesty

Often enough one hears complaints of the great dishonesty in business and ordinary life, etc.

But the sad thing is that there is nowhere such great dishonesty as in the most important sphere of all, that which concerns the soul's salvation, eternal blessedness, Christianity – and here even the most honest man is a little dishonest. And why is he so? How does it arise? It is because every man is afraid of eternity, of this immense power, and of having to do with it in all seriousness. And just because we are all afraid at this point, it is a kind of mutual human honesty that we should all hold together in being dishonest. *XI¹A 326*

The 'voluntary'

The voluntary is essentially for Christian reality the knot which can hold. But just because this knot has long ago been loosened, the thread of Christianity has been lost.

1. The voluntary, as everyone understands, is a thousand times harder than what comes from circumstances or external power, where without any responsibility one can use one's whole power simply to endure.

2. The voluntary really expresses the true fear and trembling and respect for the divine majesty – whereas obligatory poverty, for example, expresses nothing.

3. The voluntary produces the double conflict which is the sign of every Christian reality – to be hated, maligned, abhorred, to have to suffer through being willing to suffer. It would not occur to anyone to persecute someone who was living in poverty against his will; but there is no one so hated as he who freely gives up that in which men naturally live their life.

4. From a Christian standpoint only the man who is marked by the voluntary can be entrusted with a command. The man who lives in compulsory poverty or suffering, and so on, is far from being hard enough, he does not stand firmly enough;

his life shows that if he could only escape, then he certainly would much prefer it.

But is it not appalling beyond all measure that men have so reduced Christianity to their level that for generations decent and in other respect virtuous men, who are even noted among men for their Christianity, should assume in good faith that the voluntary is something childish, immature? What the heroes of mankind have shrunk under like worms, and yet have withstood, what another group of eminent men have despaired over – this is now assumed in good faith to be something childish to be smiled at. From the Christian standpoint is this not more frightful than if one lived in such a way that precisely the decent people assumed in good faith that to be honourable was childish?   *XI¹ A 327*

'Time' is the sophistical

16 August 1854

Can an eternal blessedness be decided in a moment of time? Can the eternal be decided in time? Philosophically, the question may properly be put to Christianity, and a negative answer given. Of course it does not follow that Christianity must abandon its position, for Christianity itself declares that it is against the understanding, that it is paradoxical; a conception which one does well to hold firm in face of all the mythological views of Christianity, that it is a mythology, which one must question to see whether they themselves do not betray a mythological view which itself claims to be against the understanding. In general, all objections to Christianity are in virtue of the understanding – but without understanding enough to halt at this sign where Christianity itself declares that it is against the understanding. The *summa summarum* of all objections is a ridiculous amount of trouble for nothing.

Philosophy, then, can deny that the eternal can be decided in time.

The popular view is that it is much too bold of philosophy to

deny the principle, and thus Christianity, with so little ceremony. It has been thought that seventy years are much too
few, and that many many more years would be required.

Here is where the sophistical nonsense begins.

If something eternal can be decided in time, then seventy
years or ten years or five minutes are equally enough, and
nothing is gained with 170,000 years – except an escape for the
man who cannot think.

If something eternal can be decided in time, then seventy
years are more than enough. Nor can the decision be made by
a man in his thirtieth year, say, ceremoniously saying to
himself, Now you have still forty years ahead of you, and you
have to use them for an eternal decision. No, it cannot be done
like this. Nor is it true, because existence (which knows well
enough what it wants) has arranged things in such a way that
nobody knows if he will live for another hour – and it is this
very disquiet which Christianity thinks is integral to bringing
about an eternal decision.

For an eternal decision in time is the most intensive
intensity, the most intensive leap.

But men continually look for an escape, they continually
turn for help to the sophistical in time. With the help of time,
in fact, by giving things time and by giving the impression
that the longer the time the nearer one is to an eternal decision,
men know very well that they are escaping from decision, and
that decision approaches just when one intensively denies
time – the shorter the time the nearer a possibility of an eternal
decision – and that is why death is such a help in relation to
an eternal decision, for here time is short . . .

Therefore when someone makes the popular and plausible
suggestion that seventy years are too short a time and that a
much longer period of years is necessary, one could answer
him with the words of Abraham to the rich man. 'They have
Moses and the prophets, they do not believe them, neither
will they believe if someone should rise from the dead' [Luke
16. 29–31]. Nothing is more certain. It is indeed possible that
one rising from the dead would give them a superstitious shock,
but that is not the same thing as believing. And so one must

also add that the man who thinks seventy years is not long enough, that the error lies here and not in himself, will certainly never come nearer to an eternal decision, not even if he lived 170,000 years.

This can also be seen from the way men live. Their so-called striving in the course of the years is nothing more or less than a continual regression. *XI¹A 329*

The human – the divine

Man is 'a social animal', and what he believes in is the power of union.

So man's thought is, 'Let us all unite' – if it were possible, all the kingdoms and countries of the earth, with this pyramid-shaped union always rising higher and higher supporting at its summit a super-king, whom one may suppose to be nearest to God, in fact so near to God that God cares about him and takes notice of him.

In Christian terms the true state of affairs is exactly the reverse of this. Such a super-king would be farthest from God, just as the whole pyramid enterprise is utterly repugnant to God.

What is despised and rejected by men, one poor rejected fellow, an outcast, this is what in Christian terms is chosen by God, is nearest to him.

He hates the whole business of pyramids. For as God is such infinite love that his father's eye easily sees how this human notion of pyramids can easily become cruel towards the unhappy and rejected and the like in the human race (whom therefore the God of love takes care of), so he is also too infinitely wise in his majesty not to see that if this idea of a pyramid received the least approval from him, as though it had some truth, just the tiniest bit of truth in it, that men with the help of the pyramid might get higher, come a little nearer to God, then they would not give up the thought of building the pyramid one day so high that they would think of being able to thrust God from his throne.

That is why God pushes at the pyramid till everything collapses. A generation later man begins with the pyramid again. *XI¹A 330*

The free-thinker – the Christian objection

The free-thinker says: If only there were no priests with their Christianity.

The Christian objection is: If only the priest was not there, with his Christianity – which makes Christianity impossible. (+)
XI¹A 332

[*In the margin*] (+) The free-thinker wants to be rid of the priests with the idea that he will then be rid of Christianity. You short-sighted man, with your superifical view! In truth the priests do not have such an intimate relation to Christianity. No, the Christian objection understands the matter better, it wants to be rid of the priests in order to have Christianity. *XI¹A 333*

'Father, forgive them, for they know not what they do'

[Luke 23. 34]

This does not contain the Socratic view that sin is ignorance.
XI¹A 334

Strength – weakness

When a girl's lover dies or is unfaithful to her, and she says it will be the death of her – and a year later is married; then men say, who would have believed that she would have been so strong.

The truth is that she was weak.

But the strength of the idea is regarded as weakness, and material strength as strength. It is called strength if a man

I   129

has strength to live entirely without ideas, it is called strength if a man is strong enough to make sure of profit everywhere, and so on.   *XI¹A 337*

The Christian thesis

is not *intelligere ut credam,* nor is it *credere ut intelligam.*

No, it is, Act according to the precepts and commandments of Christ, do the will of the Father – and you shall have faith.

Christianity does not lie in the least in the sphere of the intellect.   *XI¹A 339*

The Christian demand

Christianity continually aims at suffering for the sake of the doctrine, suffering at the hands of men.

If fasting and so on is the general practice (and therefore honoured by the judgement of men), it is simply not Christian in the stricter sense.

No, the characteristic Christian suffering is to suffer at the hands of men. This is connected with the fact that as a consequence of Christianity to love God means to hate the world, or with the fact that in consequence of Christianity there is enmity between God and men.   *XI¹A 341*

The New Testament

A girl of sixteen: it is her Confirmation day. Among the many tasteful and fine presents she also receives an elegantly bound copy of the New Testament.

And this is what is called Christianity! In fact no one expects – and rightly – that she will read it, any more than the others, not even in some quite primitive manner. She receives this book as a consolation for her life, 'Here indeed you will find consolation if you should need it' – but of course no one expects her to read it, any more than other girls, least of all in a quite primitive manner: for then she would discover that here indeed are all the horrors beside which everything else that happens in the world is little more than a jest.

But this is Christianity. So too is this fooling around with Bible Societies, which distribute New Testaments by the million.

No, I could be tempted to make Christendom another proposal: collect every single New Testament there is, take them all out to an open place, or to the top of a mountain, and then, while we all kneel, let someone address God as follows: 'Take this book back again. We men, as we are now, are not fit to deal with this sort of thing. It only makes us unhappy.' This is my proposal, that like those Gadarenes of the Gospel we beg Christ to depart from us [Luke 8. 37]. That would be an honest and human way of talking – different from the disgusting hypocrisy mouthed by the clergy, that life would have no value for us without this priceless treasure of Christianity.

XI¹A 347

Christianity a fortress

Imagine a fortress, absolutely impregnable, furnished with provisions for an eternity.

Then a new commandant arrives. He has the idea that it would be best to build bridges across the trenches – in order to attack the besiegers.

Splendid! He has transformed the fortress into a village – and naturally the enemy took it.

So with Christianity. The method was changed, and of course the world triumphed.   *XI¹A 349*

The truth

Every man fears the truth more than death – this is the truth about all the hypocritical nonsense about loving the truth

131

and being so ready to follow it, if only it were possible to understand it, and so on.

No; by nature man is more afraid of the truth than of death – and this is perfectly natural: for the truth is even more repugnant than death to man's natural being. What wonder, then, that he is so afraid of it?

Attentiveness to the truth requires *being aside* (Christ took him aside [Mark 7. 33]), aside from the crowd. And this in itself is enough to make a man fearful and anxious – more than in face of death. For man is a social animal – only in the herd is he happpy. It is all one to him whether it is the profoundest nonsense or the greatest villainy – he feels completely at ease with it, so long as it is the view of the herd, or the action of the herd, and he is able to join the herd. For man is an animal who can become spirit, a fate which as an animal he is more afraid of than of dying. He is an animal – and going aside aims at turning him into spirit.

And this being aside, when a man wants to enter into the truth, is more precisely to be understood as being exposed to ridicule, contempt, maltreatment by the others, by the herd – which means an even greater isolation than the first.

This, then, is why men alter the concept of 'truth'. The truth means to run with the herd and then, they add, this is also what love means. And this has become Christianity in our time.   *XI¹A 352*

The meaning of existence

Everything concerning the history of Christianity and so on is chatter and nonsense; moreover it is knavery, aiming at dethroning Christianity as absolute power.

The meaning of this existence is that we should be examined, be examined for eternity.

And God has so arranged this existence that it is impossible in this world to be related in truth to truth without coming to suffer – and eternity judges everyone according to whether he has been related in suffering to the truth.

Man's concern, on the other hand, is to get hold of the truth without suffering. Man, every man, has some feeling for the truth, but truly he is not willing to suffer for it, nor is he willing to understand that suffering is bound up with the truth.

So man's concern is to get hold of the truth without suffering, which is impossible.

Such, then, is existence and its examination. If I were a pagan and had to speak Greek, I should say that God has arranged everything for his own entertainment; he amuses himself like a man who puts a piece of bacon in a mouse-trap and watches all the tricks of the mice to get the bacon out without being trapped – so God amuses himself at the leaps and springs and contortions of these millions of men to get hold of the truth without suffering. All these millions – alas, yes; for the divine has majestic proportions, and millions are needed to make just a few pieces, centuries are needed to let errors have their fun.

. . . When, therefore, there is a single person who wishes a little more honestly to risk himself for the truth – even if he too would prefer to have the truth without suffering for it: then Providence takes pity on him and helps him really to suffer. Of course he cries out, Alas, and woe is me! But nevertheless it is loving of Providence, if it is certain that one can only be related to the truth through really suffering and that eternity decides whether one really has suffered for the truth, and rejects all the sophists.   *XI¹A 353*

The truth

is a snare: you cannot have it, without being caught. You cannot have the truth in such a way that you catch it, but only in such a way that it catches you.   *XI¹A 355*

To be loved by God – to love God

What Alcibiades said of Socrates, that in the end from being a lover he became the beloved, also express God's relation to a man: in the end God becomes the beloved.   *XI¹A 356*

The examination of existence and the judgement

The question which existence, if one may put it thus, poses to man, and the different answers to which divide men into two qualitatively different classes (the animal, and those who are kin to the Deity) is: Are you willing that another man, or other men, should be martyred with all possible torments in order that you may have a materially good life; or are you yourself willing to be sacrificed for others?

He who answers yes to the first question is *eo ipso* an animal, this is no less bestial than when Ole Kollerød sits and eats with the knife with which he has murdered another man. The bestial thing is to devour, to want to live off, another man, off his torments and sufferings. This is the immense mass of perdition. This mass is great, fearfully great, at all times, but the false teachers have a great responsibility for its being as great as it is.

The other class of men answers no to this question.

And now they are asked the other question: are you yourself willing to be sacrificed for others?

If a man is unconditionally willing, joyfully certain that God asks this of him out of love, then he is really related to God.

But even if a man is not so strong that he is willing to be sacrificed for others in the full flood of enthusiasm, if there is nevertheless some readiness in him, then God helps him sufficiently to sacrifice himself.

If the question were put to a better man: are you willing that another man should be sacrificed for you with every conceivable torment? – he would answer, if my salvation and blessedness are in some way dependent on this, then I accept. But in that case I must also be permitted to say that this other man is quite different from myself; he is different in quality from me. I must worship him as a supra-human being.

This is the relation to the God-Man.

But analogously to the God-Man, though on a lower plane, the apostles too were sacrificed, and the witnesses to the truth. Here Catholicism is in a certain sense right in wishing to worship the saints; for a saint is of a higher quality than the man who wants to have a materially good life at the expense of the sacrifice of another.

Protestantism is the crudest and most brutal plebeianism. The Protestant refuses to recognize any difference in quality between the apostle, the witness to the truth and himself, even though his existence is entirely different from theirs, as different as eating from being eaten . . .   *XI¹A 358*

A measure for existential specific gravity

. . . In the physical world there are measuring instruments. If one took a barrel of water, and put some colouring in it, and tried to sell it as brandy, for example, then it would be tested and the result would be: it is a lie.

Similarly it would be desirable to have an instrument for testing existence. If there were such an instrument, we would be amazed to see that in Christendom we have not made a start, but existentially have remained in paganism or Judaism.
XI¹A 361

God – we men

We men think that Adam's fall is far, far in the past, and forgotten. Now we are fine people. For God Adam's fall is today.

We men imagine that the killing of Christ, that infamous

act of the human race, was 1,800 years ago, far in the past, forgotten. Now we are fine people. For God it happened today.   *XI¹A 362*

Man

according to Christianity is a fallen spirit, who has been punished by being degraded to being an animal.

Yet it is necessary to have spirit in order to grasp the humiliation properly; the trivial and the bestial are perfectly happy to be animal, that is to say, they do not really notice it.

If Christianity had not come into the world, then man would probably never have become aware of this sad secret; for Christianity is required to explain the true state of affairs to man, that he was originally something quite different, and how infinitely low he has sunk in having become an animal. Such a thing would never have occurred to man of himself, and only the most eminent individuals outside Christianity have ever had an inkling of it.

It may now be seen in what sense Christianity is good news, and how bestial Christendom is. Christianity is the good news which opens man's eyes to a misery which the natural man has no conception of. Christianity is the good news which turns this earthly existence into the greatest misery, and then into the most anxious effort, in fear and trembling – and in this way Christianity is the good news about eternity.

Does this resemble the Christianity of Christendom?

XI¹A 363

To unite is, from a Christian standpoint, trickery

We are always hearing 'Let us unite, in order to work for Christianity'. And this is meant to be true Christian zeal.

Christianity is of another view, it knows very well that this is trickery, for with union Christianity is not advanced, but weakened; and the more union there is, the weaker Christianity becomes.

Christianity always requires just one person; but it strains him to the utmost. And that is what we men want to be rid of. But in a dishonest and cheating way we turn the matter as though true Christian zeal consisted in uniting, and the more the merrier. (+)   *XI¹A 368*

[*In the margin*] (+) With the achievement of union real Christian conflicts (what men are most afraid of) of course are abolished (to suffer at the hands of men). And that is why we hear, 'Let us unite in order that – with Christian zeal and solidarity!!! – we may work for Christianity.'   *XI¹A 369*

O Socrates

you were and are the only thinker in purely human terms.

The so-called Christian philosophers – how confused they are! Take the celebrated Augustine! At one place he argues with the Donatists as follows: what do a handful of men like you imagine you are over against the whole Christian church, as though a handful of men possessed the truth? O Socrates, can we call him a thinker? He argues about the truth from numbers. And a Christian thinker! Whereas Christianity rests upon the reality of the single person.   *XI¹A 371*

Fear of men – fear of God

The conflict Christianity constantly aims at is, in fearing God more than men – that is, the conflict is with fearing men more than God. The conflict is not in fasting or celibacy or the like – no: if you fast from fear of men, then this is not Christianity; and if men try to intimidate you into giving up fasting, then it can be Christian to fast.

God is the only sovereign. To express this he chooses as his envoy a quite simple man – this is the greatest possible distinction. And then he demands of this his ambassador and apostle that he express the truth that the great power he has the honour to represent is unique. And he is to express this unconditionally, in face of kings and emperors and the public and the Pope, and what the devil are all these human authorities called which intimidate men. And to make matters complete, in order to give unconditional expression to the extent to which he is the only sovereign, God joins with men in beating his own ambassador – and yet out of love, yes, out of love, oh infinite Love.

Christianity has only once been proclaimed unconditionally in the fear of God – by the God-Man.

When Christianity is entirely proclaimed in the fear of men it ceases to be Christianity.

Here is the falsehood in the whole of Christendom. As soon as Christianity is proclaimed unconditionally in the fear of God, everyone falls away. When Christianity is proclaimed entirely in the fear of men everyone is a Christian – and it is self-evident that this makes a fool of God, and there will be a reckoning to follow . . .   *XI' A 372*

Judas Iscariot

Christ himself spoke the terrible words of him: 'It would have been better for that man if he had not been born' [Matthew 26. 24].

But though everything has been done in Christendom to paint Judas in the blackest possible colours, I should like to say that I could imagine him a whole quality worse.

Judas Iscariot would then not be (as he probably was in reality) a despairing man who in a moment of folly sells his master for a paltry thirty shekels (and the smallness of the amount is itself some extenuation, as is also in a certain sense his terrible end).

No, Judas is a man of a quite different mould: quiet, and with a very different view of life and profit. So he goes to the high priests and says to them: 'I am willing to betray him.

But hear my conditions. I am not so interested in getting a large lump sum which I could squander in a few years. No, I want a fixed annual payment. I am a young man, healthy and strong, with very likely a long life ahead of me, and I should like to have a comfortable and enjoyable life, married and with a family. This is my price.'

On my view this is a whole quality more abominable. Nor do I really believe that such an abomination could be met with in ancient times, it has been reserved for our sensible time.

It is easy to see that I have represented Judas a little like a professor, who in tranquil security leads a tasteful and enjoyable life – thanks to Christ sweating blood in Gethsemane and crying on the cross, 'My God, my God, why hast thou forsaken me?'

It is his tranquil life in complete heterogeneity with this which makes the professor such an abhorrent figure.

Alas, it is in vain that you hope to have an effect on the professor. When I am dead all that I have said will be grist to the mill of the professor . . .   *XI¹A 374*

'Get behind me, Satan! You are not on the side of God, but of men'
[Matthew 16. 23]

So Christianity is so exalted that even the most well-meaning man (and Peter was surely well-meaning) is not a misunderstanding or a mistake, no, he is of Satan.

Then what is 'Christendom', what is it but something that is not even as honest and humanly well-meaning as Peter?

So Christendom is the invention of Satan.   *XI¹A 375*

First the kingdom of God
[Matthew 5. 33]

Christendom interprets this – with erudition! – as first money, *virtus post nummos.* But this is Christianity all the same, and it is even regarded as a rare Christian honesty and true

Christian seriousness if one gets a little declamation on Sundays for one's money, *post nummos.* In the end the *post* disappears, and the proposition now runs, First money – and you are swindled by getting nothing at all for your money. When this point has been reached, I am convinced, or rather it lies in the nature of the thing, that this will be declared to be true Christianity, the objective sound doctrine.

XI¹A 379

About myself

If my contemporaries could understand how I suffer, how Providence, if I may dare to say so, maltreats me, I am certain that they would be so profoundly moved that in human sympathy they would make an attempt (as sometimes happens with a child which is being maltreated by its parents) to wrest me free from Providence.

Yet this would be a misunderstanding. For what I rest in is that it is of love, yes, of love, that you do this, infinite Love! I know that in love you suffer with me, more than I, infinite Love – even if you cannot change.

Yet my contemporaries cannot understand this. Even if I were to speak, they would not understand – even if I were to speak, yet for safety's sake things are so disposed that in fact I cannot speak, since I understand that things are so disposed that those to whom I should speak cannot understand – still another cruelty, my contemporaries would say, if they could understand.

Like those in the bull of Phalaris whose cries sounded like music – yet even worse, God bars the way for those he makes use of. For all their suffering is understood by their contemporaries as pride, which means that their contemporaries take delight in heaping more suffering on them – because of their pride.

Yet so it must be, o infinite Love! If such a man could make himself understood – and then in a weak moment forgot himself and told tales out of school: what an irreparable loss!

Therefore, o infinite Love, you watch to prevent such a thing happening.

XI¹ A 382

The law of existence according to Christianity

The law (which again is grace) which Christ has established by his life for man's life is that you have to do as a single person with God. Whether you are clever or simple, highly gifted or only slightly gifted, it does not matter in the least: relate yourself as a single person with God (oh divine grace, willing to have to do with an individual man, with each single man!); dare as a single person to have to do with him, he will adapt everything to your capacities and possibilities.

So first have to do with God; not first with 'the rest'.

But the fact is that to exist, existence, has something immensely frightening for a poor man. So he is afraid – he does not dare to set himself first in relation to God, the animal in him thinks, 'It is cleverer to be like the rest.'

Every existence which thinks first of being like the rest is a wasted existence, and since from a Christian standpoint it has happened through one's own fault it is a forfeited existence.

These millions, the law of whose existence is 'first be like the rest', this mass of aping – materially they look as if they were something, something great, something immensely powerful. And materially they are indeed something; but ideally this mass, these millions, are zero, they are less than zero, they are wasted and forfeited existences.

A sparrow, a fly, a poisonous insect is an object of God's solicitude, for they are not wasted or forfeited existences. But a mass of aping is forfeited existence. After God has taken such pity on men, shown such grace, as to desire to be related to each single person – and since this is precisely what grace is, he may ask this of us – when men then prefer to be like the rest, we have *lèse-majesté* against God. The mass of imitators

141

are guilty of *lèse-majesté*. The punishment is to be ignored by God.

From the Christian standpoint all lecturing means a wasted and forfeited existence. The professors can become more and more skilled in falsehoods, it is no help, their existence is still forfeited.

To be like the rest is the law for all earthly and temporal cleverness.

From the Christian standpoint this is a cleverness which is so clever that it makes a fool of itself for eternity.

Ah, it is with sorrow that I write this. In melancholy sympathy, though myself unhappy, I loved men and the mass of men. Their bestial conduct towards me compelled me, in order to endure it, to have more and more to do with God.

So the result has been that I have undeniably come to know what Christianity is; but this truth gives me pain.

XI¹A 384

Primitiveness

Every man has a basic primitive disposition (for primitiveness is the possibility of 'spirit'). God knows this best, for it is he who has created it.

All earthly, temporal, worldly cleverness tends to destroy its own primitiveness (+). Christianity aims at following it.

Destroy your own primitiveness, and in all probability you will get through the world well, perhaps even be a success – but eternity will denounce you. Follow your primitiveness, and you will fail in the temporal world; but eternity will accept you.

XI¹A 385

[*In the margin*] (+) By primitiveness Christianity of course does not mean all that trumpery of intellectuality, being a genius, and the like. No, primitiveness, spirit, means to stake one's life, first, first, first the kingdom of God. The more literally a man can take this in his actions, the greater is his primitiveness. *XI¹A 386*

Christendom

In Christ God offered to enter into relation with the human race.

But what did the human race do? Instead of entering into relation with God they transformed it into the *history* of how God in Christ entered into relation with the apostles, or the history of how God in Christ entered into relation with men. In brief, instead of entering into relation with God, they have turned it into a historical matter which they repeat in diluted form from generation to generation. . . .   *XI¹A 388*

The wrong turning in Christendom

. . . Yet, from a Christian standpoint, this talk about our fathers' faith is a misunderstanding, at all times a misunderstanding: for this can never be described as something decisive. For the Christian the only thing that matters is the New Testament, with which every generation has to begin. And the confusing factor, which has produced 'Christendom' and led Christianity back to Judaism, is that in the course of time each generation, instead of beginning with the New Testament, has begun with 'our fathers' faith', with holding fast to our fathers' faith. Always this knavery of bringing in history and the category of the human race instead of ideality and the single person, which is the Christian category.   *XI¹A 392*

Change of scene (Christianity – Christendom)

The Saviour of the world, Jesus Christ, sets everything, absolutely everything in motion, both in heaven and on earth, in order to make 'reality' the scene – and this he calls Christianity.

Christendom starts up everything, absolutely everything that man can hit upon, in order to prevent reality being the scene, it hits upon everything possible to shift the scene, to set it at an artistic distance from reality.

The first is to introduce Christianity into the world; the second is to conduct it out of the world.   *XI¹A 394*

Unrest – reassurance

Christianity represents the matter thus. An eternity lies before you – your fate is decided in this life, according to the use you make of it. Perhaps you have thirty years, perhaps ten, perhaps five, perhaps one, perhaps only a month, a day: terrible unrest!

Christendom arranges something different for itself. The priest assures you (that is, if you assure him his fixed income, otherwise you won't get a word out of him) that an eternity lies before you, millions, billions, trillions of years. Time for infinite effort! This life is only a beginning, what are seventy years compared with an eternity, not like five minutes – if you waste them, what the hang! Amen!   *XI¹A 399*

The apostle

. . . What torture! If a man is really to be the instrument of God, for the infinite will that God is, then God must first take all his will from him. What a fearful operation! And it is natural that no one knows how to examine so painfully as one who is omniscient and omnipotent. Certainly with other forms of torture there are doctors present to estimate how long the tortured man can hold out without losing his life. Yet mistakes can happen, and the tortured man can die before their eyes. This never happens with one who is omniscient. And certainly there are also means at hand to strengthen the tortured man, so that he can hold out still more, but his strength is lessened every time, and death comes nearer: only one who is almighty can give absolutely new powers every second.

144

And here too is torment: for since despite every suffering it is something indescribably great to be God's instrument, so the apostle has always the further effort to make – to be thankful without cease for this infinite benefit.

So one thing is reserved for the apostle, to be able in truth to love God. Alas, with what sort of love do the rest of us love God!

We say that as God's creatures we must love God – and the only one who truly loves God is the apostle, he who, that he might become an instrument, has been absolutely annihilated by God.

To love God because he has created you is to love yourself. No; if you will truly love God, this must be shown by your gladly and adoringly letting yourself be quite annihilated by God, that he may unconditionally promote his will.

XI¹A 400

Infinite love!

You imprison a man – and then you make a fool of him.

Yes, but you do it from love, and so you do not make a fool of him, o infinite love.

No, no, no, you will not get me to believe otherwise of you; you – once again – you do not make a fool of me, you are infinite love!

It is true, you wish to make a fool of me, you wish to test if you can make me believe that you are anything but love, which, if it happened, would cause you, o infinite love, more pain than me – so you do not make a fool of me, o infinite love!

XI¹A 405

Strange contradiction

There is nothing human envy naturally is so much directed against as the extraordinary.

And yet no one becomes the truly extraordinary except through man's maltreatment.

Therefore envy maltreats a man in order to prevent his becoming the extraordinary, and no one becomes the extraordinary except through man's maltreatment – therefore it is envy which produces the extraordinary. *XI¹A 410*

'*Two women will be grinding at the mill; one is taken and one is left,*' etc.

[Matthew 24. 41]

What a fearful separation and isolation! What a difference from paganism and Judaism, where the family and then the town and then the province and then the country participate in the individual, so that, for example, when a man distinguishes himself then immediately the family, the town, the province and the country share in his fame! Whereas Christianity means the separation of the individual, paganism and Judaism mean the supreme power of the category of the race and the generation.

But in Christendom everything is understood in a pagan and Jewish fashion, in Christendom one is a Christian through being in a family, however remotely, along with someone who is a Christian. One is even a Christian through being descended from Christians at a great remove. One is a Christian in a way in which it is impossible to be a Christian.

The apostle says that faith comes from hearing [Romans 10. 17]; but this other way means to be a Christian from hearsay! *XI¹A 421*

Another side from which Christianity can be seen

Christianity is that which God must suffer on account of us men.

This is to be understood as follows. One who is loved naturally understands this to mean that the lover is changed to be like the beloved in will and in his views. One who loves understands that loving means to be changed to be like the beloved, to become what the beloved might or does wish.

146

Now there is in God, if one may so put it, the contradiction which is the source of all torment: he is love, and yet he is eternally immutable. So he cannot be changed – and yet he is love. Therefore in one sense he must make the beloved unhappy – and yet he is love.

To be love and to be immutable in such a way that there can be no question of sparing the beloved; immutably to see everything conspire against the beloved, to see him forsaken, hated, persecuted, without helping him – and yet to be love!

When Christ cried, 'My God, my God, why hast thou forsaken me?' it was terrible for Christ, and this is how the text is generally understood. But it seems to me that it was even more terrible for God to hear it. How terrible to be unchangeable! Yet no: the terrible thing is not this, but to be unchangeable in this way and then to be love: what an infinite depth of unfathomable sorrow!

Alas, what have I, a poor man, not experienced in this regard! This contradiction of not being able to change and yet of loving! Alas, what have I not experienced! This helps me, from a great distance, to have a faint notion of the suffering of the divine love. *XI¹A 422*

'Shut the lid'

These words are from an old hymn. Shut the lid, that is, the lid of the coffin, shut it properly and firmly, that I – as a child is infinitely happy when it is nicely tucked up – may be in peace, well forgotten.

Shut the lid, shut it properly – for I do not lie in the coffin, no, what lies in the coffin is not I, but is that which I so infinitely desire to be rid of, the body of sin, this prison garb, which I have had to wear. *XI¹A 423*

The man – the woman

The woman was taken from the man's side – but from the Christian standpoint is the man's relation to the woman not to be compared with what we call making a digression?

The man was made for eternity, the woman leads him into a digression.

Without the woman the man is weaker in this world, he has a weak side which the woman covers up, and united they are stronger for this life. But from the Christian standpoint the weakness, which is that of the solitary, the weakness for this life is indispensable for strength for eternity.   *XI¹A 426*

Socrates – Alcibiades

Why did Alcibiades weep when Socrates spoke? ('When he speaks my heart beats more violently than that of the corybantes, tears stream from my eyes.')[1]

Alcibiades was surely a man who knew how to express himself, to choose the significant expression. Now if his view of Socrates had as its starting-point the fact that Socrates was an ironist who was an incomparable leg-puller, then it would be strange to speak thus of him. In that case Alcibiades should rather have said that one could split one's sides with laughing when Socrates spoke.

Then why did Alcibiades weep? It is easy to see that Socrates like the true ironist used irony to conceal ideals. But sometimes he also revealed them. And it was this which moved Alcibiades so profoundly.

Alcibiades wept, tears streamed from his eyes, his heart beat violently – quite simply, because Socrates brought him into the distress which a light-hearted intellectuality of no character can experience at the hands of a man of character Alcibiades had sufficient ideals and intellect to be grasped and captivated by the ethical ideal which Socrates put forward. But he could not conquer the lower element in himself. Hence

[1] Plato, *Symposium*, 215d *f.* RGS

148

the tears and the heart-beats. If it had become a matter of ethical action, Socrates would have said, then the tears and the violent heart-beats would have ceased.   *XI¹A 428*

The deceptive with Socrates

The deceptive with Socrates is that his irony is so witty, his intellectuality so eminent, that one is tempted to forget completely that at the same time his actions are a matter of life and death.

You read Plato's *Apology* and are enchanted: how infinitely witty he is, how pointed every word, how absolutely right – alas! and we who are corrupted by the accursed nonsense that the great thing is to be an author, we are tempted to read him as though he were an author, a witty author who might carry off the palm in the newspapers – but he is playing for life and death.

My life shows something similar, in a smaller measure. For my personal existence is worth much more, it is much more exhausting than my writings . . .

. . . How true and how Socratic is this view of Socrates, that to understand, truly to understand, is to be! For us more ordinary men these things are distinct, and remain so: it is one thing to understand, and another to be. Socrates is on such a high level that he abolishes this difference – and that is why we cannot understand him, in the deepest, Socratic sense. I can point to him from a distance, but I doubt whether if I had been his contemporary I could have borne with him . . .   *XI¹A 430*

Christianity (authority)

Christianity came into the world on the basis of authority, its divine authority; therefore the authority is superior.

But for a long time now the situation has been quite changed around: one seeks to prove and establish authority on grounds of reason.

And this is supposed to be the same religion.

When Christianity came into the world mankind had long despaired of making sense of this existence, they had despaired of finding the truth – then Christianity came with divine authority.

Augustine, for example, always turns the matter thus, that the perfection of Christianity consists precisely in authority, that Christianity has the truth in the most perfect form, namely, authority, that if one had the same truth without authority it would be less perfect, for authority is perfection. Alas, Augustine was still able to teach what mankind needs – authority, what men who were weary of philosophers' doubts and the misery of life had learned when Christianity came into the world.

But now the matter has been turned around. A so-called philosophical Christianity has discovered that authority is imperfect, at best something for the plebs, and that perfection consists in getting rid of it – in order to restore the situation to what it was before Christianity came into the world.

And theology seeks to establish the authority of Christianity by reasons, which is worse than any attack, since it confesses indirectly that there is no authority.

So the thing has gone on for a long time, from generation to generation – and everything is fine, students become ordinands, ordinands become clergy or professors, they get married and have children at the expense of Christianity, their living is assured: how infamous!

What is now called Christianity is really nothing but making a fool of God.

Oh, it is such a terrible thought, whether eternity will not in fact reject as eternally lost these generations and these millions? *XI¹A 436*

To love God is to hate what is human

The human is the relative, it is mediocrity, only with mediocrity is man happy. God is the unconditioned. To love God is impossible without hating the human.

But in truth hatred of the human, as Christianity thinks of it, is not original to man; no, it is human wretchedness and meanness which torture it out of the man who originally loved men, and in a certain sense continues to love them, namely, in the idea, in accordance with the eternal, but not in the sense of letting himself be overcome by mediocrity.

This may sometimes be seen when a man who feels very happy is inclined to what we call loving men. It is much rarer, as in my case, that a man who feels unhappy, and realizes he must submit to his unhappiness, thinks he must be able to do good to others.

That was my case. But men's meanness and wretchedness provided an ill reward for the good intentions that I in my sympathetic melancholy had towards them. This taught me, it compelled me, to seek to come nearer and nearer to God, it made it impossible for me to hold out without entering upon the Christian way, namely, of loving God in opposition to men. I see well how Providence has been with me in this . . .

XI¹A 445

'History'

This too is a part of human confusion, to believe that a young man is to be formed by history. Good heavens, what is history? Let us be honest and not abandon ourselves to the human presumption that the human race is something so important and significant that its history is so educative.

History is a process. Only on the rarest occasions is a tiny drop of idea added to it. And the process consists in transforming this idea into twaddle – for which sometimes centuries and millions multiplied by trillions of men are required (and this is carried out under the pretext of perfecting the idea which has been added).

And this is what is so important that it is to form the young man, presumably by perfecting him in due course in twaddle.

And every decade new discoveries are made which aim at dragging if possible everything into history, so that every grocer can find a place in history, just as in a daguerreotype we all get included.

No, Omar was right: burn everything, for either it is in the Koran or it is a lie.

From the religious point of view the infinitely important thing is to save primitiveness, if possible to have the young man retain the impression that he is the only man in the whole world. And what historical culture tends to do is to drown the young man in that ocean of twaddle of the millions. From the religious standpoint salvation lies in the single person, while the human race, of course, thinks that it lies in the race.

XI¹ A 446

Enthusiasts

Lessing justly says, somewhere, that the word *Schwärmer*, enthusiasts, comes from *swarm*, and therefore indicates the social, the desire to flock together – and in this way he cannot be called a *Schwärmer*.

A solitary *Schwärmer* is something so remarkable, a phenomenon as rare as a meteorite, that there could only be one – Socrates.

A solitary *Schwärmer* is as strange as mixing oil and water, or talking of a chaste voluptuary or a social solitary, or keeping a liquid in a bottomless jar! Wonderful Socrates! To keep the greatest enthusiasm in the most eminent reflection and wisdom – as wonderful as keeping liquid in a bottomless jar. For the rest of us this will not work, if the jar has no bottom the liquid runs through – and as our reflection and wisdom are developed the enthusiasm drops off . . . *XI¹ A 448*

Duty to God – duty to oneself

As duty to God went out, duty to oneself came in.

It is characteristic enough: duty to God means an effort towards the absolute, which is undeniably the most embarrassing thing possible – so enough of it!

In compensation for this a new kind of duty arose, duties to oneself, in other words, advancement for all that is low and egoistic in man; this was advanced and became 'duty to oneself'. It was strange that it was so long before this discovery was made, since it lies so near to hand – for one is nearest to oneself.

Some examples of duties to oneself: a man falls into the water, another comes past: now it has always been the rule that the other does not have the courage to save the man. But before the discovery of duties towards oneself what happened was that the second man skulked off and confessed to himself that he was a coward. Now, on the contrary, he does not skulk off at all, but he stalks off full of dignity. This is duty to oneself. Eating and drinking have always been regular habits, but after this discovery they mean something else: they are duty to oneself. To see that one scrapes some money together was always the rule, but now it is also something meritorious – it is duty to oneself. In brief, such men of duty as we have today were never to be found before, their whole life consists of sheer fulfilment of duty. What a splendid discovery – duties to oneself! What the moral philosophers have hitherto sought in vain, a way of presenting duties that will persuade men to do them, has now been achieved, namely, by making a duty of what men like doing and will do in any case.

My proposal is that since duties to God have now gone out we should now abolish duties to our neighbour as well, and treat the whole of ethics under the rubric of duties to oneself.

$XI^1 A$ 451

The great haul of fish

'You will catch men' [Luke 5. 10]. In 1800 years there have now been caught kingdoms, countries, peoples, etc. etc. a whole continent has become Christian, and has been so these many hundreds of years: an immense catch, a wonderful fulfilment of the Lord's prophecy!

Suppose that a fisher received the order to catch pike and carp, and he caught a million roach: what an immense catch! Or if he got the order to catch whale and then he caught a million herring: what an immense catch!

The method which has been increasingly followed in the course of the centuries is as follows: the standard for being a Christian has been lowered, so all the more have been caught. Instead of whales, herring have been caught – but in millions. Instead of herring, sticklebacks have been caught, but in innumerable millions – instead of whales. The prophecies of the Lord have been strangely fulfilled – 'but when I come again, will I find faith on earth?' [Luke 18. 8]. *XI¹A 454*

To be the first

To gain eternity without risking anything is impossible.

But to risk means quite simply to have no others before oneself.

O Socrates, when a man is solitary in this way, then we stand by the 'if'!

'To risk everything on an if', you say. My friend, if you do not take a risk on an 'if', then you take no risk: take away the 'if' and you take away the risk. You cannot really have any objection to risking on an 'if', for this is just what risking is. If therefore you have any objection, then it must be against risking itself. Take care that you are not disappointed, by claiming that you have nothing against risking, you are quite ready for that – only not on an 'if', which is just as though one were to say, 'I have nothing against swimming, on the contrary I should love to swim – only not in water.'

So a shudder seizes the man, and he reaches out to grasp the others: I must have some certainty before I take the risk, he says. Again, to be certain before one takes the risk is putting the cart before the horse, or filling your mouth with flour before you speak. No, if your mouth is full of flour, you must first get rid of it before you can speak. And so with taking a risk. If a man is certain about something, then there is no risk, if he is to take a risk he must first get rid of the certainty, as one who as a child was certain, or thought he was, must get rid of the certainty in order to be able to take a risk. So first get rid of the certainty, in order to take the risk – so far is it from being true that you must first be certain before you can take a risk.

But a shudder seizes a man, he wants to be certain: he reaches out to grasp the others.

The others! And even if these others were millions through trillions of billions of centuries, then one would think one would dare to take the risk. O my friend, nothing is more certain than this, that if you build on this certainty, then you will be fooled for eternity.

This is the cunning of existence, if you wish (yet 'spirit' cannot exist in any other way): the utmost human certainty is just what fools us most certainly for eternity – and the very least human certainty is just what provides the possibility of eternity . . .   *XI¹A 458*

Existence an examination

. . . In my childhood I heard a great deal about great joy, sheer joy in heaven. And I believed it and thought of God as happy in sheer joy. Alas, the more I think about it the more I come to imagine God as sitting in sorrow, for he most of all knows what sorrow is.   *XI¹A 459*

Immortality

One of our poets (Ingemann) is of the sentimental view that even insects are immortal.

The man is right, and one could almost be tempted to say that if such men as are born nowadays *en masse* are immortal, then it does not seem unreasonable that insects too should be immortal.

This is right tea-table gossip, so cheery and so touching,

real priests' chatter, for they always excel in cheerily watering down every idea till it is nothing at all, or even something disgusting! Immortality was once the lofty goal which the heroes of mankind looked up to, humbly confessing that this reward was so excessive that it was quite incommensurate with their greatest efforts – and now every louse is immortal! . . . $XI^1 A 463$

God in heaven

If it were permitted to talk of such things, I should say that it is lucky for God that a thousand years are for him as one day, otherwise it would be terrible to endure these centuries upon centuries, these throngs of millions, where not the slightest advance is made or where we retrogress by leaps and bounds. $XI^1 A 466$

The temporal – the eternal

The temporal is a snail's pace, spreading out in time and space; the eternal is the intensive which hurries to meet death. $XI^1 A 468$

The north

That the north is the least favoured part of the world may be seen from two things, amongst others. First, the inclement climate renders impossible the kind of carelessness about one's livelihood which is found in the warm lands. For the same reason the latter attain more easily to a philosophical ideality which does not divide man so that with the help of philosophy he becomes a professor of philosophy and a tradesman. Secondly, it is only in the north that we find the prosaic outlook which in so many ways falsifies the nature of women, and sets problems which simply could not arise in the south:

that the woman is a person who is also useful and profitable. Originally it was not thus, but woman was a luxury, she was company, she was for decoration and show, and the like. Only in the north she has also to be useful, and that is why it is in the north that the question of her emancipation arises.

XI¹A 469

Jest – seriousness

. . . The serious fact is that you cannot truly have to do with the eternal without becoming more and more embittered with the temporal, with your animal existence.

'But in these circumstances you will have no one at all who will want to have to do with the eternal.' My friend, you must not tell me this, I did not invent Christianity. If you have any objection to make, you must turn to his majesty, God in heaven. *XI¹A 472*

The fear of death

was taken away by Christianity, and the fear of judgement was substituted. This was a sharpening, but also progress. And one cannot impress upon oneself too much the fact that in the life of the spirit real progress is always a sharpening. There is in fact no spiritual progress where matters become easier: anything that makes things easier is *eo ipso* not progress, however much it is acclaimed as such. *XI¹A 479*

Sad change in 'man'

Once man understood little, but that little moved him profoundly. Now he understands much, but it does not move him, or it moves him only superficially, like a grimace.

Is this then progress? Or is this much understanding, which makes no impression on the man himself, does not move him –

is it not something like a harlot, corresponding to a woman who is tastefully made up and initiated in every invention of cleverness and coquetry to please a man – but is lacking in love? *XI¹ A 480*

Christ and his apostles

Certainly there is a difference between the apostles' teaching and that of Christ, or between the apostles' Christianity and that of Christ. But nothing can be more mistaken than the view of the *Wolfenbüttel Fragments* that Christ's aims were entirely earthly, and that when the sorrowful fate of his life and death had taught the apostles that all was lost they transformed him into a fictional figure, and represented him as one whose chief thought was the desire to suffer. Christ would then really be an optimist, and the apostles the 'compulsory-voluntary' inventors of pessimism.

But nothing can be more mistaken: and it is a poor sort of pessimism which one is compelled to invent.

No, Christ understood pessimism better. And the difference between Christ and the apostles is that Christ expressed absolutely absolute pessimism, which will have nothing to do with the wretched and sinful world except to be slain, sacrificed. The apostle on the other hand adumbrates the first possibility of a new optimism: hence the founding of a community. Of course I should not suggest that the apostle is to bear the responsibility for what became of that possibility in the course of the centuries, especially in Protestantism, especially in Denmark, where Christianity (*sit venia verbo*) does not retain the least vestige of a long-lost likeness to Christ's Christianity, but on the contrary is exactly like the drinking-song of Jeppe on the mountain: 'merrily merrily round and around'.

Besides, when Christ almost gives the impression, in the earlier part of his life, that his intention was to found an earthly kingdom, it must always be remembered – what I have emphasized elsewhere – that this is essential for radical pessimism. But what do men understand by pessimism, these wretched creeping creatures that are called men nowadays, who are so eager to get a little happiness in the world that of course they could have no inkling of what pessimism is, nor that it first seeks to win everything only in order to throw it all away? This is the passion of martyrdom; then let us think of it so intensified as it is in the God-Man, and we can have a dim notion of this pessimism. The kind of pessimism which is invented by men who wanted to be happy and then failed is not pessimism, but a kind of optimism, an attempt in the given circumstances to come off as well as possible. And with this kind of pessimism one flatters oneself to be able to measure the passion of martyrdom in the God-Man!

No, true pessimism always has the mastery of the earthly.

XI¹A 482

About myself

Once my situation was that I had to bear the torment which I can call my thorn in the flesh: sorrow, a sorrow of spirit on account of my dead father; sorrow of heart on account of the girl I loved and everything connected with that. So I thought that in comparison with men in general I could be said to be prettily heavy loaded.

In the interval I found so much joy in my work that even this weight which is sorrow at one's sin could not make me call the life I led one of suffering.

Now in addition to all these previous things I have material cares and the maltreatment of the mob to bear.

Without falsifying or spoiling the concept I should say that my life is a kind of martyrdom, only of a new type. What I suffer as a public person is best described as slow death, being trampled to death by geese, or as that painful killing by degrees practised in distant lands when you are delivered up to insects, where the culprit is first smeared with honey to give the insects a proper appetite – so my fame is the honey which gives the insects the proper appetite.

Then come, revision of history! Everything is in order, and

nothing is lacking, not even that I have *voluntarily* exposed myself to this, and that it did not simply come upon me.

XI¹ A 484

The race – the single person

The category of the race – the crowd, the number, abstractions – has never been so overwhelming as in our time; and never has the single person been so strongly emphasized as with me, for even Socrates had disciples. The two things are related, and are connected with the divine majesty.

For God's majesty is not of the kind, when rebellion becomes stronger, to lower the price: no, he raises it. Take an illustration. If a man took a big thick stick to beat ten men, and these ten were reinforced by another ten, then the truly majestic thing is to lay aside the thick stick and take a quite thin one to beat the twenty men: so far is true majesty from yielding.

Just because the rebellion is so qualified and so powerful, then use is made – how majestic! – of the nearest approach to nothing.

Alas, in a certain sense it is a terrible thing for the poor man who is to be used in this way, to be constantly maintained at the nearest approach to nothing; and this, moreover, in every sense, in order that the majesty can be properly seen as, with the increase of the rebellion, it becomes, if I may put it thus, more playful, thus showing the sure superiority of its infinite power. In a certain sense it is a terrible thing for the poor man – and yet it is love which is at work, You infinite Love!

XI¹ A 486

I – third person

To be 'spirit' is to be 'I', God will have those who are 'I'; for God desires to be loved.

Man's interest lies in introducing objectivity everywhere, this is the interest of the category of the race.

'Christendom' is an association of millions – all in the third person, without any 'I'. *XI¹A 487*

To believe – Nicodemus

If to believe were a secret inwardness, then Christ must have approved of Nicodemus, who certainly was a man of secret inwardness [John 3. 1 *ff.*]. *XI¹A 488*

Judaism – Christianity

Every suffering where the help comes in this life, so that the suffering ceases, is Judaism.

Christianity remains to the very end in suffering – then eternity. *XI¹A 496*

The measure of the spirit

This is how we speak: a man says with feeling, I am not a single man, but a man with a family – perhaps a large family. In the realm of the spirit a single man is more.

This is how we speak to God: someone steps forward and says, we are not a few individuals, we are a people. In the realm of the spirit an individual is more for God: this is just what Christianity is, that every man can be that individual.

How ironical to think that every man is made to be an Atlas, to carry a whole world – and then to see what we men in fact are! Alas, how sad that we ourselves are guilty for what we are! *XI¹A 498*

The point – the mass – the intensive – the extensive

11 October 1854

An image: the centre is a point, the target itself is a large body. Yet only hitting the centre is a proper hit, just to hit is not a proper hit. So only the intensive is really living, extensive being is really not being at all. The extensive is false being, its being consists merely in devouring the intensive. Only the intensive has being in itself, the extensive lives from or in eating, in sucking the blood of the intensive (as the shades in the underworld suck the blood of the living).

As writing in the sand or the ocean leaves no trace behind, so all existence which does not become spirit disappears without a trace. *XI¹A 500*

Politics – Christianity

Politics consists of never venturing more than is possible at any moment, never going beyond what is humanly probable.

In Christianity, if there is no venturing farther out, beyond what is probable, God is absolutely not with us; without of course its following that he is with us wherever we venture farther out than what is probable. *XI¹A 502*

Philosophers on the throne

is what Plato wanted. Our time teaches us that a dramatic poet on the throne is a suspicious thing.

I mean Louis Napoleon. As a poet he understands that during the review in Boulogne it will have an incomparable effect if a courier comes bounding up at that moment with the news of the taking of Sebastopol. Well, well, how splendidly things fall out!

The consequence of course is that next day all France has a hang-over, as after a prolonged carouse.

But Napoleon is first-rate at prostituting the human race. This generation of wind-bags deserves to have a wind-bag *en gros* as emperor. And how splendid, too, that all men's great inventions (the railway, the telegraph, etc.) tend to develop and support charlatanism. In this way perhaps men will come to themselves again! *XI¹A 507*

– Alas, that was how I understood it: I thought that I should have your help, O God, in loving men. You understand it differently: you used men against me in order to help me to love you. *XI¹A 509*

The reliability of numbers

is of course a fraud, they are unreliable; and yet this is what is offered you in the world, calculated to fool you, so that you become part of the numbers.

There are millions of Mohammedans – but look more closely and you will see that they are Mohammedans of this type: 'Yes, I am like the rest' – Mohammedans in the sense that if they had been born in Christendom they would be Christians. There are millions of Christians – what a reliable fact! Yes, it is so reliable that if the same men had been born in those other lands they would be Mohammedans.

If there is a certain truth in the saying that man has been given words in order to conceal his thoughts (or as I should say in order to conceal the fact that he has no thoughts), the truth, namely, that he was not given them for this purpose, but that is how he uses them, something similar can be truly said about numbers. Numbers are used in order to conceal the emptiness of existence, they put you in a state of exaltation, like opium, and so you are tranquillized by the immense reliability of numbers running into millions. Yet in truth millions are just as unreliable, every bit as unreliable, as one. But one man does not have a stupefying effect, as millions do: with millions we can be sure, everything is reliable! . . .

This again is connected with the fact that man is a synthesis. He is both an animal creation and the possibility of spirit. But the animal needs no higher certainty than numbers. To feel the impulse to another kind of certainty than that of numbers introduces spirit. That is why Providence has so arranged things that this impulse to spirit (for truth's sake) immediately meets with bracing opposition. For

numbers naturally take this kind of thing amiss and call it
arrogance. *XI¹A 512*

The divine – the human

are related to one another in the most polemical way, according to the teaching of Christianity.

When Peter, very well-meaning, wants to hold Christ back
for *human* reasons, Christ says as categorically as possible,
'You know only the things of men, this is Satan's suggestion,
get behind me, Satan' [Matthew 16. 23].

On the other hand, when Christ speaks to the Jews of God
and of himself (e.g. in John 8) then the Jews cry out that he is
possessed of Satan, of the devil, he is a Samaritan. And Christ
says of the Jews that they are the devil's sons [John 8. 44].

The human, then, is the relative, the mediocre, which
brings happiness, up to a point. From this standpoint the
Absolute is the devil, for the Absolute is a veritable plague
for this human mediocrity, which egoistically wants a materially good and enjoyable life, and does not want to hear of the
Absolute: for the Absolute is sheer unrest and effort and
torment.

That the Absolute is the divine, that what causes such
torment and trouble is the divine, can only be grasped by man
after he has given himself to it, and learned from the Absolute
itself that it is the divine. If man persists in the merely human
view, then the Absolute is the devil, or God is the evil, as is
said in the latest French philosophy, that is, he is guilty of all
man's unhappiness; if only we could get rid of the Absolute,
empty our heads of all ideals, things would surely go well.
But God makes us unhappy, he is the evil.

On the other hand, from God's standpoint it is precisely this
mediocrity which wants material enjoyment which is devil-
possession, it is of the devil. The extreme things we men say
of the wildest sins are perhaps from God's standpoint still
more true of the sensual enjoyments of mediocrity: they are
of the devil, for seen ideally this mediocrity is even more

distant from higher things than the worst sins. Where there is unrest – and it is always to be found with great sins – there is a possibility of higher things; but where there is no unrest then the distance from 'spirit' is greatest.

Mediocrity is the principle which shapes the *compact mass* of the human race. And what the Absolute, and therefore God too, must demand as the first condition for entering into relation with men is that he separate them out. And again it is a fact that great crimes make the relation more possible than mediocrity, for great crimes isolate . . .   *XI¹A 516*

Christianity – Christendom – God – Man

This is the position – I can well repeat it once more.

According to Christianity salvation means to become spirit, to be saved from the human race; but to become spirit means to become the single person: isolation is a *conditio sine qua non*, an unavoidable condition.

Scarcely is this word about salvation heard, salvation for men, than humanity, so to speak, replies, 'Splendid, let us now unite' (there we have it!), 'in order that united we may aspire to this high good.'

But as I have shown elsewhere,[1] by uniting men defend themselves against God, the idea, the Absolute, ideality – and so also against 'salvation'.

So countless many unite – and thus are fully secured against Christianity. And this is 'Christendom'.

Since there is a qualitative difference between God and man it is self-evident that it is difficult for them to come to an understanding with one another, even with the best will on man's part. And unfortunately man always presents himself along with 'numbers'.

If (to put almost facetiously something that costs me so much suffering, which however I do not regret) – if God in heaven were to open his window and say: 'I need a man, get

---

[1] *cf. XI¹A 248.* RGS

165

me a man', then humanity would reply: 'I shall immediately make the necessary dispositions, I shall assemble a few hundred thousand men and women, then you can have as many men as you wish.' But God asked for one man. And 'man' cannot get this into his head, that one man is more than millions, and that by getting hold of millions he really gets less.

It is only with great difficulty that one can get this faith in millions out of man's head, for it is part of his animal disposition. Every one in whom the animal disposition is preponderant believes firmly that millions are more than one; whereas spirit is just the opposite, that one is more than millions, and that every man can be the one.

Everyone in whom the animal disposition is preponderant always has this faith that he is more when he is with his family, and what families are in a small way millions are in a big way, they are families. But it may easily be seen even in small proportions as when, for example, there is talk of working for an idea, that man does not say most who says, 'Yes, I am willing, and not myself alone, but with my family.' No, that man says most who says, 'I am at your service, I am just a single man.' For in relation to the idea a single man is more than a man with a family. But this predominance of the category of the race is firmly embedded in us, in the very words we use. Hence the man who really said least said 'not merely myself but also my family', and with these words 'not merely' he gives you to expect that what follows is really more, even though it is less, for the family means a subtraction. And the man who said most says, 'I am only a single man' – 'only' – and yet it would be less if he brought his family too.

XI¹A 518

Christianity – man

Does it occur to any child that he needs to be educated? Or if you took several children and let them live together, grow up together, would it occur to them that they needed to be educated? Would anything else occur to them but that they were just fine as they were?

But a higher view, that of their parents, sees that they need to be educated, and so sets a standard for the child.

So with man. Of course it occurs to no man or community of men that they are profoundly corrupted. This is quite simply impossible, for one cannot be profoundly corrupted if at the same time, on one's own, without external help, one can see that one is profoundly corrupted.

But something higher (Christianity) undertakes to proclaim to man that he is profoundly corrupted, and so sets up a standard for him.

Yet nowadays Christianity is not proclaimed in this way. One takes the natural man's natural views of life, his hankering after enjoyment is regarded as the truth. So some of the promises are taken from Christianity, and put together so as to fit into the enjoyment of life.   XI¹A 522

Existence of spirit

To live in such a tension that one's life is not merely blameless before the law but by human standards extremely strict and pure, and yet to speak of one's body as this 'body of sin' (as Paul [Romans 6. 6]) – this is the life of the spirit. And as 'what is not of faith is sin' [Romans 14. 23], whenever the body is not docile to the spirit, and even at the least point or for the shortest moment does not will what the spirit wills, it is the body of sin.

But no one has the least suspicion of this kind of thing in our time, when all existence is mediocre, and Christianity is regarded as living in harmony with the flesh.

And it is understandable that just because the spirit is implicated the body in turn becomes more unruly. The body, so to speak, is also in its way a kind of good fellow. When it is permitted to run along its own groove, that is, in a level mediocrity, then it hardly gives any trouble. And this favourable result of such a method of treating the body is regarded as a proof that the method is the right one, or, as is said, the truly Christian one.

Yes, in a sense it is true, what the free-thinkers assert, as well as the orthodox in an indirect fashion: Christianity is myth; yes, it is myth, fable, that men have lived by such a standard, it is myth since this 'people of boys' [Isaiah 3. 4], called Christians today, are the truly human, even the highest condition of humanity, since they represent the latest stage in the increasing perfectibility of the human race. If we did not possess the mammoth's bones, we would of course also assert that the historical account of such animals is also a myth, a fable – at least all the animals belonging to that species would say so. *XI¹A 524*

Christendom

is a disguise. This whole business of priests and professors gives the appearance of being work for infinity: but it is finitude, quite simply it is the same as every other trade. It is just the same as when Morten Fredriksen turns up as a Russian officer, enters fine society (without renouncing his thief's nature) – then suddenly a police officer notices him and says 'Hi! That's Morten Fredriksen!' So with priests and professors, disguised as servants of infinity and of the idea: the police recognize them immediately, and know that they are grocers and innkeepers in disguise. *XI¹A 529*

The Word of God must be preached to the people – the medium (the clergy)

'The people' always represents the good health which can give birth to something good. What has become something in the world, or is derived from this, is in general weak already, even corrupt, for everything human is frail, and the generations grow rapidly corrupt.

That is the reason – along with many others – why God's Word is and must be preached to the people.

But in order to preach it there must be men. These are then the medium through which God's Word reaches the people. This medium is the clergy.

Now it is easy to see that if this medium were quite without any selfishness, this would be perfection, for then God's Word would reach the people for all practical purposes direct, the medium being no disturbance at all.

But it is in this medium that the evil has always resided, and still resides.

Catholicism has rightly seen that it was good for this medium to belong as little as possible to this world. Hence celibacy, poverty, asceticism, etc. This is certainly right, and is calculated to get rid of selfishness in the medium. But what happens? Satan enters the clerics, and in spiritual pride they hit on the idea of being something other than a medium: they want to be the intermediary authority between God and men, as recompense for their earthly renunciation.

Protestantism sees this defect, and to prevent this spiritual pride it comes up with the idea that the clergy must be like everybody else. So we have a completely worldly clergy, functionaries, dignitaries, men with wives and families, more than any others trapped in all the twaddle of temporality. And these are supposed to be the medium through which God's Word is to be heard! Yes, if this medium is intended to increase noise, mattresses would do as well! No, such a clergy, such a medium bars God's Word, or when God's Word sounds through it, it becomes something quite different.   *XI¹ A 532*

Has the whole of Christendom not arisen through a confusion?

Christianity entered the world when Cæsar Augustus enrolled all the world for taxation: one is almost tempted to believe that Christendom has made a mistake and confused the two events, thinking that it was Christianity which entered the world in order to tax everyone.   *XI¹ A 534*

Numbers – the idea

The idea is always related to one: one man is enough, and from the Christian standpoint everyone can be this one.

Eternity does not count numbers, it is quality, and so it is not numbers, though it is a number.

When two unite in order to be related to the idea, you have the beginning of numbers, for two count.

In the end numbers are so overwhelming, when they have become millions, that the idea has vanished and can be advertised for in the newspapers.

This is the position. In every case it is necessary to call a halt and change this deceitful use of language – 'uniting in order to be able to serve the idea, the truth, better, or in order the better to be able to be spirit'. No, so far as the idea and the spirit are concerned numbers do not help, they subtract.

But men unite, because they cannot endure to be simply one. Indeed that is another matter! But let us say just how things are, let us get to the truth of the matter and not weaken in advance, putting the idea under lock and key, and making it impossible to be related to spirit.

Sociality is part of the definition of man as an animal: and it is the cunning way (in every case an instinctive cunning) in which being joined together has been related to spirit which has rendered Christendom spiritless or caused it to be abandoned by the spirit, and to such an extent that it is under lock and key: for if men confessed that joining together was a result of weakness they would then be related after all to the spirit.

XI^1A 536

Arthur Schopenhauer

It is indisputable that he is a significant, a very significant writer, and it must be gladly and gratefully acknowledged that his whole existence and history are a deep wound for the philosophy of the professors.

But nevertheless, in my opinion he is a disquieting sign. For, strictly speaking, he is not what he thinks he is, even if it is undeniable that it would be of the utmost benefit if he were. He is neither a radical pessimist nor quite exempt from sophistry.

He is not a radical pessimist. Certainly a genuine pessimist in his whole character is what our effeminate and characterless time requires. But look more closely, and you will see that Schopenhauer was not a man who had the power to be successful and to win recognition, and then threw it away. No, perhaps even against his will he was forced to let temporal and earthly recognition go. But then to choose pessimism can easily be a kind of optimism – from a temporal point of view the cleverest thing one can do. So he undertakes to give asceticism, etc., a place in the system. This is where he may be seen to be a disquieting sign of the times. He says, not without great self-satisfaction, that he is the first to give asceticism a place in the system. Oh, but this is just professors' talk: 'I am *the first* to give it a place in the system.' Moreover is the fact that asceticism now finds a place in the system not an indirect sign that its day is over? There was a time when men were ascetic in character. Then there came a time when the whole business of asceticism was forgotten. And today a man boasts that he is the first to give it a place in the system. But this very way of busying oneself with asceticism shows that in a deeper sense it has ceased to exist for him, much the same as Judaism is no longer a religion for the many writers in our time who depict the old orthodox Jewish family life in novels. Schopenhauer is so far from being a pessimist that at best he represents the 'interesting': he makes asceticism interesting in some way – the most dangerous possible thing for a time which is avid for pleasure, a time which will be damaged more than any other by distilling pleasure from asceticism – namely, by reflecting upon it without involvement, by giving it a place in the system.

Nor is Schopenhauer quite exempt from sophistry. With all the roughness one could desire he lets fly at those tradesmen, the professors, and at the lucrative philosophy of professors.

Very good. But what is the difference between him and the 'professor'? In the last resort only that Schopenhauer is a man of means. But ask Socrates what he understands by a sophist and you shall see that he answers that it is surely that a man profits sufficiently from philosophy to be stamped as a sophist, but that it does not follow that not making a profit is enough to decide that a man is not a sophist. No, the sophistical element is in the distance between what one understands and what one is; the man whose character is not in harmony with his understanding is a sophist. But this is the case with Schopenhauer.

True, he says it himself, and that is so far laudable, but that is not enough. And though he says it himself, he seems to forget it when he lets fly at the professor's philosophy. But he should remember it, if he is to remain true to his own confession.   *XI¹A 537*

Do you want to be powerful?

Surely everyone wants to be, yet hear how the truly powerful man should speak.

'If someone asks me what full power it is that I possess, then I reply, the only true power. For to suggest that power means to be at the head of 500,000 men and 1,000 cannon is merely comparative power. Suppose another faces him with 600,000 men and 1,500 cannon? No, my power is the only true power – and when I think about it in this way, it seems to me so easy to achieve that it is inexplicable that every man is not that which he so infinitely desires to be. For this is my power: if they want to ridicule me, I am ready! If they want me to be imprisoned, I am at their service! If they want to execute me, I am waiting. And I will happily pay all the expenses of the public trial: for human justice is a wearisome waste of time, and as a writer has said, defender and accuser are harlequin and pierrot. So just say the word, just a hint from the authorities and I shall take a carriage and fetch the executioner myself, and the two of us will set off – no priest is necessary, nor warders nor police – but if the request is made that it should take place where the crowd can be gathered I shall not object, only I shall ask the authorities to reflect that if a public execution is intended as a deterrent, then it would certainly be best that mine should be as secret as possible, lest it achieve the opposite of the desired effect.'

Well then, have you any desire to be powerful, or do you not want it? Alas, we live such a pitiable life nowadays that we are all spoilt with reading and hearing this kind of thing, and perhaps admire it as a poet's fiction – but it never occurs to us to follow it up in the slightest. That is why it is even dangerous for a man of character to have this poetic power, for it can easily happen that his poetic power is taken from him, and as for his character – no one cares about that. The poetic power along with character is dangerous just as, for example, it is suspicious in logic to illustrate the laws of thought by interesting examples: it is easy for the important point to be forgotten.   *XI¹ A 538*

Infant baptism

It is easy to see that this is really connected with the knavish cunning with which mankind has tried to cheat God of Christianity by turning it into Epicureanism.

Take away the illusion of infant baptism, and straightway we have genuine Christian conflicts: to be father and mother, themselves as Christians hoping for eternal blessedness – but to leave it to the child to decide, when its time comes, if it wishes to be one.

This demands an effort, a tense effort, which will make people a little less eager to marry and marriages more serious; an effort which Christianity is by no means anxious to remove, but which man wants to remove at all costs.

So infant baptism was invented, and now we can say that little ready-made Christians are put into the world, who are straightaway all right for eternity, and there can be proper pleasure in the idyllic enjoyment of the comforts and joys of family life.

Oh, it is abominable to have falsified Christianity so vilely! In the end it has been so turned around that its purpose seems to be to awaken the desire in men to have children.

XI¹A 546

A Protestant minister

That such a figure should be a teacher of Christianity is just as ridiculous as to see a chest of drawers dancing. The chest of drawers – of course in itself it is a very respectable piece of furniture, I certainly do not mean to disparage a chest of drawers – is deficient in just those qualities which are required for dancing. So too with the Protestant minister in respect of being a teacher of Christianity. He is deficient in all the requisite qualities, and possesses the wrong ones: he is a married man, a father, a functionary, a dignitary, a knight, he goes about in long clothes, and so on: as a chest of drawers very respectable and estimable, but a chest of drawers is not suitable for dancing, and he is not suitable to be a teacher of Christianity.

XI¹A 548

The Model

In Protestantism a point has been reached where the desire to follow the Model is regarded as downright blasphemy.

How may this be explained? Presumably because the life of the Model is basically regarded in its outcome – and so there is some truth in saying, 'I have no desire for this kind of end.'

But in truth the life of the Model was not the outcome of his life: but his life was to be, as Scripture says [Psalm 22. 7] a worm and no man, and he too speaks of it thus as sheer misery and suffering. How vile to say, in face of this, 'I am too *humble* to desire this kind of fate.'

But this human language is false from beginning to end. If

God proclaims 'joy', the language immediately comes along and takes the word 'joy', and derives from it the meaning of Christianity as 'enjoy life'. And so too with the Model. The Model represents the highest existence. But wait a little, what does the highest existence turn out to be? Sheer misery, need, being a worm, *ecce homo*. But what does man do, with the help of his tricks with language? He takes the words 'highest existence' and says, 'I am too humble to desire or to will this highest existence.'

And this is Christendom, a society of Christians – who cannot be described in terms of what the apostle said about the heathen [Romans 1–3], since bestial and savage excesses have been replaced by a lying way of life which is even viler. In a certain sense I could be tempted to say that by means of the New Testament it is impossible to get in a right attack on the corruption of Christendom; for the New Testament is essentially concerned with the demoralization of Judaism and paganism, but naturally not with that which has been brought about by the abuse of Christianity. And yet it is easy to see that this must be the most frightful of all, for the more powerful the remedy, the more dangerous the consequences of abuse.

XI¹A 550

Christendom

Instead of all the impudent twaddle which – after first having (oh *lèse-majesté*!) degraded Christianity to the status of a simple historical phenomenon – then hit upon the idea that Christianity is perfectible – just as if a drop of attar of roses were to fall into the ocean, and the ocean were to maintain that this addition brought about perfection, that it is now going ahead (impudent effrontery): no, as the ocean to that drop of attar, so the world in relation to Christianity is only able to destroy, to corrupt it:

Instead of all this impudent twaddle the truth is that Christendom is apostasy from Christianity.

The sad thing is that one thinks of apostasy in terms of a

ceremonious and genuine renunciation of Christianity. Oh my dear friend, the world is not so honourable and good; no, lies are its element, and so the apostasy takes the form of lies, apostasy is the lie of seeming to be Christianity.

I have already said that every demoralization is related to health, and that Christianity being the truth, demoralization tends towards lies. After asceticism one does not have simple desires, but unnatural lusts – and after Christianity has appeared, as the truth, one no longer has simple paganism, but the lie of being a Christian, one has a subtle form of paganism through the dishonourable acceptance of one side of Christianity as a gain for an epicurean life; and this lying style of life is painted up to be Christianity. . . .

Christendom is apostasy from Christianity. The handful of better Christians who do exist, so far from being beneficial, rather do damage, through not having had the energy and character to make the true state of affairs clear, and to venture their life. So they do not help, but are just added to the total, much as in a riot of ten thousand people ten policemen might be present with their badges of rank: they do not help, and strictly speaking they must be added to the total, so that if the total number of rioters were to be given accurately one should have to say there were ten thousand and ten. There is a difference, however: the policemen are not able to make a resistance: but every Christian is able to get out of Christendom's falsities, emphasizing what he is to the uttermost – and if he does not do this, then it is quite in order to count him in with the mass of corruption. *XI¹A 552*

A real relation to God

As I have said elsewhere, a real relation to God is of such infinite value that even if it lasted only one moment, and the next moment one were kicked and derided, cast off, pitched far away, forgotten (which is, however, impossible, for not only is God love, but these relations are remembered eternally, so that the end must be that one lays hold of God again) – it is nevertheless of infinitely more value than all that the world and men have to offer.

But a real relation to God is also quite different from becoming a professor *of*, getting married at the expense of, living *on*, that is, *with* a family (of, on, with), living on the fact that another has had a real relation to God in the only possible way, in terrible torments and sufferings.   *XI¹A 553*

The sacraments

It is essentially in virtue of the place assigned to the sacraments and the use made of them that Christianity has been led back to Judaism. And what Pascal says is very true, the truest thing that has been said about Christendom, that it is an association of men who by means of certain sacraments free themselves of the duty of loving God.

By means of baptism one is – objectively – the people of God, and by means of infant baptism into the bargain; just as by means of circumcision one is the people of God.

So the following of Christ has been completely abolished. The sacrament is something objective, and every serious person must feel the need for something objective. Many thanks! And by means of this objectivity the whole matter of eternity is settled once for all in the easiest and cheapest manner possible – and now we have the whole of our life to be happy and joyful and enjoy this life, and then we have eternity after that, so that the enjoyment can go on *ad infinitum*.

The sacrament of the Lord's Supper is used like the sacrificial offering in Judaism: everything is calculated to set one at rest – objectively and rapidly – in relation to the matter of eternity, and then we live our own lives, enjoying existence, multiplying and filling the earth.

This is Christianity. And that it is New Testament Christianity is proved by the fact that Christ was present at a wedding in Cana. All honour to Christendom!   *XI¹A 556*

To treat Christianity as a science

is to change it into something past, or to express that it is no longer something present.

Science, theory, always comes last.

Take another example. To turn the grammar of a living language into a science is never really successful, but only that of a dead language, because the direct present existence of a living language makes science difficult.

In times when Christianity was present as a religion and a faith – although then too an attempt to turn it into a science was made, this was not really successful, because Christianity was still in existence, and hence was not an imperfection.

It has been reserved for our time to have a philosophy which boasts that Christianity has been entirely resolved into science: that is, Christianity has ceased to exist.

But turned around as our language in its trickery always is, we do not say, what in fact is the truth, that Christianity has ceased to exist. No, we say 'What immense progress! Now Christianity has entirely become science!' *XI¹ A 557*

To be spirit

Flesh and blood, or the life of the senses, and spirit are opposites. So it is easy to see what being spirit means: it means being free to will that which flesh and blood most shrink from . . .

Now what do flesh and blood shrink from most of all? From dying. Therefore spirit is to will to die, to die to the world.

Now it is easy to see that to die to the world is suffering of a higher potency than dying. For dying is merely to suffer, but dying to the world is freely to engage oneself in the same suffering; moreover dying is a fairly brief suffering, whereas dying to the world lasts the whole of one's life. . . .

XI¹ A 558

The situation is the decisive factor

When Christ says to the leper, or to the two blind men (Matthew 9. 28), 'Do you believe that I can help you?' and they were healed in virtue of their faith, and when we now say, 'I believe that Christ can help me', the two things by no means correspond to one another. For now Christ is no longer in the humble form of a servant, and in his incognito, which was the offence required in order that faith could be faith.

And yet in Christendom we make a pretence of nothing, we speak of believing as if it were the same thing to believe that God can help us and to believe that this individual man with whom I am talking, in his humble servant's form, the sign of offence, that this man can help me. *XI¹A 562*

A symptom

If something is in process of disappearing, or has disappeared, from life, this can be known from its becoming the object of another kind of interest, for example, a speculative or an aesthetic or an artistic interest.

Thus it is characteristic of our time that a more and more popular theme for a novel (as with Goldschmidt among us) is the depiction of the struggle of genius with reality. This means that it no longer occurs to anyone to try to realize this kind of thing in real life (Goethe, for example, clearly falsified his genius into talent). But we still want to have it, and so it is provided in novels.

Short-sighted people are deceived, and think that it is always a good thing to have it in this way, perhaps they even think that in this way genius comes nearer to us, or we come nearer to it. Ah, they are deceived, it means that it is really departing from us. The more artistically complete the novel is, the less does genius enter into life, the more are men just pampered and spoilt by busying themselves with the enjoyment of this sort of thing through their imagination. To believe that art helps us to enter into reality is just as misguided as to believe that the more artistically perfect a sermon, the better it is able to transform life. Ah no: the more aesthetic is its effect, away from the existential. *XI¹A 570*

, *'How can you speak good, when you are evil?'*

Matthew 12. 34

In a certain sense one must say that it is a kind of wickedness, this dissimulation which hinders what Christ adds, that out of the abundance of the heart the mouth speaks. The passage is therefore probably not to be understood as though Christ were reproving them for not speaking out of the abundance of the heart; or it must be understood only in the negative sense that they did not speak good, that this very dissimulation was the abundance of the heart out of which the mouth spoke evil (in good words). *XI¹A 571*

❤ The law and the gospel

The way in which Luther speaks of the law and the gospel is not Christ's teaching.
[*In the margin:* as, for example, in Luther's sermon on the Gospel for the third Sunday in Advent.]
Luther distinguishes two things: the law and the gospel. First the law, and then the gospel, which is all mildness and so on. In this way we end with Christianity as optimism, its aim being that we should have things good in this world.
That is to say, Christianity becomes Judaism. The law corresponds to what in the Old Testament was tempting and trying by God. Then comes the gospel, just as in the Old Testament the trials ceased and everything was joy and jubilation.
But as I have often said, every existence in which life's tension is resolved within this life is Judaism. Christianity means sheer suffering in this life, it is eternity.

It does not help if we men get furious ten times over and say, no man can endure this. It does not help: God is not impressed. And the error in Luther's sermon is already to be seen in the marks it bears of concern for us poor men, which proves that he is unable to maintain Christianity at the pitch which it has in the New Testament, and precisely in the gospel: the pitch of the Absolute. . . . *XI¹A 572*

Sorrow at one's sin

True sorrow at one's sin is to better oneself. One can forget sin, or try to forget it perhaps in new sins, so that the one drives out the other; or in distractions – but it is in vain. True sorrow and true forgetfulness are in bettering oneself.

XI¹A 574

Religious suffering

If a dray-horse or a farm-horse were to see the instruments of torture which are used on a show-horse, it would shudder. So the natural man would shudder to see the instruments of torture which are used for religious suffering, which are a part of reaching blessedness.

To this extent it is undeniably disgusting and abhorrent to see the falseness of this gang of merry professors and priests, who live by laying forth what is regarded as being religiosity, uncommonly profound religiosity, for the congregation's religiosity consists in now and again listening to them laying it forth. This is charming, just as true as tea made from a piece of paper which once lay in a drawer beside another piece of paper in which some dried tea-leaves had once been wrapped, from which tea had already been made three times.

Yet it is wrong to complain. For when eternity is at stake – these professors certainly do not live in and for eternity, so fairness demands that they should have it all the better in this world. *XI¹A 579*

Christendom

could be regarded as a sheer misunderstanding, a wrong turning, which introduced the historical in place of the primitive. And this historical element has now become an immense screed, just as in some fairy-tales every part is introduced by all that has gone before.

That is what I have so often drawn attention to, that men shrink from the effort to be the primitive I – and so they remain in the third person, and are at ease in the historical and in marking it out.

But can one be immortal in the third person, or in virtue of the fact that others have become immortal?   *XI¹ A 587*

God's majesty

I have shown elsewhere how God's majesty is secured against what otherwise would be the ruin of majesty, namely, numbers, and that God is inversely related to numbers: the greater the number the less the relation with God.

Now from another side I want to show his majesty: he does not need, like other majesties, police and a guard to punish offences against him. No, he is much better secured. For the position is that to sin against God is to punish oneself. So sure is God that his enemies will be punished! Perhaps someone will think that this means making all punishment natural punishment, thus abolishing all positive punishments. This is a frivolous objection. But let us take care. What makes it seem, with the crimes which do not carry their own punishment with them, that the sinner can escape, if justice does not catch him in time, is that the time of a man's life is limited, so that he can escape punishment by dying. But God has eternity before him. So we have the principle that sinning brings its own punishment, the sinner does not escape, when eternity lies before him. Therefore to sin against God is to punish oneself, and thus God's majesty is secured. And not only that, but the punishment a man suffers (his sin) he must

also repent of into the bargain, if he desires to have an understanding with God. What an immense distance of majesty!
To be thankful for a gracious punishment is the most a man
can think of. But a sinner must repent of his punishment,
suffer the punishment and then beg forgiveness for it: what
majesty!   *XI¹A 589*

. . . In a time when everyone is hankering after originality,
there suddenly arises an originality so qualitative that it
must be sheer suffering to be this originality.

This is my case. Yet I do not complain of my contemporaries, for the same thing would happen to me in every age.

Merely quantitative originality, by being related to a given
situation, is recognized and understood without further ado.
(And the less the originality the more rapid and assured the
recognition.) Qualitative originality must really demand
faith. But men never want to make this effort. And when this
qualitative originality awaits its result in posterity – yes,
then it is fêted. But it no longer needs faith. Thus a qualitative
originality must always come more or less to suffer. For it
simply cannot begin with its result. And men are never
capable of more than believing in virtue of the result. They
are not capable of believing, they are only capable of hankering
– to be fooled!   *XI¹A 593*

Scandal

Mediocrity will perhaps find consolation in thinking that if
one does not take Christianity too seriously (a charge of which
it is undoubtedly not guilty) at least one has the merit of not
causing a scandal.

No thank you: if exaltation can be guilty of causing scandal
by taking Christianity too seriously, mediocrity is guilty all
the time.

Mediocrity merely recalls (what for the rest it may never
dare to appropriate for itself, for Peter was as far removed
from mediocrity as possible) – it merely recalls what Christ

says to Peter, 'You are a stumbling-block to me' [Matthew 16. 23].

And how often, in more modest circumstances and proportions, has one who in truth desired the truth found occasion to say to that accursed, wretched, hearty and scoundrelly mediocrity which wanted to hold him back, 'You are a stumbling-block to me.'

You see, o mediocrity, that you perhaps least of all are exempt of the guilt you thought you were absolutely secure against – namely, of causing scandal. Could this thought not help you, could it not stab you awake and provoke you to get out of your groove?   *XI² A 1*

The absolute – the relative

The law for applying the relative is, Look out, look out. The law for applying the absolute is, Shut your eyes, be blind, in faith, for God in heaven's sake do not look out, as the raven lost the cheese through listening to what was being said, so you will lose the absolute if you look out, no matter whether it means looking out in fear for oneself or looking out in so-called participation.

That is why Christianity has quite disappeared, for what has applied a little Christianity has always followed the law of looking out.

But the world is so wretched, lying, as Christianity teaches, in evil, so that if you want to look out, you will have to say all the time, 'It is something if one can get men to live a little more decently than they do' – and so you fall off, and do not apply the absolute. Or it is something to get some people in some way to follow a softened-down Christianity – and so you fall off, and do not apply the absolute.

XI² A 2

To forgive sins

is not only divine, in the sense that no one but God can do it, but it is also divine in the sense that no one can do it without God's help. Men, if they really could forgive sins, are not up to it – no, how poverty-stricken, niggardly, sullen and restricted is their forgiveness, so that the sinner may well say, No thank you, I prefer to ask to be punished, and take my punishment, and be spared your wretched and miserable forgiveness, which perhaps in any case, if I should be truly saved and become something excellent, would come knocking at my door again and in the form of envy present me with an account for its forgiveness.

How different is the divine forgiveness! The human tendency is basically to expose sin, to get to know something bad about a man – then we know that he is not different from the rest of us. The only kind of forgiveness which is in any way practised is reciprocal discharge. God rejoices to forgive sin; as he is almighty in creating from nothing, so he is almighty in reducing to nothing: for to forget, to forget in almightiness is surely to reduce to nothing. $XI^2 A 3$

Spiritual sins

How far the world is from being spirit can also be seen in the fact that just those sins which are regarded by Christianity as the most terrible are not regarded by the world as sins at all, but almost as admirable – for example, cunning, malicious wrong-doing, disingenuousness, and so on.

What the world regards as sin, and makes a great fuss about, is either theft and everything to do with the security of property, or sins of the flesh, which it is probably true to say Christianity regards as the most pardonable. A man who lives day in day out in cunning and fraud, but otherwise is extremely cultured and belongs to the best circles – if he were unlucky enough to get drunk, alas, it would be an irreparable loss, and he himself would judge it so severely that perhaps, as one says, he would never forgive himself; whereas it would never occur to him that he needed to be forgiven for all the cunning and fraud and dishonesty, for all the spiritually terrible passions which dwell in him and are his life.

XI² A 6

God is love

Transformed into a catchword, and concocted into childish nonsense, this is what has certainly confused Christianity and made a galimatias of Christendom.

The law of love is quite simply what is well enough known: to love is to be changed into likeness with the beloved.

But this law holds only for the ascending scale, not for the reverse. Example: if a man is superior in reason and wisdom, then the law for his love in relation to one who is much his inferior in reason and wisdom is certainly not that he should be changed into likeness with the latter. To love in this way would be absurd; and if he is really superior then it does not happen in this way. No; the law is to wish to do everything to raise the beloved up to oneself, and if the beloved wishes it then the law for his love is to be changed into likeness with the beloved.

This law is respected in every possible circumstance, it is everywhere valid.

In Christendom an exception is made with one alone: with God in heaven; he is supposed to be, in a childishly nonsensical way, pure love, in other words, sheer nonsense; here something is supposed to be valid which is denounced as egoism and deceit, when the one who is superior is not changed into likeness with the less reasonable, here this is to be valid, that is to say, here one supposes that there is an exception, for God is pure love: that is to say, sheer nonsense. . . .

No, that God is love of course means that he wishes to do everything to help you to love him, that is, to be changed into likeness with him. As I have so often said, he knows well how infinitely painful this change is for a man, he is willing to suffer with you, yes, he suffers in love more than you, he suffers all the heart's sorrow of misunderstanding – but he does not change.

But as an older person, wishing to win a child's love, introduces the matter by endearing himself to the child in the child's understanding, and to that end brings the child cakes and the like, so Christianity also offers something attractive.

This attraction is the proclamation of the forgiveness of sins. No man who does not have enough self-composure to be sorry for his sin, to see that it is there that the mischief really lies – no man without that much of the eternal in him can really come to love God, God cannot have dealings with him, he cannot, if I may dare to put it thus, try to capture him.

So the forgiveness of sins is proclaimed with – if I may dare to put it thus – a splendour without parallel.

And here Christianity really begins. For from this point the transition is made to loving God, or to being changed into likeness with God. And so there begins what I describe thus: God must make you unhappy, from the human point of view, if he is to love you and you are to love him.

Now Christendom – like a child who eats the cakes and turns his back on the giver – has achieved the supposed masterstroke of accepting the divine splendour, and using it as a stimulating ingredient for living in its own way in enjoyment of this life. This is a scoundrelly act, which is of course the most foolish possible, for it is the most foolish of all things to try to mock God.   *XI²A 8*

– My life is an immense strain: I feel so alienated, so different, from what occupies men in general. Day in day out I notice my heterogeneity, in almost every contact, in the most different ways. . . .

As I say, the strain lies, among other things, in my being so completely different from other men. Either they live purely for finite ends – and this is the class of men I like best, with whom I could also have got along very well, if the gutter press had not spoiled things; or else they pretend to live for something higher – only this is mere mystification. In each case my way of living for the idea is as different from men's life as speaking Hebrew is from speaking Danish: we do not merely not have the same aspirations, but in a certain sense we do not even have language in common, in so far as they make a false use of language.

Think of a criminal, whose life is different from that of other men. But then there are usually other criminals, and they unite to form a world for themselves. But imagine that you are the only criminal: would this not mean an immense strain?

On the other hand, take the highest, take the God-Man: to live in this way, to know that he came to cast fire upon the earth [Luke 12. 49]. This is not a matter of setting fire to a house or two, but of setting fire to the human race: to be a man and live among men, and yet to be so different from being a man – now I am able to have a faint idea of this fearful strain.

At the same time this also lets me see what nonsense all this is with these millions of Christians and thousands of priests: for if a man must undergo such strains as I do in order to get just a faint idea of Christ's suffering, what is the value of what the priests preach, who are in the van, and whom the people follow? *XI²A 11*

Isolation

That Christianity is absolutely bound up with isolation (the single person) may also be seen in the fact that Christianity's presupposition is always the consciousness of sin, that it begins with proclaiming the forgiveness of sin.

But consciousness of sin is absolute isolation. Even the most primitive originality is not so isolating: it is only anticipation in relation to others, it does not reach the most intimate depths of personality. Even the worst human misfortune or suffering does not isolate so much as this, the very fact of being a man means that the others participate in this, which ends with death, and does not reach the most intimate depths of personality.

Sin alone is the absolutely isolating factor. My sin does not concern anyone else but myself, and it concerns the most intimate depths of my personality.

So one can see what nonsense it is to speak of peoples and states and lands and other abstractions as Christian, which means little children being Christian. The point has been reached where Christian is defined without any reference to the *sine qua non* of Christianity, namely, isolation, the single person. *XI²A 14*

The Saviour of the world

When one thinks of the insipid, nauseating and syrupy idea of the Saviour of the world which is worshipped and put up for sale by Christendom, it makes a strange effect to read his words, 'I come to cast fire on earth' [Luke 12. 49], come to make a division which can burst the most sacred bonds, bonds hallowed by God himself, between father, son, husband and wife, parents and children, and so on. *XI²A 15*

A quite special kind of preaching

is entrusted to me, and how demanding to the nth power!

Wherever I look, the law for preaching has hitherto been that if men have been willing to accept the word of the preacher, and say to him, 'What is it you wish of us, do you wish us to do as you do?' then the answer has invariably been, 'Yes!' It is different for me. If all the millions of men alive today were to come together to me, with the greatest willingness, and were to say 'What is it you wish of us, do you wish us to do as you do?' then I should have to answer, 'No!' There is not a single man alive who has a task in common with me; and among the millions there is again not a single one – as I see it – who has a task in common with any other – and this is precisely what I have to proclaim. The difference is like that between gathering and scattering: all other preaching tends towards gathering men, mine towards scattering them, making them single persons.

This much is easy to see. He who replies yes to that question (shall we do as you do?) is perhaps himself an individuality, but his preaching is not that of individuality. He obviously has a doctrine, and his preaching essentially does not make individualities of men, but copies.

My preaching preaches individuality by way of reduplication.

But how am I to be even remotely understood in a time where all the tactics tend to gather men, and where consequently no one has an inkling of the tactics which tend to scatter them, and how this requires a qualitatively different effort from the other?

Nevertheless this is the way that the human race should go.

And my task is, being myself an individuality and preserving myself as such (which God in heaven also watches over in infinite love), to proclaim the infinite reality which each man has in himself, when he remains himself before God. But in this way I do not have a scrap of doctrine – and doctrine is what is wanted. For doctrine means lazy imitation for the student, and the way to material power for the teacher, for doctrine gathers men. The preaching of individuality means to be happy with a reward in oneself – to be sacrificed to men.

What I have to preach is in the strictest sense the service of the spirit. Everything that is preached with the tendency to gather man is related in one way or the other to the determination of men as animals. That is why it is all so simple. For when everything is reduced to mere generality, when one reckons not with individualities but with copies, then one soon has thousands – alas, in a certain sense there are enough of these. But the preaching of individuality is so slow, that even one is a lot, and one could even be content with none at all – which in another sense the true individuality easily can, since he is himself the individuality.

My preaching is as though someone should say: what a wonderful sight the starry heavens are! And if those thousands of men were ready to listen to his words and say to him, What do you wish us to do, do you wish us to learn your discourse by heart? must he not reply, No, no, no, but I want every single one of you to look up at the night's starry heaven and, each in his own way – and he can do it – be uplifted by the sight.

But alas, man is an animal creation, and the comfortable desire for imitation is like his second nature. That is why it is so tremendously easy to gather him together into a herd, and the preacher will get thousands who will learn his words by rote – and perhaps become professors of his words – but for ten thousand perhaps there will not be a single one who himself looked up at the night's starry heavens. Yet the preachers themselves are only too often to blame that everything becomes an imitation, for it brings them earthly and temporal profit. Be dishonest, if you will, about the starry heavens, and pretend that it is not the heavens that are the splendour, but your idea of them; recruit your staff from trumpeting knights of industry – and in no time you will have a crowd ready to pay through the nose for your splendid teaching. But if you are honest about the starry heavens, and say, what is the truth, that it is they which are splendid and that every man in his own way could see the splendour, and that for him his way is infinitely more worth than yours for him, or his for you – yes, then there is no more room for financial speculation or for animal gatherings in a herd. . . .

XI² A 19

An apostle – my insignificance

An apostle's task is to spread Christianity – to win men for it.

My task is to take away from men the illusion that they are Christians – and yet I serve Christianity.

Christianity has now existed for 1,800 years – let me be

shown whether this thought has ever been raised before in Christendom.

My life, like everything in the sphere where I am at home and for which I work, is the sphere of paradox: the positive is known by the negative. Ah, certainly my life is sheer melancholy, like a night (hence those words in the Diapsalmata of *Either-Or* are completely fitting: 'When I die I shall be able to say, *"Du bist vollbracht Nachtwache meines Daseins"'*);[1] certainly my life is torment and suffering, and God torments me, lovingly and from love, in what gives me most suffering of all. Yet this negative is a sign of the positive, it is a primitivity which is related not to my contemporaries but to mankind; and its great significance is properly expressed by saying that for my contemporaries I am superfluous. . . .   *XI² A 21*

Indignation

In all seriousness I demand of everyone who wants to have to do with me that he bind himself to pay double as much as before in church contributions.

Nothing weakens the impression of moral pathos more than bringing money into the picture. Thus if a man wishes to express indignation by refusing to pay any contributions to the church, it can all be explained by saying that he wants to save the money. No, I ask for double contributions to the church – but keep away from the church.

The punishment I should wish for the priests is to give each of them ten times as great an income as they have – but not a single man in church. But of course, like everything that comes from me, according to the words of Bishop Mynster, this is 'much too high'. I fear that neither the world nor the priests would understand this punishment. Yet it is the truest punishment, and entirely in keeping with the idea.

If someone – let us make the experiment in thought – if

[1] From '*Enten-Eller*', *Samlede Værker*² I, 29: *Either-Or*, Doubleday Anchor ed., 35 ('Thou art perfected, night-watch of my being'). RGS

someone were to prove completely (not in the sense in which I speak of Christianity as not existing at all) – no, if he could prove that Christ simply never existed, nor the apostles, that the whole thing is fiction, and if nothing was done by the state or the public, if no show was made of confiscating all these livings, I wonder how many priests would lay down their offices? If the matter were not so serious, it is infinitely ludicrous that the parsons quite tranquilly go on living off Christianity with their families.

Yes, in the end of the day what most sustains Christianity in our time is not so much the cleverness of the government, and the like, as fear of an immense financial revolution. And it is also quite certain that not even the bankruptcy of ten Rothschilds would cause such a revolution as Christianity going out of business.   *XI² A 22*

Twaddle – ill-treatment by ridicule – public persecution

If I had time, I think I should write a book of instructions for future officials of Christianity; for this is the way we must go, and here is where the evil lies; and it is a good thing that an official should have in advance as concrete an idea as possible of the suffering and the danger.

What makes such ill-treatment so infamous and trying is that it has no real factual foundation, it has nothing one can get a hold of, but it is always carried out under cover of being nothing at all. This in turn causes many, who would otherwise for very decency restrain themselves, to think that they can join in here, or at least can get some pleasure out of such a thing happening to someone. And the man concerned cannot well speak of the treatment he receives, since its purpose is to deprive him of the idea he has of himself. . . .

For my part I do not complain. For in the course of time the whole thing comes to mean something different for me, it becomes a welcome opportunity for a loving understanding with God. Gifts from God should surely be the dearest for a man; and if it should happen now that, *si placet*, he oddly chooses, *si placet*, that his gifts come in the form of torments – then no matter, it comes from him!

But even if it were not so, I would not complain; as a psychologist I am content. It would be a queer doctor who complained about an illness he had to do with that it was malignant! No; my wish has been to get to know men, and I could never have been better placed for this, and it has been infinitely valuable for me, teaching me, indeed, that men are very little worth. *XI²A 23*

Baptism

If Christ had approved of regarding baptism as it is now regarded by Christendom, as an analogy to circumcision, an *opus operatum*, he would scarcely have used the word 'baptism' metaphorically, as, for example, when he speaks of being baptized with a baptism: 'Can you be baptized with the baptized I shall be baptized with?' [Mark 10. 38], where he is speaking of his Passion. *XI²A 25*

The public

is that which is the emptiest of ideas, indeed it is the very opposite of the idea. For the public is numbers.

This is also why, as is shown in our time, and what Poul Møller was so well aware of, without being able to explain it – that Jews in particular make good publicists. The Jew in general lacks imagination and heart, but he does have abstract intelligence. And numbers are his element.

For the publicist the struggle of ideas in public life is neither more nor less than an affair of the Stock Exchange. As in the quotations of stocks and shares, so what concerns him is merely to know what opinion has the numbers on its side. He believes that numbers are ideas – and this is the very culmination of absence of ideas. *XI²A 26*

Unrest

As the fisherman when he has cast his net makes a noise in the water in order to chase the fish in that direction and make a good haul, as the hunter with his beaters covers the whole ground and disturbs the game so that they are concentrated at the point where the guns are placed: so God, who desires to be loved, catches men with the help of unrest.

Christianity is the most intense, strong, and greatest possible unrest. No greater can be conceived, it aims (just as Christ's life did) at disturbing human existence to the very depths, at shattering and breaking everything.

So God makes use of unrest, he applies unrest in order to catch men who wish to love him. But the difference from the fisher and the hunter is that God does not apply unrest in order to catch all the more. He does it not for the sake of numbers but for the sake of intensity: that is to say, when the greatest possible unrest is applied there exists in a man, in the tension, an intensity which brings him to real love of God.

But what man loves is rest, security. Yet it is certain that no one can become a Christian in rest and security. Nor is it less certain that no Christian can remain in rest and certainty. Where a man becomes a Christian, there is unrest; and where a man has become a Christian, there will be unrest.

XI² A 29

Temptations of thought

The tactics are quite simple: remain entirely indifferent to them, the most absolute indifference to them is victory over them. What such thoughts desire is to make you afraid, they wish to make you afraid till you are so pusillanimous that you imagine you are responsible for them, they want to penetrate you with fear and so saddle you with them that now you listen to them, and dwell on them, and so on – and all under the torment that you are responsible. If you once imagine all this,

195

then Satan is loose. So remain absolutely indifferent! Be more indifferent to them than you are to a little rumbling in your stomach or the like. Or get angry, as you get angry when someone stands ringing at your door-bell at an inopportune time and you rush out and say 'What's all this going on?' and so on; that is, get so angry that you cannot be afraid; for being afraid is just what you must avoid.

You fight temptation best when you flee and escape. But this cannot help with temptations of thought, for they follow you. So here the tactics must be not to be afraid, be quite calm, absolutely indifferent.

Temptations of thought (which are entirely normal when a man makes a real effort, as with the effort to be a Christian, as also in the effort involved in the sphere of imagination) do not arise nowadays at all among Christians, especially Protestants, especially in Denmark. And this is even regarded as progress. Ah, it is a progress backwards, of the same kind as that cure the doctor in *Barselstuen* speaks of: 'The patient is dead, but the fever has entirely vanished!'[1] So the temptations have vanished, but of course so has Christianity.   *XI²A 30*

A view of Christianity

which, so far as I know, has never been suggested before is that Christianity is the invention of Satan, calculated to make men unhappy by means of the imagination. As the worm and the bird seek out the finest fruit, so Satan has turned his attention to those who are outstanding, in whom imagination and feeling predominate, in order to lead them astray by means of the imagination, and so cause them to make themselves unhappy, and if possible others along with them.

This view has something in it. It is also certain that when this height has once been reached, where it can be said that the matter of becoming a Christian is really beginning, then every single step is so demanding, so dangerous, that it is like a constant 'Red or black' – a choice between God and Satan.

---

[1] Comedy by Holberg, Act 3, scene 5. RGS

To be a Christian, merely to approach it, implies such an ideality that it is constantly a question of God or Satan. . . .

$XI^2 A 31$

'A better future'

It is surely naïve and undialectical to let oneself get enthusiastic at the thought of a better future, a future when one will be understood better – as though things did not always remain essentially the same, namely, bad, or if there is a change then it is for the worse.

A better future, and better understood – that means a future in which admiring professorial rascals and priestly riff-raff turn the dead man's life and work and witness into profit for themselves and their families. Is this a better future? Is this to be better understood?

Take the highest of all: which misunderstanding has been the greatest, which must be most abhorrent to Christ – that of the Jews who put him to death, or that of Christendom which has made a profit out of him? Surely Christendom's, it is only Christendom's which must be abhorrent.

And yet it has always been so with all the militant *men* I have read about (with the sole exception of Socrates), that they get enthusiastic at the idea of a better future, when they will be better understood.

This idea does not rouse the slightest enthusiasm in me, and I think that to require such an encouraging thought (an illusion) is an indirect proof that one is not at rest in one's enthusiasm in and for itself. In any case this idea does not rouse any enthusiasm in me, on the contrary, what can provoke me most of all is to think of that scoundrelly posterity. The misunderstanding of my contemporaries is nothing like so embittering nor, if one will, so hopeless: no, everything is hopelessly lost, one's life is suffocated in misunderstanding, only when the misunderstanding is characterless and thoughtless admiration. $XI^2 A 32$

Temptations of thought

are related, as I have said, to the imagination – purely rational types do not know this kind of thing.

One may best compare such thoughts with wind. Like that, they are nothing, but they can give trouble enough so long as they persist.

And to continue the metaphor, as those who suffer from some abdominal complaint must take care to have a good evacuation every day, so a good evacuation in action which engages the character is the best means for dealing with such thoughts. It is really in the time before one has to act, when one cannot come to terms with oneself or reach clarity about one must do, that such tormentors make their appearance, just as dawn and dusk are the time for ghosts. These thoughts are possibilities, they are the production of what is possible – and the best remedy for them is reality.   *XI²A 33*

Christian revision

What money is in the finite world, concepts are in the world of spirit. It is in them that all transactions take place.

Now when things go on from generation to generation in such a way that everyone takes over the concepts from the preceding generation, and then uses his day and his time in order to enjoy this life, to work for finite ends, and so on, then it happens only too easily that the concepts are gradually changed, and become something quite different from what they originally were, they come to mean something quite different, they become like false coinage – while all the time all trans- actions happily continue to be carried out in them. This, however, does not affect men's egoistic interests, as when false coinage is issued, especially when the falsification of concepts tends to buttress human egoism, in such a way that he who is really deceived is (if I may dare to say) the other interested party in the matter of Christianity – namely, God in heaven.

Yet no one has any desire to undertake the business of revising the concepts. Everyone understands more or less clearly that to be caught up in the business in this way is much the same as being sacrificed. It means that your life is laid hold upon in such a way that you cannot do what man naturally desires – to busy himself with finite ends. No, the human thing is to sit as lightly as possible to the concepts, and then – the sooner the better – to enter into the concrete matters of life; or in any case not to be too fussy about the concepts, not so fussy that you cannot go full tilt into the concrete matters.

Yet with every decade a revision becomes more and more necessary.

So Providence has to take possession of an individual who can be used for this purpose.

A reviser of this kind is of course something quite different from that whole band of chattering priests and professors – yet he is not an apostle either, but rather the very opposite.

What the reviser requires is just what the apostle has no need of, namely, intellectuality, in the highest degree, and in addition an immense acquaintance with every kind of trickery and falsification, almost as though he himself were the craftiest of all scoundrels – for his job is precisely to 'know' falsehoods.

Just because this knowledge is so immensely ambiguous that the greatest possible confusion could arise as a result of it, the reviser is not treated as the apostle. Alas, no! The apostle is a trusted man, whereas the reviser is placed under the strictest control. I have always just one image for this, but it is very telling. Suppose that the Bank of England realizes that there are false notes in circulation, which are such good imitations that the Bank despairs of detecting them, or of securing itself against future imitations. Despite all the talent there might be among the personnel of the Bank or the police, there is just one man with the absolute talent in this matter – but he is already condemned, a criminal. So they use him, but not as a man they trust. He is put under the most terrible controls; with the threat of death hanging over him he has to sit and deal with all that mass of money, and he is searched each time, and so on.

So with the Christian reviser. If the apostle's task is to proclaim the truth, the reviser's task is to unmask falsifications, to let them be recognized and thus impossible. If the apostle's personal character is one of noble and pure simplicity (which is the condition for being the instrument of the Holy Spirit), that of the reviser is his ambiguous knowledge. If the apostle is in a unique and good sense entirely in the power of Providence, the reviser is in the same power in an ambiguous sense. If the apostle, with all his efforts and labours, possesses no merit in the eyes of God, all the less may this be said of the reviser; nor could he (supposing it to be in any way possible) ever acquire this merit, for he has something negative to pay off: thus essentially he is a penitent. But essentially they are both sacrificed, and both are chosen in grace by Providence. For it is no disgrace that one is chosen to be a reviser. And as the apostle comes at the beginning, so the reviser can naturally come only at the end, since he presupposes the spread of Christianity. And if the apostle derives his name from his mission, coming from God and going out from there, the reviser's task is to penetrate the falsifications and to lead back to God.

There can be no more apostles; if they could come again, Christ too would be able to come again, but in a different sense from his second coming. Christ's life on earth is Christianity. The life of the apostle means that now Christianity is there, and from this time onwards you men have to take it over, on your own responsibility.

So men took it over. And if it is an eternal lie that Christianity is perfectible, one thing is certain, that men have developed an increasing perfectibility – in falsifying Christianity.

In face of this falsification God cannot, even if he wished, and even if there were no other obstacle, make use of an apostle, because Christendom with its falsehoods has put itself at such a distance from God that there can be question of his turning, if I may dare to put it thus, in confidence to men.

No, since Christendom is a falsification, and since nowadays sin is chiefly cleverness, so from the side of Providence – whom man by his falsehood has put at a distance from himself – everything is mistrust: there no longer come joyous emissaries from God, any more than we greet the police as such; no, there come only connoisseurs in dishonesty, and even these, since they are essentially part of the general dishonesty, are treated by Providence as ambiguous creatures.

Nowadays Christendom is pleased and happy. Often enough the situation is depicted as though a new era were about to begin, and new apostles about to come. For Christendom has of course done a splendid job, it has learned and appropriated so perfectly all that the apostles set going, that now it is possible to go on from there. The truth is that Christendom has made as scurvy and dishonest a job as possible, and to expect new apostles (if there were any truth in the idea at all) would be sheer effrontery. *XI² A 36*

'*To speak in tongues*'

[I Corinthians 14. 2 *ff.*]

Consistent as Christianity naturally is (so consistent that I am far from having grasped how consistent it is – so that it does not occur to me to speak of it as almost everyone nowadays speaks, like a critic of something he feels superior to) it also acknowledges that it has its own special language. Speaking in tongues is the Christian language, which is entirely different from the difference between one language and another, different from all human language, being a qualitative difference based on a difference of concepts.

The more I look at this matter, the more I see that the confusion is not just in Denmark, or just in Protestantism, or just in Christendom, but in the nature of man and the thieves' slang we men speak.

The Christian language makes use of the same words as we men; in this respect it does not desire any change; but it uses them in a qualitatively different fashion from us: it uses them in the reverse fashion. For Christianity indicates a sphere additional to or higher than the sphere in which we men naturally live, and in this sphere the common language of men is reflected in reverse. For example, Christianity says that loss of earthly things is a gain [Philippians 3. 7], and that to possess them is a loss. We also use the words gain and loss. But we simply do not take the sphere of the spirit into account, and so we understand by gain and loss just the opposite of what Christianity understands by them. So we let Christianity chatter on, then afterwards we preachify its words in our own language, and we call it Christianity.

As in music we speak of transposing a part for a different voice from that for which it was originally written, so the Christian language is entirely and at every point qualitatively different from our language, even though we use the same words. It was a master-stroke of Christendom to transpose Christian language back into the old wretched stuff – and in this way we are all Christians.

And so we await new apostles, for now mankind has polished off the task set for it by the apostles: what effrontery!

XI² A 37

That there should be epochs in Christendom

Once New Testament Christianity was reduced to the simply historical, and men imagined next that Christianity was perfectible, it was a quite straightforward discovery that there were various epochs. The epoch of the Son was New Testament Christianity, and now the epoch of the Spirit is at hand.

No, no: Christianity in the New Testament *is* Christianity. And Christianity is life's examination. God wishes to be loved: this is the test. But the result is that Christendom as a whole is to be regarded as rejected.

By way of compensation Christendom has been inexhaustible in inventing nonsense and tricks.

An epoch of the Spirit! If there were any meaning in this

kind of talk, then it would have to begin with the apostles. But to have it beginning later, in the progress of Christendom (there we have it: the progress of Christendom!): in Christian terms there is absolutely no meaning in speaking of progress from generation to generation. Every generation begins at the beginning, the examination is the same. Then when the generation has descended to the tomb, eternity sees how many there were in it who passed the divinely instituted examination. Then the next generation can begin.

But man's trick is always to put forward numbers, so that he can hide among them. The single person hides by taking refuge in the mass of his contemporaries, the contemporary generation. And in order to hide still better, each generation hides in the sequence of generations. And when they are thus hidden, like all cowards when they think they are safely hidden, men become impudent and insolent enough to talk about the progress of Christianity, and about a new epoch, the epoch of the Spirit. Indeed it looks like the Spirit! The most cowardly cramming together, like sardines, or like a herd of beasts, impersonality from first to last. If this period, our time, is the age of the Spirit, then it must get its name (*ad modum lucus a non lucendo*) from being so spirit-less, so that the age of the Spirit is characterized by being entirely free of Spirit. Among all the millions of men who are nothing but 'the public' there is not a single one who has the courage to have to do alone with God; there are not even many who even have any conception of what this means: and it is this collection which is supposed to be the age of the Spirit!   *XI²A 38*

The hidden attack on Christianity

What has done much harm to the cause of Christianity is that, in virtue of the respect it now enjoys, the attacks on it have for a long time been surreptitious.

I give an example from Lessing, who cannot be acquitted of guilt in this connexion.

In a recent book by Professor Schwarz, *Lessing als Theologe*, we hear once more the assertion, in particular regarding *Nathan the Wise*, that what Lessing abhorred above all was fanaticism. And of course, on the other hand, he was no enemy of Christianity.

This is how the example works: the concept of fanaticism is set up, it is furiously attacked, and everybody thinks this is wonderful. And as for Christianity, justice is done to it.

But wait a moment. When fanaticism is defined we learn that what constitutes it is its exclusiveness, that there is a definite set of conditions for salvation, a single and exclusive set of conditions outside which there is no salvation. Further, we learn that fanaticism is recognized by its zeal to save others and its condemning of others.

But if this is the state of affairs, then Christ is the greatest of all fanatics. Then why not put the attack in this way: Christianity is fanaticism, Christ is a fanatic?

This has caused incalculable harm: with a deep bow, empty respect has been paid to Christianity, and at the same time it has been deprived of all its characteristics which are branded as pernicious aberrations. This in turn has made the defenders of Christianity step out of character and transform Christianity. If the attack upon Christianity had been direct, the matter would have been clear, and would have constrained the defenders to remain in character. But what does happen is that the attackers of Christianity bow respectfully before it, and its defenders in reality attack it. Lessing attacks fanaticism – but Christianity, oh heaven forbid that he should have anything but respect for it. The defenders of Christianity show clearly that Lessing is right, and that Christianity is not fanaticism. And if you look more closely, you see that the result is that Christianity has ceased to be Christianity, and that gradually something quite different from New Testament Christianity has replaced it. The point is that the defenders should in face of Lessing have given matters an entirely different turn: they should have said, No thank you, Christianity is fanaticism. A Tertullian would have done it. But in our time this seems far too lofty and far too bold. When the attacker is so polite as to express his respect for Christianity, it does not occur to the Christendom of our time to repulse him and compel him to go over to the attack: for the many who are financially interested in Christianity thank God that they are not attacked. *XI² A 39*

'*I came to cast fire upon the earth*'

[Luke 12. 49]

How fearfully true are the utterances of Christianity! 'To cast fire upon the earth.' Yes, for what is a Christian? A Christian is a man who has taken fire.

This appears again at Pentecost – the Spirit is fire, tongues of fire rest on them.

The Spirit is fire. This is current usage. An example from a quite different world, which just because it is different casts light on the general usage. In Kruse's adaptation of *Don Juan*, Don Juan says of Elvira, 'In her eyes there burns a fire as from another world,' and that is why 'his heart thumps when he sees her'.

The Spirit is fire. Hence the phrase 'to be burnt to spirit' (in Baggesen).[1] But alas! in the fire which Christianity wishes to light, not all are burnt to a spirit, some are burnt to ashes, that is, in the fire they do not become spirit.

The Spirit is fire, and Christianity is incendiarism. And by nature man shrinks from this fire more than from any other. For even if a man has suffered from ten fires, provided the desire of life does not die out in him he can still perhaps prosper and enjoy life. But the fire which Christianity kindles is not intended to burn down a few houses, but to burn down the desire of life – to burn it to spirit.

The Spirit is fire. Hence the saying, as gold is purified by fire, so the Christian is purified. But fire does not just mean the fire of 'tribulation', that is, something coming from outside. No, a fire is kindled in the Christian, and with or in this fire is the purification. So there was diabolical ingenuity in the

---

[1] Jens Baggesen (1764–1826), Danish poet, with considerable interest in philosophical and religious questions. RGS

most fearful and revolting cruelty practised on some of the early Christians, when they were burnt as torches on the road. One can almost hear the contempt of those inhuman emperors, as though they were saying: 'Christ wished to cast fire on earth, so let the Christians serve as torches.' *XI²A 41*

To preach true Christianity, New Testament Christianity

is in a sense beyond man's powers, divine authority is required, or rather, a divine lostness in the Absolute.

Let me take myself. Nothing is more certain than that I am really attentive to what Christianity is. Nothing is more certain than that, in order to remain attentive, I must be, humanly speaking, unhappy in the depths of my being.

But when I have now to turn to men in order to proclaim Christianity to them, things are different, immediately my human sympathy bars my way – for it is clear that to become a Christian means, humanly speaking, to become unhappy.

This is the point: can I bring it over my heart to make men, humanly speaking, unhappy? There's the rub! That I should be unhappy concerns myself alone. But others – and that I should make them so! So the whole situation is changed, and in having to proclaim Christianity I am very near to saying, forgive me, oh forgive me for making you, humanly speaking, unhappy. I say something similar in another way, when I say, 'You yourselves are to blame that the price of being a Christian is forced up so high', for what I am speaking about then seems to be not a good, but almost an evil, and this again is connected with true Christianity, making a man, humanly speaking, unhappy.

It is different with the apostle, he is absolutely lost in the Absolute, blind to everything else, in a certain sense he simply does not see, humanly speaking, what he is doing, namely, making us men, humanly speaking, unhappy.

For the rest we may see once more here the distinctive character of the sphere, in which the positive is recognized by the negative, Christ is the Saviour of the world (the positive) recognized by the negative, that he, precisely he, makes us men, humanly speaking, unhappy. It is easy to see that this belongs to the sphere of paradox, and is naturally something entirely different from the galimatias about the Saviour of the world, which Christendom excels in. *XI²A 45*

Sanguis martyrum est semen ecclesiae
[Tertullian, *Apology*, 50]

If these words mean that for every witness unto blood there come many who are not willing to give their life, then from the Christian standpoint they are untrue. It is the martyrs who are the true church, the rest are the envelope. But in this situation it is not the church that increases, but the envelope.

Even in these words the idea of expansion is really too much accentuated. It looks as though Christianity were a human affair connected with expansion, instead of what it is, a divine affair connected with intensity. . . . *XI²A 47*

– But then there is an eternity, with no winter cold or summer heat or paralysing storms, or the countless stings of a thousand torments; nor is there – what perhaps causes as much pain – the envy of men, their pettiness and triviality and wretchedness; nor is there – what perhaps causes even more pain – well-meant misunderstanding: no, in eternity it does not happen that what you did from love looks like cruelty, no, there it is understood in all clarity that it was love: there is blessed peace. There it does not happen that what you did in humility looks like arrogance, no, it is understood in all clarity that it was humility. God be praised. There it does not happen that what you did in self-denial looks like a crime and is punished as a crime, no, there it is understood and settled, in all clarity, that it was self-denial. Blessed reward, I do not ask for a greater.

Yes, this is how things are. But if someone – yourself, say – should come to read these words, are these not two entirely different things, one, to be inflamed with the poetic beauty of such words, and the other to be warmed by the very thought itself? As I have so often said, the poetical is a dangerous gift both for a man himself and for others, and what should be a transformation of character can remain an aesthetic blaze.

And yet such is the state of affairs in Christendom that it would almost be regarded as the chief pre-requisite that every priest in the land should possess this kind of eloquence. Yet if this were so, it would not in the least follow that there would be a single Christian.   *XI² A 48*

Falsification

At different times there has been an outcry that the doctrine was falsified, at some points, at many points, at as good as all points. It may well be so. But the falsification of Christianity is much more dangerous than this, and it goes much deeper: what has been falsified is the very concept of a Christian.

The New Testament understands a Christian to be a swimmer who expresses the divine demand that has been proclaimed to him by leaping out into the deep; that is, he steps straight into the midst of reality, in order to learn now whether he has faith, and in order to practise and learn what it is to be a Christian. This is what God desires. As soon as a man does this, God in heaven says: It is well, this is what I await, and only trust in me, I shall not let you go.

But in Christendom, in steadily increasing millions from generation to generation, a Christian is a molly-coddled swimmer of the kind who does not want to go into the water, it is a collection of such swimmers who are land-lubbers deluding themselves that they are swimmers, who think that to leap into the water would be dreadful presumption, would be tempting God; what the priests din into them with all their might, as is natural – for it is important for their livelihood – is that nobody should leap out into the deep.

And meanwhile God sits and waits in heaven: he neither can nor will have to do with someone who does not leap out into the deep, he does not have to do with anyone who utterly seriously – plays at Christianity.

Christendom's guilt is really that it makes a fool of God, considers that he is a fool, it lets him sit and wait in heaven and so plays at Christianity in common, or in theatres built for the purpose, called houses of God – very apt, if it is in the same sense as one defines a storm-house as a house intended to keep storms out.

No, God does not need a house – the world of reality is what he wishes to be with, the world of reality, where – in defiance of the New Testament – the rule is still that 'one must take the world as it is'.

This falsification is the worst of all, far more dangerous than the falsifying of the doctrine. And that is why no one wants to meddle with it. For people prefer to have falsification of doctrine, since here the conflict is about objectivities. And the objective always covers over the subjective.

No, the falsification is to be found in the subjective.

XI² A 50

Spirit – appearance (*phenomenon*) – God's nearness – God's farness

God is Spirit. As Spirit God is related *paradoxically* to appearance (phenomenon), but paradoxically he can in turn come so near to reality that he is right in the midst of it, in the midst of the streets of Jerusalem.

It is impossible for God to be directly recognized. His majesty is so great that the boldest invention of the boldest imagination as the directly recognizable expression of this majesty would not be in the least suitable for God. For his majesty is qualitatively higher, and is therefore only paradoxical; indeed, if he were directly recognizable he would be essentially ridiculous. If I were a German professor I should here exclaim that I was the first to have drawn attention to how God could be ridiculous, in that paganism is essentially ridiculous, so far as in relation to God's direct recognizability one must say either that what I see is not God, or that if it is God, then it is ridiculous. The human has by nature no analogy to this majesty, whose height is such that it cannot be expressed by anything recognizable, but it can only be recognized paradoxically. If I were to suggest a feeble analogy, I should say that at certain times in human history, when everything was in confusion, there have arisen rulers who have ruled, if I may say so, in shirt-sleeves. This is a much higher majesty than that of an emperor who is directly recognizable: here is something paradoxical, that the rulers are recognized because they go about in their shirt-sleeves. It follows from this – and we should not omit it – that if one imagined such a ruler later getting established as an emperor who was directly recognizable as such, then one should have to laugh (the comical nature of direct recognizability) if he thought he had become something more, for in fact he had become something less.

Therefore God can be related only paradoxically to appearance, but then he also comes so near that he can stand in the midst of reality before our very noses.

The law for God's nearness and farness is then that the more the phenomenon, the appearance, expresses that God cannot possibly be there, the nearer he is. And inversely, the more the phenomenon, the appearance, expresses that God is quite near, the more distant he is.

The more the phenomenon, the appearance, expresses that God cannot possibly be there, the nearer he is. So in Christ. And just at the moment when the appearance expressed that not only was it impossible that this man should be the God-Man – no, when the appearance expressed that men even denied that he was a man (see, what a man!), at that moment God's reality was the nearest it has ever been.

The law for God's farness (and this is the history of Christianity) is therefore that everything that strengthens the appearance makes God distant. At the time when there were no churches, but the handful of Christians gathered as refugees and persecuted people in catacombs, God was nearer to reality. Then came churches, so many churches, such large and splendid churches – and to the same degree God is made distant. For God's nearness is related inversely to the appearance, and this increase (churches, many churches, splendid churches) is an increase in appearance. When Christianity was not a doctrine, when it was a few poor propositions, but these were expressed in life, then God was nearer to reality than when Christianity became a doctrine. And with each increase and embellishment, etc., of doctrine, God removes himself the more. For doctrine and its spread mean an increase in the direction of appearance, and God is related inversely to appearance. When there were no priests, but the Christians were all brothers, then God was nearer to reality than when there were priests, many priests, a powerful priesthood. For priests are an increase in the direction of appearance, and God is related inversely to the phenomenon.

And so the point has been reached when Christendom has gradually become almost the greatest possible distance from God – and all in terms of the claim that Christianity is perfectible and that progress is the rule. And this is the history of Christendom: by strengthening the appearance it puts a distance between itself and God, or else (as in certain circumstances one speaks of removing someone in a refined manner) the history of Christendom consists of removing God more and more, in a refined manner, by building churches and splendid buildings, by elaborating monstrous edifices of doctrine, along with an endless horde of priests.

So Christendom practically means the greatest possible distance from God.

And if I say this to someone, I know that there is not one of those who claim to care about such things (for of course those who do not care about such things will send me packing) who will not reply: But we must do something; in relation to the numbers of people there are certainly too few priests, let us get another thousand (wonderful – in order to get farther away from God!) and a great many more churches (wonderful – in order to get farther away from God!) and get the doctrine even more precise, with the help of a permanent committee of priests and professors – wonderful, in order to get farther away from God!

No, no, no: if you seriously wish to have God nearer, then to death and the devil with all that lying company of priests and professors, who publish *en masse* an excellent commentary on the text: Seek first the kingdom of God [Matthew 6. 33], risk yourself in the very midst of reality, risk – and at the very same moment God is there, and believe and be assured that with a quite different certainty from when a doctor, rung up in the night, leaps from his bed, in the very second that a man really takes a risk for God's sake, he is there, he is immediately present, he who is infinite love.

So ready is he, infinite love, so ready to have to do with a man that he has written love-letters in his Word, and wooed us, and said, Come, come. And now he sits and watches whether there might not be a single man who is ready to take the risk.

And absolutely every man can take the risk, and God is ready to have to do with absolutely every man who takes the risk. But of course he, infinite love, is also majesty, and he really knows: with terrible sharp-sightedness he sees whether one wants to profit by him, or to take a risk. So if some creature in a velvet gown spouts solemn phrases about loving God and tries to fool him, then God surely sees with fearful clarity that such a man understands in a quite special way the words about seeking first the kingdom of God. . . .   *XI²A 51*

[*In the margin*] The least possible place or phenomenon: a poor, solitary, needy, abandoned man – this is the place for God, to such an extent is he negatively related to the phenomenon; and God must make this man, humanly speaking, even unhappier if he is to be present in him – to such an extent is he negatively related to the phenomenon. He must have the least possible phenomenon, and then he must deny it over and above everything.   *XI²A 52*

God – the appearance

To assume that God is directly related to the appearance (if this did not conflict with God being spirit, and with the whole standpoint of Christianity) would also lead us into the difficulty of having to assume that this world is a fine place. The sensual man, who thinks that this world is a fine place, also thinks that God's nearness is directly related to the appearance: the more phenomenon there is, the nearer God is. But Christianity teaches that this world is in the grip of evil, and therefore it follows that God is related paradoxically to appearances, only in a tangential fashion, as to something one can only touch, and yet enter into decisively, yet not in continuity with it. *XI² A 53*

God's Majesty

This is what I have often said, that the whole confusion in Christendom is bound up with the loss of the idea of God's majesty, of what the majesty of the spirit is. So the guilt of Christendom is *lèse-majesté*, the God of Christianity has really been degraded to having no more than a human reference, or in men's understanding a reference which does not allow him to be more than a superlative of human majesty, which in turn means that the worship he can demand and wishes to have becomes something else, namely, what is most suitable to men – the bustle of finitude, in finite understanding the struggle for his kingdom as though it were a kingdom of this world; instead of the worship which is related to the absolute, which is undeniably the most demanding of flesh and blood.

God is pure subjectivity, entire and sheer subjectivity, without any trace of the objective in itself; for everything which has this kind of objectivity enters thereby into relativities.

This has been entirely forgotten. Hence the general view in Christendom (which is very near to the old pagan view) that

God is not concerned with trifles, and on the other hand that there is something which is in and for itself so important that it must concern God, attract his attention, and interest him, one may say, whether he wishes it or not.

Both views are alike unchristian. But it is the latter view I want to dwell upon, in so far as it is *lèse-majesté*, the other view will be illuminated *en passant*.

The pagan thought that trifles were too little to concern God, An individual man does not concern God, but a people, let us say, a people's affairs and the like, here is something whose importance in itself must concern God. From the Christian standpoint, on the other hand, God is such infinite majesty that nothing in and for itself can concern him, except as it pleases his majesty. Hence the most insignificant matter can concern him, just as much as what we men call the most significant of all, because whether God is concerned or not does not lie in the object but in his good pleasure – he is infinite subjectivity.

That the lower view of God's majesty is in fact *lèse-majesté* can easily be seen if we consider human majesty. Take the mightiest emperor who has ever lived. It is quite true that there are a great many things of which one must say that they could not concern him in and for themselves. But whether things do occupy his attention depends on the good pleasure of his majesty. But since even the mightiest emperor is not pure subjectivity, but has objectivity in his world, he is subject to the law that circumstances can arise in which events and the like are so significant and decisive that his majesty must be concerned with them whether he likes it or not. Here is the limit to his majesty, and it is *lèse-majesté* if one suggests that God can be in such a position.

And yet men live in Christendom entirely under this persuasion. The single person entirely despairs of existing for God – let us unite, let us become the many, a whole people, an immense undertaking – and yet the truth is that this does not concern God in and for itself more than the most abandoned, poor and stupid man: if it does so concern God, then it is only because it is his good pleasure. One might say, 'In so

far you could spare your troubles with these great under-
takings which are intended to interest God – for God is interested only in what he pleases, he who is pure subjectivity:
sheer subjectivity is interested in nothing else but what he
pleases.'

If a war should break out, not just in Europe, but if Europe
went to war with Asia, and Africa, America and Australia
found themselves compelled to join in, then in and for itself,
by itself, this does not concern God in the least, but it would
concern him that a poor man should sigh to him, for thus it
pleases his majesty, and this would affect him subjectively.

But now suppose that all the emperors and kings of Europe
should issue an edict, commanding all the thousands of
ordained hired servants (I mean the priests and parsons) to
implore the aid of heaven *officially*. And suppose that an
immense united religious service were organized, with 100,000
musicians and 50,000 organ-blowers, and a million ordained
hired servants to implore the aid of heaven *officially*. This
would not concern the divine majesty in the least. But if a
poor man walking along the street sighs in his inmost heart
to God, that concerns him, it concerns him indescribably,
infinitely, for thus it pleases his majesty, and this would affect
him subjectively.

And why would the other thing not concern him, the
immense official din which could be heard miles away, and
could consequently penetrate up to heaven – why should this
not concern him in the least? My friend, whatever idea you
may otherwise have of God, you surely do not doubt that he
is what could be termed a 'connoisseur', a fine connoisseur,
he who is sheer subjectivity, and precisely being subjectivity
is bound up with being a connoisseur. Hence, indeed, the
common view that women (who in comparison with men are
predominantly subjectivity) are fine connoisseurs, who can
straightaway distinguish between the official and the personal,
who know that the official is really a piece of effrontery, a
ceremonious way of making a fool of someone. So what an
infinite distance it is from God when an emperor, by means
of an edict composed by a minister of state, commands 10,000

ordained hired servants to bawl officially to God, what an
infinite distance in comparison with a poor man who sighs in
his inmost heart to God. . . .   XI² A 54

God's majesty – God's cause

As I have said, Christendom is guilty of lèse-majesté, God has
been degraded to being a mere superlative of human majesty,
as a consequence of the way Christianity has been served.

For how is Christianity served in Christendom? Is it not
simply as politics? By a clever use of human means? Therefore
God has a cause in the human sense, and is degraded, reduced
to a purely human majesty.

But where is there in this the least resemblance to the
precepts of Christ in the Sermon on the Mount? Is there any
trace of the thought that it is blessed to be persecuted? No,
suffering is just what is avoided by every possible means, and
this is praised as *Christian wisdom*. Suffering is avoided by
every possible means, so that the cause of Christianity is
abandoned or altered. Is this the commentary on the *blessedness* of suffering? For we do not read that we must submit to
suffering, but the words are 'Rejoice and be glad' [Matthew
5. 12]: this is the blessedness. Where is there the least recollection of Christ's precept, 'If one would take your coat, let him
have your cloak as well' [Matthew 5. 40]? Or is the commentary of Christendom on these words not rather, 'When
you have taken the coat, take the cloak as well'? Where is
there the least recollection of Christ's precept to be entirely
heedless of the morrow, like the lilies and the birds [Matthew
6. 26]? Or is the commentary of Christendom not that to study
theology is the surest means to a livelihood?

No, but entirely as though God were a human majesty
who longed to spread his influence and become the most
powerful of all, that is, entirely in political terms, is the way
that Christianity has been served.

But God in the New Testament, the God of Christianity is
infinite majesty: he does not have the least shred of a cause

216

in the human sense. And that is why he asks to be served in a quite different way, namely, scorning the use of human means and human cleverness, and refusing human help. Earthly understanding can naturally not grasp this kind of thing, it is something sublime of which it has no conception, something infinitely sublime which does not have a *cause* in the human sense.

But just because God is infinite majesty in this way, he does not have a cause in the human sense. So he has absolutely no use for the gang of politicians in silk and velvet, who kindly desire to serve Christianity and God by serving themselves. No, God has no use for politicians, only worshippers can serve him. Worshippers: and to worship means to scorn human cleverness, because it is a blessed thing to suffer for God.

When Christianity is served in this way it is qualitatively different from what it has become in Christendom, a flat, trivial, general cause just like every other political affair.

As Christianity was served in the earliest time, it was understood to be so infinitely sublime that the whole of existence, angels and devils and so on, were interested in the event. Whereas a cause which is served by human means, where one does not risk going farther out than the politicians, naturally sinks to the level of a mere bagatelle *ad modum* a European war and the like, it is just a piece of nonsense that we men undertake amongst ourselves.

The supra-human only appears when a cause is served in contempt of human means and human cleverness. But serving in this way means that the cause one serves is not a cause at all in the human sense.

No, humanly speaking God does not have a cause at all; spare yourself the trouble, God is just not exposed, so that it is not important that you should exert your cleverness on behalf of him and his kingdom; he does not aspire in the least to extend his power, for it cannot be extended. No, God wishes to be worshipped; and to worship means to give him such reverence that you look to him alone, scorning human means. To worship him means that you do not seek by human aid to avoid suffering; it means looking to him alone, and finding that it is blessed to suffer. . . .   *XI²A 55*

[*In the margin*] This is the rule: in relation to an absolute, or in serving an absolute absolutely, suffering is unavoidable in this world which is a conditioned world. This rule must be held to. Cleverness would very much like to make it appear that the cause is the same, only that cleverness knows how to avoid suffering. But this is a lie, the cause is not the same, it is not the absolute, for no cleverness can discover a way in which suffering can be avoided, when one is really to be related absolutely to an absolute.   *XI²A 56*

'*Journalists – hirers-out of opinions*' (*Schopenhauer*)[1]

This expression of Schopenhauer's is really valuable, and he himself understood its value (+). He shows that whereas in an outward regard most people would be ashamed to wear a second-hand hat or coat, this is not at all the case in matters of the spirit. Here practically everybody goes about in cast-off clothing. The mass of men have of course no opinion, but – here it comes! – this deficiency is helped out by the journalists, who live by hiring out opinions. And of course, as he rightly adds, what they would like to have is of the same quality as the costumes hired out by the fancy-dress suppliers.

For the rest, the matter is perfectly natural. Gradually, as more and more men are torn out of the state of innocence in which they are not in the least obliged to have an opinion, and 'obliged' (it is every man's duty, the journalists say) to have an opinion – what are the poor men to do? An opinion becomes a necessary article for the whole great public – and to the journalist offers his services in hiring out opinions. He works in two ways: first, he impresses upon us with all his power that it is necessary for every man to have an opinion, and second, he recommends his own assortment to us.

[1] *Die Welt als Wille und Vorstellung* ii, vii, conclusion (*Sämtl. Werke*, iii, 98, Leipzig, 1922.) RGS

The journalist makes men ridiculous in two ways. First, by making them believe that it is necessary to have an opinion – and this is perhaps the most ridiculous side of the matter: some unfortunate decent citizen, who could have such a good time, is now taught to think that he must have an opinion. And second, by hiring them out an opinion which in spite of its airy quality is put on and worn as – a necessary article.

XI²A 58

[*In the margin*] In a sense it is almost disagreeable to me to have come to read Schopenhauer. I am indescribably scrupulous and fearful about using expressions and so on of others, without making it known. But his terms are at times so akin to mine that perhaps I end, with exaggerated fearfulness, by ascribing to him what is really my own.   *XI²A 59*

Spiritual power – material power

To become and to remain a spiritual power is very difficult, and dangerous besides. So men prefer, as easier and more profitable, to become a material power by simple addition. This art is practised more and more generally in our time, to the detriment of spiritual power, which in future will find it more and more difficult to penetrate. If men lived out their lives as in earlier times, fending for themselves in a naïve routine, it would be easier for spiritual power to get a hold of them. But nowadays there are parties and numbers and material power everywhere. As the discovery of gunpowder altered the conduct of war, so too this change, in which material power is everywhere predominant, could change the struggle of the spirit. But this cannot be done; for if the spirit changes and becomes like its opponents, then it ceases to be spirit. The consequence must therefore be that it becomes more difficult for spirit to penetrate. For as I have said, gunpowder changed war, it abolished personal bravery, and in the same way men tend, in relation to spirit, to abolish personality – that is, to abolish the spirit, and to make personality impossible, that is, to make the spirit impossible.

In material matters the change was irresistible. When a nation goes to war with cannons, there is no help for it, but the other nation must also acquire cannons, or submit. We may depend upon it that the same thing will happen in the realm of the spirit. If it does, it will mean that the spirit will have ceased to exist. *XI² A 62*

Ambiguity

Everything Christian is ambiguous, a reduplication. And this is what sets up the tension, as well as making understanding with others so difficult.

How straightforward and easy is understanding with others when being happy or suffering is unambiguous!

But that suffering means blessedness is an ambiguity. One cannot complain about suffering in a straightforward way when it means blessedness. And one cannot be understood, either when one speaks of blessedness or when one speaks of suffering, for the one is always implied in the other, and only the unambiguous is to be understood in a straightforward way.

Here one may also see that Christianity is intended for a-sociality, it is intended to shut us off in the relation of the single person to God. *XI² A 65*

Man and woman in relation to religion

In a certain sense a woman is by nature better suited to real religious service. For a woman's nature is to give herself entirely. But on the other hand she explains nothing. Strong masculine intellectuality, joined to feminine submission: this gives true religiosity. A woman's resignation is essentially related to interjections, and it is unwomanly if it tries to be more. But on the other hand strong masculine intellectuality

is directly related to immense selfishness which must be slain
in submission. *XI²A 70*

Time – eternity

The temporal retards and broadens, and is therefore essentially
related to *chatter*; eternity is sheer haste and intensive, and is
related essentially to *action, to the transformation of character*.

In the temporal world the main thing is to be able to
chatter, to have a diabolical gift of the gab. And this is true
all along the line, from the merchant extolling his wares, and
the man whose words are aimed at womenfolk and the agitator
whose words are for the public, to the poet, the orator and the
scholar: for this too is chatter, it is not the transformation of
character.

But eternity looks at action and transformation of character.
Every change in the direction of chatter is of no help for entering into eternity. If a man who has talked bawdy changes to
pious talk, it does not help, there is no essential difference.

But on the temporal view it is precisely the defect of action
that it is so brief – there is simply nothing to talk about, there
is no delay. That is why temporality likes poetry, for it lingers
and does not become action; and why it likes learning, which
helps to shirk action. If eternity were master there would be
no long-windedness, which temporality loves – for it loves the
appearance, and delays, and chatter. *XI²A 76*

Bishop Mynster

Mynster can be said to have been as ominous a figure as
possible for me, not because he was not what I needed, but
because he conjured up the semblance of being what I needed.
What I needed in the episcopal see of Zealand was a character,
and the misfortune for me was not that Mynster was not such a
character, which would not be saying much, but that he refined
all his other pleasures by cunningly succeeding in being taken

for a man of character, a man who governed; whereas he was only a Sunday orator, and for the rest a worldly-wise eudemonist.

So as long as he lived I could not attack him. For my charge against him was precisely that he did not govern, this was an optical illusion; but he was a journalist, the public's slave as much as anyone ever was. But to whom could I say this? And on the other hand I was fighting on the government's side, and so could not very well have weakened him. In private I told him – but what did he care about this, he was only afraid of the public, for he was a coward. *XI²A 78*

Christianity is a kingdom which is not of this world

Yet it wants to have a place in this world – and here is the paradox and the conflict, it wants to have a place, but again not as a kingdom of this world.

So it is in the New Testament. Christendom, of course, has not been able to accept this, it was too demanding, so either Christianity has been turned into a kingdom of this world (Catholicism), when Christian conflicts vanish, and straight-forward recognizability, which pleases men, becomes the rule; or Christianity has been transferred to hidden inwardness, a form one may call adequate for the refusal to be a kingdom of this world, yet nevertheless not the Christian form, not the paradoxical form, and the Christian conflicts are once more avoided. It is easy enough to see that the form which most nearly corresponds as adequate for a kingdom not of this world is hidden inwardness, for hidden inwardness is a negative just like *not* of this world. But then one sees again the paradox in Christianity, namely, that a kingdom which is not of this world will nevertheless have a place, a visible and recognizable place, so paradoxically will have a place in this world, while constantly watching that it is paradoxical, and that it is not changed into becoming a kingdom of this world.

At the same time we have here an illustration of the connexion of this with all Christendom's so-called progress.

For all the talk about hidden inwardness as the true form of existence for true Christianity, which is extolled as something higher and truer than early Christianity, is in fact simply something lower. Christianity in the New Testament has more hidden inwardness than you find in Protestantism, but that is not enough for it, it wants to be recognizable in a paradoxical form, and it is at this point that all the Christian conflicts arise.   *XI²A 80*

Christianity – being born again

The view of Christianity is that everything turns on a qualitative change, a change of the whole character in time (as qualitative as the change from not being to being which is birth). Everything that is only a development of what man is originally is not Christian existence.

Christendom has as its constant concern the abolition of the paradox (for the paradox is to be born when one is already old [John 3. 7]), and thus the abolition of all effort. To this end the scene for becoming a Christian has been transferred to the tenderest age. In itself it is ridiculous to think that the paradox can be avoided in this way, for it is just as paradoxical that a child which has only been alive for five minutes only has to be born in order to be born a second time, as that a forty-year-old man should be born a second time.

But what Christendom has aimed at, and attained, is the abolition of every effort. Re-birth is pushed so far back in time that as one says of one's birth that one does not know how it was, so too with re-birth: one does not know how it was. And so one is happily and well quit of all Christianity's qualitative efforts.

It goes without saying that one is thereby also quit of all Christianity's promises: and Christianity really teaches that re-birth is eternal life, immortality.

By displacing the paradox Christendom has quite simply approached the condition of ancient paganism – embellished with Christian expressions and phrases.

Confirmation is of little help, for it too takes place in childhood, and it is almost laughable to hear the priests address the boys as little Christians. My proposal is that we introduce at Confirmation the custom of giving the boys false moustaches and beards, so that they may look like men.

XI²A 81

'Thou art not far from the kingdom of God'

Mark 12. 34

Christ says these words after the scribe had explained the commandment of love.

From this one sees that to love God means to be related to the kingdom of God.

This can serve as a counterpoise to the fraudulent doctrine of faith which we hear nowadays in Christendom.

XI²A 83

'Teach them to keep all that I have commanded you'

[Matthew 28. 20]

With these words Christ leaves the earth. If things were as they are taught in Protestantism, especially in Denmark, then how remarkable that Christ speaks of keeping all that he has commanded: this is not at all like our talk of faith alone.

From this we see that Christ must understand faith quite differently from the way Christendom has hit upon.

XI²A 84

The state of affairs in the Establishment

How basically corrupt everything is may be seen from the very fact that everyone knows it more or less clearly – but no one is willing to say it, and all men, with varying degrees of guilt, hold honourably together like conspirators in the determination to prevent its being said – how false the Establishment is.

Hence it once more comes about that a single man is enough, just one is needed to say it straight out. This is the nemesis that is hanging over such dishonourable conduct, that one man is enough; if it is just said and heard then everything is changed, fire is cast upon the places of the Philistines.

But for this reason it can of course be dangerous to be the man who says it; indeed, perhaps the danger is the greatest possible, just for this reason.

When the struggle is between a clearer insight and one which is less clear, though honest, then it seldom becomes really fierce. But when one knows that things are in a bad way, where everything is done to conceal it and to prevent its being said, then it can become the most frightful crime to say it.

Take an illustration: go to a merchant who thinks that his business is going very well – but you know that he is bankrupt; inform him . . . he will certainly not be very happy to hear you, but he will give in. Then again, go to a merchant who has known for a long time that he is bankrupt, and has himself done everything he could, in every possible underhand way, to conceal the fact that he is bankrupt – show him that he is, and he will fight you tooth and nail.

The fact is that where it is knowledge that is lacking, the truth is not an accusation against the character; but where knowledge is already present, the truth becomes criminal.

The dangerous conflicts never arise where there is merely a lack of knowledge, but always where those who are really involved knew very well themselves that they were fighting for a lie. And the most dangerous conflicts of all are those in which the persons really involved drag a crowd of men with them; of whom to a certain extent it may be said that they lack knowledge and so to that extent are not entirely dishonourable. . . . *XI²A 85*

Will – knowledge (*Christendom*)

Christianity in the New Testament has to do with man's will, everything turns upon changing the will, every expression (forsake the world, deny yourself, die to the world, and so on, to hate oneself, to love God, and so on) – everything is related to this basic idea in Christianity which makes it what it is – a change of will.

In Christendom, on the other hand, the whole of Christianity has been transferred to intellectuality; so it becomes a doctrine, and our whole concern is with the intellectual.

If this is not a scoundrelly trick, then I don't know one! Anyone with the least human knowledge, that is, self-knowledge, knows very well it is a change of will that hurts a man. And it is at this point that Christianity aims its mortal blow. But Christendom dexterously avoids the blow – and transfers everything to intellectuality.

How abominable! And to think that it is carried out by millions of people, that children are brought up in this way, so that a father in Christendom palms this lie on his child in the highest and holiest of matters.

It is dreadful! When a layman has to be present at a dissection he is sick; so too the student when he has to make his first dissection. But not so the old hand; and yet it can sometimes happen that a cadaver can be so loathsome that even he is sick. If a man from the ordinary run of people were to possess the knowledge of crime such as a policeman has, he would be overwhelmed – but an old police officer is never overwhelmed in regard to crime; and yet it can sometimes happen that the affair can be so dreadful, and with such horrible ramifications, that even he can feel overwhelmed. I can truly say that I possess an innate flair in respect of crime; I too am old and hardened; but in truth this matter of Christendom overwhelms me with its horror. The corruption in Russia, where every official is corrupt, is only a feeble image of the terrible state of affairs in which this lie is mixed into every possible situation that we are Christians, that we have Christianity, while we lyingly call that

Christianity which is the very opposite of New Testament Christianity.

How abominable, that it is bound to happen that, if a man in Christendom really wants to be a Christian, he must first experience the shock of thinking for a time that God in heaven seems to be the most abominable of swindlers. For from his childhood a lie has been inculcated in him concerning what Christianity is. The child is sent out into life with the illusion that 'God in heaven will surely help you; whatever happens, he will not fail to help you.' And in the New Testament things are very different: what God wills is that you should love him. And this means that from the human standpoint you will come to suffer terribly – just because you have come to do with God. For what is the New Testament? It is a handbook for him who is to be sacrificed. How vile it is to bring up a child in this Christianity which is the general one in Christendom, whose effect is either that the child fools his life away in the same twaddle, or that he must some time experience the horror of thinking that God is a seducer who, in the crucial moment, just when a man has most need of him, is changed and becomes the very opposite of what the child had been deceitfully told to believe. . . .

But if the kind of Christianity in which a child is brought up were New Testament Christianity, then the New Testament would have to show that Christ spoke chiefly of his death as a sacrifice, sparing others, and spoke with the utmost reserve and caution about discipleship. But instead of this matters are quite the reverse, he speaks of his death as a sacrifice only one single time, and then only conditionally; but what he really teaches is discipleship. *XI²A 86*

To live comparatively

The law for the existence of those who are merely numbers is that they live comparatively. One also sees from this that a number is a sophistication, something that spreads out, but when seen more closely dissolves into nothing.

To live as well as the rest is called happiness. Whether every-one's life is sheer misery or a really worth-while existence does not concern in the least the man who is one of a number: it is enough to live like the rest.

To behave just like the rest – this is the right thing. It means nothing to those who are just part of the number if this behaviour is as perverse as possible; if they are just like the rest, that is the right thing. To have the same religion as the rest is to have the true religion, and so on, and so on: the great thing is this 'like the rest'.

'Like the rest.' In this phrase is contained the twofold characteristic of being a man in general: (1) the social, animal creatures related to the herd, like the rest, and (2) envy, which the animals, however, do not have.

This envy is quite characteristic. An animal has no envy, because every animal is simply a copy. Whereas man is the only species of animal where every copy (κατα δυναγιν is more than the species, is an individuality made to be spirit. Now numbers naturally cannot become spirit, but they retain this characteristic which distinguishes them from other animal creatures, namely, envy. If man were just a copy, he would not have envy. But even the man who most lowers himself in order to approach that lofty goal towards which the race strives, especially with the help of the daily newspapers, the goal of becoming a copy – even this man is so different from the rest that he is distinguished *vis-à-vis* the animals by envy.

I say that it is especially the daily newspapers which labour at degrading men to be mere copies, and nothing is more certain. As in a paper factory the rags are worked together into a mass, so the newspapers tend to smooth out every individual difference in men, all spirit (for spirit is differentiation in itself, and consequently also from others), in order to make them happy *qua numerus* by means of the life which is peculiar to the number – in everything like the rest. Here the animal creature finds peace and rest, in the herd, and here envy is set at rest.

If the newspapers reached their lofty goal it is a question

whether the number would not suddenly feel the need for some to be not quite like the rest – in order that envy could have a little to live off.

In a certain sense I could wish for men to be punished through the newspapers reaching their goal and making everyone into copies – a fearful punishment: a million men entirely like one another. It could be presented in a moral tale and called 'Envy punished'. And the punishment, of course, would be the most agonizing boredom.   *XI² A 88*

Christian courage

(which also corresponds to the fact that the truth was in one man, in Christ, over against the whole race) is to be found where a single person withstands the resistance of the number, where there is heterogeneity of concept and of character with the number. The range of the single person is in proportion to the size of the number; the longer he holds out, the more inward is his relation to his world.

This moral courage in the range of concepts, of truth and spirit, is qualitatively different from all other courage. A brave soldier going out courageously and alone against even 1,000 enemies, or against guns, into certain peril, and the like – all this kind of courage does not have in it the conflicts of ideas.

Christian courage begins where ideas are at stake.

Paganism therefore did not really know this courage. Paganism, like the merely human in general, rests on the principle that numbers constitute the concept. (Socrates is an exception, he is the only one who understood that the task was that of the single person against numbers.)

Christianity introduced the concept of spirit and thus established the conflict of the single person against numbers; the truth can be in a single man, absolutely alone, against and in opposition to everyone, absolutely everyone.

This conflict is the most intense possible. Hence, wherever there is this conflict, existence itself is concerned. For a concept is so capacious that it can contain millions, indeed everyone. Therefore the man who fights in the realm of concepts, and wishes to change them, fights with the possibility of millions.

And this conflict is fearfully demanding: to maintain that these countless men, in many respects lovable men, all of them, are living in untruth! Ah, how human rather to give in and oneself to live in untruth! But here is where the Christian struggle is, Christian courage, fighting against the impulses both of fear and of compassion.

If I were to speak in pagan terms, I should say that existence is like an immense giant who lies quite quietly and amuses himself at men, as we men can amuse ourselves with watching birds or domestic animals: so the giant lies quite still and amuses himself at men playing their games, at John and Jean looking at one another, falling in love, getting married, becoming parents of a numerous brood – everything fine: existence remains entirely quiet. Yes, even if someone were so advanced as to play the game of being regarded by the rest as one who really had to do with ideas (as for example Bishop Mynster played at Christianity), existence would still be quite peaceful; for this does not really concern him, it is only a game.

But at the moment when one man has to do with ideas in all seriousness – then existence arises. And in order to defend itself, that is, in order to examine this man, the conflict takes place. The conflict of the single person with numbers.

And among all those who have really had to do with existence, and really touched upon ideas, there is not one, not even the most courageous of all, who has not shuddered for a moment at this *tête-à-tête* with existence itself, and at this conflict with numbers in the battle of the idea.   *XI² A 89*

A piece of arithmetic

One hundred thousand million men, of which each is like the rest = one.

Only when one turns up who is different from these millions or this one, do we have two.

In the world of numbers unity is what counts; in the world of the spirit unity does not count, but difference counts, which means that there is no counting.

. . . One must learn not to be afraid of numbers, one must learn that numbers mean nothing, just as the child learns not to be afraid of ghosts. 'See my child, it isn't something to be afraid of, it's nothing, there's no one, or it's nothing, it's just night mists' – so one must learn not to be afraid of numbers. . . .

For 'spirit' everything is reversed. In the world of sense one adds up, and it becomes a large number, in the world of spirit one adds up and the large number vanishes as in a conjuring trick. For numbers are a mystification, they are the mystification which pretends that there is more than one. One thinks more rarely of the kind of mystification in which one disguises oneself as the many.   *XI² A 90*

Humility – insignificance

Because Christianity always lays claim to humility, relating everything to humility and its tasks, the man of mediocre insignificance immediately thinks, 'This is something for me', and does not reflect that Christian humility, like everything Christian, contains a dialectic, so that its humility presupposes a pride which holds itself higher than human pride, but then humbles itself.

Examples: 'Do not aspire to high things, but cling to what is humble' [Romans 12. 16]. Splendid, says mediocrity, that is something for me, I don't wish to be king, I am content to become a privy councillor, or a prosperous citizen, a true Christian, who does not aspire to high things. That's all very well: but look more closely at what Christianity understands by the humble, and you will see that in another sense such an aspiration, when taken seriously, is denounced by man as the most horrid pride, as arrogance, as aspiring to something that is higher than being king and emperor. 'Do not sit at the first place' [Luke 14. 8]. Splendid, says mediocrity, I don't hanker after such things, I am content to sit in the middle of the table or even towards the bottom of the table – I am a true Christian, who does not sit at the head of the table. Wrong again. If a man is really serious about humility which humiliates itself absolutely, you will see that it will be denounced as the most horrid arrogance, much worse than that of wishing to sit at the head of the table. As in the story stupid Gottlieb is always mistaken,[1] so mediocrity will in all eternity be mistaken about Christianity.

But it must always be kept in mind that Christianity is not in the least concerned with differences between man and man. Difference means varying talents. No, no, no, it is offered absolutely to every man. But it demands the passion in him to stake everything. 'Do just this!' says God. 'I will do the rest.' Therefore the apostle James says, 'If anyone lacks wisdom, let him pray for it' [James 1. 5]. And therefore Christ used quite simple men as apostles, just in order not to cause the confusion that Christianity might be supposed to be essentially related to genius and talent.

But 'man', who is a past master in trickery, or has an inborn instinct for it, has naturally pretended that he did not understand this matter of Christianity being equal for all, for the demand for a change of will does not please him.

So the equality of Christianity for all men has in turn been reduced to insignificance. No thank you! Certainly Christianity is alike for all men in the sense that genius and talent are nothing but foolish tricks – but nevertheless it is so far from being the egality of mediocrity and insignificance that what Christianity demands (and what every man can, if he will – and it is here that the equality is to be found) is so great and altogether so rare that among a score of talents you do not find a single Christian. Yet everyone has the possibility of being a true Christian. *XI² A 91*

<hr>

[1] See *Puss-in-boots*, by Tieck. RGS

The numerical

Let me take an illustration. Suppose – and let us not skimp the number – that there were 100,000 words in Latin declined like *mensa*; suppose that they were written, one below the other, on an enormous sheet of paper – and all in order to impress a grammarian. Would it impress him in the least? No, not in the least. *Mensa*, he would say, is the declension, the rest, the combined number of them, is a matter of indifference, it would even be a waste of time for me to get to know the whole list. Only with *dominus* do we reach the second declension, but *dominus* does not follow *mensa*. In a dictionary, he would say, these 100,000 words have their significance, as vocabulary; but they have no grammatical significance. Or (to change the picture somewhat) if *mensa* thought of putting itself at the top of this list of 100,000 words in order to impress a grammarian, would he be impressed? Not in the least. My dear *mensa*, he would say, what concerns me is the declension, and you misunderstand yourself and your significance if you suppose that you are more significant because you are at the head of a list of 100,000 words that are declined like yourself. In fact you are mad, dear *mensa*, if you suppose you can put yourself at the head of what is nothing. For the 100,000 words are grammatically equal to zero. You are not therefore at the head of anything, it is just something you make yourself and the 100,000 imagine, or they do it to you.

And thus with numbers. Only the illustration does not express (and to this extent is unsuitable) that in the realm of words it is accidental which word is the paradigm among the 100,001 words. In the realm of the spirit it is not accidental who will provide the declension; but the words which are declined on this model, the imitations, have no significance at all.

Yes, this is how it is. And yet how sad that I am the one who has to say these things, I who in my melancholy loved the mass of men so deeply, and how sad that it is these very men who have compelled me, with the aid of Providence, to be so inflexible. But one thing is certain, if order is to be kept, what matters is an eye for quality, for who is the paradigm for the declension, and complete indifference to the number of words (perhaps an immense number), which follows this declension. *XI²A 92*

Mark 15. 39

The centurion says, 'Truly this man was the son of God.' He had obviously misunderstood, like all the bystanders, and believed that Christ was calling to Elijah. And yet Christ is saying something quite different.

But is it not strange and moving that the very words of Christ which are most filled with suffering, at which the bystanders, if they had heard aright, would have had to say, 'See, he is despairing of himself' – that these very words should be misheard by the bystanders? They hear the words in such a way as to see in them the proof that he was the Son of God.

There is a profound and enigmatic connexion here: for precisely the enduring of suffering to the utmost was for God the expression that he was the Son of God. But the marvellous thing is that the bystanders mishear – and so in a much deeper sense they hear aright. It is as though God spoke through them – by means of causing them to mishear. *XI²A 95*

The divine punishment is to ignore us

. . . Although he is omnipresent, God's power is such that his relation to us can be one of ignoring us as though he were infinitely distant. But so far as a man in his overwhelming subjectivity punishes someone by ignoring his presence, he may be said to require the self-satisfaction of showing that he can ignore him; whereas God is such infinite subjectivity that he punishes by ignoring to such an extent that the punished person does not even notice it, which again from God's standpoint is the heaviest punishment, even heavier than if the sinner came to realize it. For on God's view (and one cannot really blame him for it) everything, absolutely everything, turns upon being so happy as to exist for him. So the most terrible punishment is that in which it is hidden from the sinner that he is suffering punishment . . .   *XI²A 96*

On being related objectively to one's own subjectivity

Most men are blunted I's. What was given us by nature as a possibility of being sharpened to an I is quickly blunted to a third person (like Baron Münchhausen's dog, a greyhound which wore down its legs and became a dachshund).

It is quite a different matter to be related objectively to one's own subjectivity.

Take Socrates: he is not third-personal in the sense that he avoids danger or exposing himself and risking his life, as one would do if one were third-personal and not an I. Not at all. But in the midst of danger he is related objectively to his own personality, and at the moment when he is condemned to death he speaks of the condemnation as though he were a third person. He is subjectivity raised to the second power, he is related to objectivity as a true poet wishes to be related to his poetic production: this is the objectivity with which he is related to his own subjectivity. This is a work of art. Otherwise one gets either an objective something, an objective stick of furniture which is supposed to be a man, or a hotchpotch of casual and arbitrary happenings. But to be related objectively to one's own subjectivity is the real task.

The maximum that has ever been attained in this respect by any man can serve as an infinitely weak analogy for having an inkling of how God is infinite subjectivity.

He has nothing objective in his being, as I have shown elsewhere,[1] for this would limit him and put him down among relativities; but he is related objectively to his own subjectivity. But this again is only a reduplication of his sub-

[1] See *XI²A 54*, above. RGS

jectivity, for in his subjective being there is nothing imperfect to be removed and nothing lacking to be added, as with human subjectivity: which is the reason why being related objectively to one's own subjectivity is also a corrective.

God is infinite reduplication, which of course is not possible for any man: a man can neither surpass himself in such a way as to be related completely objectively to himself, nor can he be so subjective as completely to fulfil what he has understood about himself in objective superiority. He cannot see himself absolutely and completely objectively. If he could do that, he still could not reproduce this view of himself absolutely subjectively. *XI² A 97*

A point of view for the history of mankind

If I were to say anything (although I normally do not concern myself with this kind of thing, and consider it to be unethical to concern oneself with the history of mankind, instead of one's own existence) I should present this point of view.

God has only one passion – to love and to be loved. It is his pleasure to go through existentially with men all the different ways in which one can be loved and can love.

So he himself naturally plays a part and plans everything in relation to it. Now he wishes to be loved like a father by his child, now as a friend by a friend, now simply as one bringing good gifts, now as one who tempts and proves the beloved. And in Christianity the idea, if I may say so, is to be loved as a bridegroom by his bride, in such a way that it becomes a sheer test. And now he is changed almost into the likeness of man, accommodating himself in order to be loved in this way; now the idea is to be loved by a man as spirit – which is the most demanding task of all, and so on, and so on.

My view is that God is like a poet. That also explains the fact that he puts up with evil and with all the nonsense and wretchedness and mediocrity of insignificance, and so on. This is also how a poet is related to his productions (which are also called his creations). He lets them be produced. But just as one would make a great mistake if one were to think that what the individual person in a poem says or does is the poet's personal view, so also one would be wrong to assume that what happens, simply because it happens, receives God's assent. Oh no, he has his own opinion. But as a poet he lets everything possible be produced, he himself is everywhere present, watching, as a poet going on producing, in one sense impersonally, impartially attentive to everything, in another sense personally, making the most fearful distinction between good and evil, between willing and not willing what he wills, and so on.

The Hegelian nonsense about the real being the true is therefore just like the confusion of attributing to a poet as his own the words and actions of his characters.

Only this must be firmly held, that God, if I may so put it, wills to produce poetically in this way, not, as the pagans supposed, as a pastime – no, no, here is the serious point, that it is God's passion to love and to be loved, almost – infinite love! – as though he himself were bound in this passion, in the power of this passion, so that he cannot cease to love, almost as though it were a weakness; whereas in fact it is his strength, his almighty love. To such a degree is his love not subject to change. *XI² A 98*

God is love

This is Christianity's thesis.

It is twofold: God loves, and God wishes to be loved.

True Christianity lies in the equilibrium of the two: as much promise as obligation, always as much promise as obligation.

If a man were to hold fast, on the greatest possible scale, to the fact that God is love in the sense that God loves him – and then suddenly come to see the other side, that God wishes to be loved, then he would surely be anxious and afraid. As it can be wonderful for an insignificant girl to be the object of an important man's love, who loves her with all his heart, but in another sense is immensely critical for her when she notes how serious is his passionate desire to be loved, so for the Christian: in one sense nothing is more blessed than the assurance that God loves him, as well as the extent to which God is love, that it is his being; in another sense nothing is more dreadful than to be drawn into the supreme event of this existence where God's desire to be loved is such a (in one sense) fearfully serious matter.

Christendom of course has happily tried to play the game of fooling God: God is love in the sense that he loves me – Amen!   *XI² A 99*

Christendom

Christendom is so far from being a community of Christians that, as I have shown elsewhere, it is apostasy from Christianity.

And when one looks more closely it shows such a demoralization that all the other religions are in a better condition.

Yet this is not inexplicable, for Christendom is demoralized by means of mildness, grace, the promise, God is love, and so on. The other religions do not have this mildness, they have more of the severity of the law, and therefore the demoralization is never so deep.

No, demoralization by means of mildness is the deepest. Let me draw a comparison. If a man gets gross and fat from too heavy eating, then basically this is an unhealthy fatness; but if a man gets fat from eating cakes and titbits, with a pasty fatness, it is horrible. So with the demoralization of Christendom.

Even in hypocrisy there are differences. To play the hypocrite in face of the strictness of the law is certainly hypocrisy; but to play the hypocrite in face of grace is infinitely more abominable.

To be refractory against something that bears hard upon me is certainly sin; but to make a mock of love is abominable.

XI² A 100

To play at Christianity

. . . Oh, but when one says sometimes that a child is too big to go on playing, at the most this means one or two years, and the child is after all just one; but that it can go on for hundreds of years, and that millions play at Christianity, is terrible. The proportions of existence here are so terrifying that one becomes dizzy – happily the individual has for this reason as a Christian just to watch himself. *XI²A 102*

The medium for being a Christian. The situation

Ventriloquism consists in speaking in such a way that it cannot be determined who the speaker is; the words are heard all right, but as if they were not localized, as if no one were speaking them.

But in a much deeper sense all speaking with the mouth is also – a kind of ventriloquism, something indeterminate. What deceives one is that there is certainly a visible and determinate figure using his mouth. But note well. The speech is an abstraction.

In order that speech should be in a deeper sense human speech, or speech in the sense of spirit, something else is required, in respect of being the speaker; two points must be determined; the first is the speech, or the words, and the second is the situation.

The situation is the decisive factor in determining whether the speaker is or is not in character regarding what he says; or the situation decides whether what is being said is airy nonsense, speech without real roots, which in a deeper sense is true of all speech which is devoid of situation.

And yet it is precisely this lack of situation which characterizes negatively the whole of Christendom and makes all its Christian confession illusory, a piece of ventriloquism, so that one could really just as well use a machine.

But it is this shirking which is so common among men – saying what must be said, but evading the situation. I knew a man who took a part in public life, was a member of popular assemblies, but scarcely ever uttered a word. He got along by saying to his neighbour what should have been said at the meeting. This is lack of character arising from a lack of situation.

And so with Christendom. To confess Christ is only possible for a Christian in the situation indicated by Christianity – in the real world. To confess Christ does not mean to say it on Sundays in a quiet hour, or in private conversation in a safe sitting-room, and so on. And what does not make the matter any better is the shameless confession that one is describing Christianity objectively.

To describe it objectively is another effort at ventriloquism; for it means to speak in such a way that the speaker cannot be recognized: it is a mystification in which the I is disguised as a third person, or as an abstract I.

An illustration: there is a certain word which, if spoken to the tyrant, brings you into mortal danger. So what do you do? You play the game – of saying the word, certainly, but not to the tyrant. This is how children play – and this is how such profoundly serious men as Bishop Mynster, etc., are Christians.

$XI^2 A$ 106

Ventriloquism

. . . A man's salvation lies in his becoming a person. One could even lay down the rule that a man who becomes a personality, who succeeds in getting so far, or who comes so far, is normally saved. And why? Because it is so bright around him that he cannot conceal himself from himself, as bright as if he were transparent. And householders are now saying that gas lighting in the evenings helps to prevent a great deal of evil, for light frightens evil away: and think of the translucency of light in a personality, which is entirely light.

But man naturally prefers the dusk, the un-personal, when it is too light it is too ceremonious for him, especially if it is not a changing but a steady brightness, not certain hours light, then dusk and darkness, but uninterrupted light, as clear as possible. ('Personality' is formed in connexion with sounding (*personare*); in another sense one could describe personality in terms of transparency.) *XI²A 107*

The state

That from a Christian standpoint, as Hegel taught, the state has a moral significance, that true virtue should be manifested only in the state (which I too repeated childishly after him in my thesis),[1] that the aim of the state is to ennoble man, and so on, of course is all nonsense.

The state is rather an evil than a good, rather a necessary and in a sense a useful and expedient evil than a good.

The state is human egoism in its great proportions and dimensions – so far is Plato from being right when he says that in order to know virtues we should study them in the state.

The state is human egoism in its great dimensions, combined with such appropriateness and ingenuity that the egoism of single persons interacts in mutual correction. To this extent the state is certainly a defence against egoism – by means of displaying a higher egoism which dominates all the individual egoisms, so that they may egoistically realize that from an egoistic point of view it is cleverest to live in the state. As one speaks of the infinitesimal calculus, so one can say that the state is the calculus of egoism, yet always in such a way that it is egoistically clear that the cleverest thing is to enter into and participate in this higher egoism. But this is quite different from a moral relinquishment of egoism.

The state does not reach further than this; so that to be bettered by living in the state is just as dubious a matter as being bettered in a house of correction. In the state one perhaps becomes much cleverer in one's egoism, in a well-understood egoism, that is, one's egoism in relation to other egoisms; but one does not become less egoistic, and what is worse, one is spoilt by regarding this official, authorized, state egoism

[1] see *The Concept of Irony, Samlede Værker*² XIII, pp. 327 *ff.* RGS

as – virtue. For life in the state demoralizes one even to this extent, that one is reassured in the life of a prudent egoist.

The state does not reach higher than this; and this must certainly be called a very disturbing state of affairs, considered from the standpoint of moral education and development.

So the state is constantly subject to the sophistical problem which the Greek sophists were also so busied with, that injustice in a grand style is justice, that concepts are inverted or changed in a quite peculiar manner, that what matters is to have things big. Furthermore, the state is constantly subject to the scepticism that supposes that the concept is determined by numbers, that the truth lies in the greatest number.

And to claim that the state is calculated to develop men morally, and is the right medium for virtue, the place where a man can become virtuous! This place is in truth just as peculiar for this purpose as would be the claim that the best place for a watchmaker or a stippler to work is on board ship in a heavy sea.

Christianity is therefore not at all of the opinion that the Christian should remain in society in order to be morally ennobled; no, it forewarns him that it will mean suffering.

But in the tricksters' language of men of course it is said that the state is morally ennobling – so one is perfectly secured against anyone suspecting this authorized egoism of not being a virtue.

In general it can never be sufficiently emphasized that the direct, the crude, the imprudent, and so on, are never so corrupt as the clever. A lecher who is direct and unbridled in his passions is perhaps not nearly as corrupt as one who in his lechery – observes decorum. A swindler who, as is said, fleeces another man is perhaps not as corrupt as one who knows precisely how much one can dare to swindle and still retain respect and esteem as a most respectable man.   *XI²A 108*

Numbers

Just as a man cannot endure working without a break, but needs distraction, so numbers are distraction, relief.

The error lies in distraction having been turned into seriousness. *XI²A 109*

The state – the state Church

Since the state, as I have said, is the higher egoism, or the calculus and reflection in egoism of single egoisms, it is easily seen that Christianity fell into good hands when it was taken over by the state. And how comical that that whose point is numbers should undertake to look after that whose point is the single person.

Now that this higher egoism has taken over Christianity, it probably looks on the matter thus+ : in so far as there are single persons in the community who stubbornly maintain that they are the true Christians in opposition to the rest, this is to be regarded as punishable egoism. It is my, that is, the state's, task to prosecute this egoism, for I hate all egoism, and strive to extirpate it (by means of a higher egoism). To wish to be a Christian in this way shows a lack of civic sense and civic virtue; the good citizen wishes to have nothing for himself, but to have everything in common. Consequently such men are to be regarded as criminals. But since their guilt does not concern the highest goods in the community, namely, money and the security of property, there is no need for the highest degree of severity. Nevertheless they ought to be punished. In general it means disorder and bad habits in the state when single persons are busy with particular personal matters – this alone is a crime. The state takes over Christianity, and now it demands (for the true good of the subjects, which the state never ceases to have in mind), also for the sake of order, that all should be Christians in equal measure – and this it intends to maintain energetically.

So the state. But the single egoisms, who were content and

entirely agreeable that the state should take over Christianity, have probably reasoned as follows.

To wish to be a Christian in conditions of strife, that is, of having to suffer for the doctrine, is a misunderstood egoism. Admittedly, there is for this egoism the satisfying thought that the rest are damned; but all the same it is a misunderstood egoism. Even gold can be too dearly bought. No, a sensible estimate of the relation between various egoisms shows that the most prudent egoism for us all is that we are all Christians. And so, in order to avoid all squabbling, the one right thing is that the state should take over the whole business of Christianity. That is what the state is for. When it takes it over, there is an end to squabbling, and so at the same time everything is better looked after. This may be seen in every possible connexion. If the streets are to be lit at night, certainly, every householder, singly or in pairs, could have a light and look after it themselves. But this would be a fine mess! No, let the state take it over, and we can pay a fixed sum. And so it is also right that the state should take over Christianity, take over this matter of eternal blessedness, and we can pay a fixed sum. Besides, this affords a certain security, and so has something soothing about it. Eternity, after all, is like another continent – and for a single person to turn up there, no, it is nothing for a single person to tackle a whole world. We can see this in other matters as well. Let a man here in Denmark be so unlucky as to have a lawsuit in Italy: this is much the same as losing it, for it is a single man against a whole country. It is another matter if he is fortunate enough to get Denmark interested in the matter through diplomatic channels: then everything goes well – and why? Because it is one country against another country. And so with eternal blessedness. The matter is too serious to be looked after by a single man (for Christianity, certainly, the seriousness consists precisely in the fact that it is to be attended to by a single man, that the matter is too serious to be looked after by an abstraction): no, let the state take the matter over, let it vouch for us as Christians, and that blessedness is assured to us: this is a great comfort. The other way is so horrifying: to think of a single

man, a man from the city here, as a single person – and then
this – o horror! – another world. It is not to be imagined that
it could be penetrated. But the state, that is something, that is
a power: when it gives the guarantee, one can make something
of that.   *XI²A 111*

[*Note*] (+) So it was established by the state as a kind of eternal
principle that every child is born practically as a Christian
already. As the state undertook for the Christians (*si placet*)
to look after the matter of eternal blessedness, so it also undertook, so as to make a complete job of it, to provide a supply of
Christians. And as a machine can work on a larger scale, and
more accurately, than can be done by hand, so the state has
delivered, from generation to generation, an assortment of
Christians, all with the mark of the state factory, and all
exactly the same, so accurate that the heart of every indus-
trialist must jump for joy to see to what heights of flawless
accuracy the art has been taken. The point of Christianity is
that man is spirit, and spirit is self-differentiation. Christianity's infinitely exalted thought is that every Christian becomes one by different ways and different modes – always
diversity, which is precisely what God wills, he who (hater of
all mere aping, which is absence of spirit) is inexhaustible in
differentiating. So the state took over Christianity, and the
point in being a Christian became the greatest possible factory-
made uniformity. It is, incidentally, a strange thing that the
God of Christianity and the state have in a way one thought in
common: both wish to have complete oversight – this is indeed
the task of governors. But God, as infinite concretion, has
oversight with infinite ease, he is not afraid that he may lose
the oversight when he permits differentiation; no, his majestic
certainty that he can keep the oversight is expressed precisely
by his willing differentiation everywhere. The state, which
is not quite certain, wishes to have the greatest possible
uniformity – for the sake of oversight.   *XI²A 112*

To see God is to die – to die to the world

What was said in paganism and Judaism, that to see God is to die, or at least to become blind or dumb, and the like, is expressed ethically in Christianity as a task: to die to the world is the condition for seeing God.

In both cases the expression of the majesty is that God cannot be seen like anything else, one cannot just live and see Tom, Dick and Harry – and at the same time God. No, to see God (direct) is to be put *in pausa*. And ethically the task is to die to the world in order to see God.   *XI²A 113*

Believing in God

That it is impossible to believe in God without letting one's understanding go, is easy to see, for the understanding is related to the dialectic of finitude. When I am able to understand that something is good for me, then it seems to me that I can easily believe it – but here comes the point.

No, believing in God means essentially always being equally glad about God and in God, always equally glad. For the gladness of faith is that God is love, which – if I only let my understanding go – is equally good, whether it is gladness, according to my view, or sorrow which meets me. All, all, all is love.   *XI²A 114*

Life's worth

Only when a man has become so unhappy, or has grasped the misery of this existence so profoundly that he can truly say, 'For me life is worthless' – only then can he make a bid for Christianity.

And then life can have worth in the highest degree.

XI²A 115

Theory – practice – doctrine – existing

Theory, or being busy with theories, is so far from supporting practice in the field of ethics (that is, in the field where the task concerns self-denial, the constraining of flesh and blood, and so on; for a doctor's practice, and similar kinds of practice, are different, having nothing to do with the formation of character), which would help a man to practise better, that theory at this point is simply a piece of trickery. What Talleyrand said of speech, that it is given to men that they may conceal their thoughts, can be much more truly said of the relation between theory and practice in the field of ethics. Theory, doctrine, is there to conceal the lack of practice.

Cut the ethical as short as possible – attention is immediately fixed decisively on the question, to do or not to do, and if you do not do it you are exposed in all your nakedness.

But theory, doctrine, produces the illusion of a relation to the ethical – by speaking about it. Theory, doctrine, is the fig-leaf with whose help this or that professor or priest looks so solemn that it is positively frightening. And as it is also said of the Pharisees that not only do they themselves not enter the kingdom of heaven, but also prevent others from entering [Matthew 23. 13], so the professor prevents the unlearned man by putting it into his head that it is doctrine that matters, and that he must therefore gradually see to it that he follows this up. This is of course in the professor's own interest, for the more important the doctrine becomes, the more important the professor too, the more brilliant his way of life and the greater his reputation. The cure of souls by the professor and the priest is normally a mystification, since it is calculated to – prevent people from entering the kingdom of heaven. . . .

XI²A 117

The free-thinker (things are reversed)

We have almost reached the point when the free-thinker in our time can be said to suffer persecution at the hands of the government – for proclaiming Christianity.

How true it is that when the goal is reached everything is reversed. The orthodox church does not preach Christianity, but allows itself to botch it into Epicureanism. Then the free-thinker – admittedly from malicious motives – undertakes to preach Christianity or to show what it is – and so he is punished by the government. *XI²A 119*

– I have an innate genius for two things, for being a police-man and for being a courtier. In truth what we call courtiers have no idea what it means to recognize majesty in the supreme sense, to bow before true majesty; all their pomp is related merely to the direct scale of values. But the scale which is called the scale of reversal – to move in this and express oneself in this is a quite different matter. And what we call police live under the limitation of supposing that a large number abolishes or alters the concept, that a large number determines that one dare not follow up a matter, and that a large number turns injustice into justice. But in the police service in which I serve numbers themselves are regarded as a crime, and there can be a criminal affair in which whole centuries are guilty. *XI²A 121*

The difference between man and man

There are many differences – and eternity can surely remove every other difference: but one difference between man and man it cannot remove, the difference of eternity between whether you lived in such a way that there was truth in you, that something higher existed for which you really suffered, or whether you lived in such a way that everything turned upon your own profit. The fact that you perhaps did it in a refined way only makes the matter worse.

Eternity neither can nor will remove this difference, it will not contradict itself; two such men could never in all eternity reach an understanding with one another.

Eternity can remove every other difference, of ability, of circumstances, of fate, of sex, of age, and so on, and can bring about understanding and equality between what is so different in the temporal world. But it cannot remove that other difference.

What a satire it is, then, when a man whose life has been entirely concerned with profit, a priest or the like, speaks with sentimental enthusiasm of being gathered to Christ and the saints, and almost persuades himself that he is looking with yearning towards this union. What a satire it is, for it would be the worst punishment for him to have to live in that company. *XI²A 122*

Time – eternity (reversed)

In a noble sense to become nothing in this world is the condition for being able to become something in the other world.

So the relation between the two is reversed. But ideals are then entirely abolished – especially in Protestantism, especially in Denmark. Catholicism is certainly somewhat less devoid of ideas and spirit, from the Christian standpoint, than Protestantism. It does have an idea and conception of Christian ideality, that is, of becoming nothing in this world. Protestantism is finitude from one end to the other, everything turns on finite goals with finite intentions, and the Christian element is introduced as at most a mood which (not to exaggerate) one only has on Sundays, or (not to exaggerate) perhaps only every other Sunday. There is nothing which Protestantism, especially in Denmark, is more afraid of than exaggeration. Nor can one say that it is guilty of this, unless one said it was extravagant in its extravagant fear of extravagance. *XI²A 123*

The single person (being a Christian) – the human race

. . . For true primitivity (and without this it is impossible to become a Christian) one must be literally alone, alone with God. Only then can the conflict of sympathy properly arise, for then one has the human race on one's conscience. But

when you look more closely at even the most famous conver-
sions to Christian life, you will find that this matter of being
alone before God is not taken so particularly. As in daily life
one may speak of a girl being head over heels in love and mean
at most that she has a sister or a friend with whom she talks
of her love – that is, she does not have inwardness in the
deepest sense: so too with the transition to becoming a Christian. A pagan is converted to Christianity – but he takes his
mother with him, perhaps his wife and children. A pagan is
converted to Christianity, but he has friends with whom he
talks about this inward determination of his inwardness. In
this way the conflict cannot really arise. For in the first place,
when a man's inwardness with God admits a confidant, even
a single one, this inwardness is already 50 per cent too
slack. In the second place, when a man in going over to Christianity takes his beloved with him, he makes it easier for himself
to abandon other men. But Socrates (o Socrates, unique among
men!), is it not true that he who is really concerned with the
idea fears most of all that he is wrong? He therefore by no
means tries to put things right by avoiding conflicts; no, no,
but perhaps his greatest efforts are directed towards ensuring
that conflicts can arise. He who is concerned with the idea lets
himself be examined by existence, but he is simultaneously
the examiner. He is the examiner in that he does not want to
buy at the cheapest possible price, for he knows that from the
standpoint of the idea all the talk about cheaper prices is
sheer nonsense: from the standpoint of the idea there is only
one price, the highest. This is the price of the idea, otherwise
everything collapses; at a cheaper price you are simply deluding yourself. The man who wants to become a Christian and
says to himself, I cannot do it unless I take my beloved with
me – and then is fortunate enough to talk her round into
becoming a Christian as well – has avoided the true Christian
conflict. . . .   *XI²A 125*

Flesh and blood – speech

It is often enough said nowadays that man's enemy is flesh and blood; I am more and more inclined to think that every man has a much more dangerous enemy, or at least one just as dangerous, in speech, in the ability to speak.

There was certainly a great deal of truth in the old view that the formation of character begins with silence (Pythagoras).

It is so seductive for a man – perhaps even more than the suggestions of flesh and blood, or at least equally so – to be able to use exalted expressions, to blow them up and so make it seem as though he himself were something similar or that his life were related to something similar.

When I compare, for example, Luther with Pythagoras in this respect, the comparison does not turn out to Luther's advantage, when he claims that what matters is that the doctrine should be proclaimed without falsification, that is, objectively.

No, the misuse of speech – alas, when one looks quite closely in this way, perhaps the most famous historical figures are not to be acquitted, always with the exception of Socrates – the misuse of speech, to make one seem more than one really is, without asking closely whether one is using a too exalted expression, this sin is surely even more widespread, if possible even more all-embracing than the sins of flesh and blood.

The police search the persons of their suspects – if the mass of speakers, teachers, professors, and so on, were to have their persons searched in this way, there would be a huge criminal proceeding. To search their persons – to divest them, deprive them of the dress and the disguise of speech, to search their persons by bidding them be silent, and saying, 'Hold your tongue, and let us see what your life says, let it for once be the speaker, to tell us who you are.'

To poison the wells of a land or a city is regarded as an abominable crime – but the sin of dishonest use of speech is just as dangerous; only here, alas, the difference is that men do not reproach one another much about it.

That is why mankind has sunk, and sinks even more deeply,

into dishonesty – and even world-famous historical figures who are exalted as servants of the truth, when they are examined closely, are found not to be too careful about how they make use of speech.

And this is the source of all the nonsense of Christendom. If the New Testament had been taken literally, this confusion would have been impossible.

For what is Christendom? It is a continual reduction of the price, from generation to generation, of calling oneself a Christian: first a little is taken off the price, and then the next generation in its turn takes a little more off, and then the next takes another little rebate off the previous rebate, and so on – and all accompanied by the misuse of language, in that the highest and most decisive expressions continue to be used, while all the time less and less content is given to them, less and less obligation is acknowledged to what the words are really saying.   *XI²A 128*

God's majesty – one aspect of Lutheran doctrine

All sufferings, tribulations, troubles and persecutions, and so on, are explained by Luther as coming from the devil; if there were no devil, being a Christian would be a life of sheer idleness and luxury.

This view is not true, from the Christian standpoint, and depends in part on Luther's view of Christianity as optimism. Adversity and suffering are only accidental to being a Christian, and therefore arise from an external power; so that but for this power being a Christian would be sheer joy, for in itself, in and for itself being a Christian has no connexion with suffering.

In part this view depends on Luther's failure to raise the divine majesty high enough in the order of majesty. When the state of affairs is that God's majesty is of such a kind that over against it there is such a majesty as Satan's, so powerful over against God that God with the best will cannot ward off suffering from his believers, then the sum of the matter is that God has, humanly speaking, a *cause* on his hands, and is therefore degraded.

But men love to imagine that God has a cause, for then they get busy reckoning that the price for being a Christian must be significantly reduced. If one whose majesty is ever so exalted has, humanly speaking, a cause on his hands, what then? *He is bound to make use of* men. He must turn to them. Take some analogies. If someone on the stock exchange *must buy*, the broker realizes at once that there is something to be earned, for the man *must* buy. If a man *must sell* something to the second-hand bookshop, the bookseller knows at once that there is something to be earned, for the man *must sell*. And so also when someone must make use of men.

It is this idea which has guided Christendom, and specially Protestantism, and in this way God, from being infinite majesty who humanly speaking does not have a cause, has become a majesty who must make use of men. And in the end, to get men for him, practically the same principle has been followed as that of Vespasian in relation to money: one must not smell the money. Splendid! Christianity came into the world in order to raise men to the highest ideality; but mankind has given the matter a different turn – the requirement for being a Christian has been reduced to practically nothing, for God is obliged to make use of men.

Let us compare this with Christ's answer to the man who wanted to be a disciple [Luke 14. 26 *f.*, 33]: here we learn that God, humanly speaking, does not have a cause. In the form of a poor servant, without having where to lay his head, aware of the enormous machinery which was set in motion against him – one should believe that such a man had need of men, must have need of men, and especially when they offer as much as in this story. But no, Christ maintains the price of the absolute unchanged. As he says, before Pilate and the crowd, 'I am a king' [John 18. 37], so the majesty of his answer here is as though he said, 'My friend, my majesty is such that I do not have to make use of men.' Oh, a miracle is not nearly so majestic as such an answer is majestically in character!

Later Protestantism has entirely given up the idea of the devil in the sense of a power alongside God. With this there vanished the dose of pessimism which was nevertheless in Luther's Christianity, and Christianity became pure syrup, a philoprogenitive idyll, and so on.

What is so base about the whole of later Protestantism is that it has let a whole aspect, that was so decisive for Luther, simply fall away, without thinking of substituting another explanation, an explanation, that is, of what Luther rightly maintained on the basis of Scripture, that being a Christian is bound up with suffering – it let all this aspect fall away as though it were nothing at all, and yet it continued to claim that it was Lutheran.

A Protestant parson in our time, especially in Denmark, is practically a private person, who is paid for declaiming on Sundays almost whatever comes into his head.

The necessity for the Christian to suffer does not come from the devil.

This is just where the highest efforts of the spirit, in relation to Christianity, begin – in the fact that suffering comes from God. When a man is to think of a being as pure love it is the most fearful strain for his head and his soul to realize that this love must in one sense be like cruelty. Man has not been able to endure this reduplication, so he has made a division: God is love – from him comes everything good, and only good; all the evil, all afflictions, and so on, are from the devil. Otherwise man could not hold fast to the truth that God is love, except for admitting, at most, that from him comes punishment for one's sins.

But this contradiction, that love makes the beloved, humanly speaking, unhappy – certainly from love, but certainly, humanly speaking, unhappy – this thought is like a mortal blow to man. So he looked for help by having recourse to the idea of the devil, just as one helps a child in a similar way by speaking of a wicked man who does (but one does not say this to the child) what God has done; for one wishes to cultivate in the child the thought that God is associated only with what is good and joyful.

But suffering comes from God. Nor does it stand in an accidental relationship with being a Christian. No, it is inseparable from it.

Suffering, that there must be suffering, is connected with the majesty of God. His majesty is so infinite that it can be characterized or expressed only by a paradox: it is the paradox of the majesty which is bound to make the beloved unhappy. [*In the margin:* Little majesties may be recognized by making the beloved happy (directness).] Infinite majesty! Yet it is never forgotten that this majesty is love.

Suffering depends on the fact that God and man are qualitatively different, and that the clash of time and eternity in time is bound to cause suffering.

Suffering depends on the fact that God is the examiner. But if the examination is to be serious, the examiner must push it to the extreme. So God, who examines in faith and in the love that a man has for him, must push matters to the extreme (while himself suffering in love more than the candidate). What a man would like is that it should be directly recognizable that he is loved by God. It is only seldom, very seldom, that there is a man with such inwardness that he does not wish this. But in truth the relation should not and cannot be of this kind, if God is spirit. But the examination must go to the opposite extreme, in which the beloved looks like one who is forsaken by God. This is the examination in which there can be different grades, but which is essentially the same for all.

God is the examiner. This is a very significant description. An examiner has not the least thing in common with one who has, humanly speaking, a cause. But it is clear that in this time of ours, with its endless chatter, all concepts are turned topsy-turvy, till in the end there is no word for characterizing the sublime. A schoolmaster in our time means a man who needs pupils; a doctor means a man who needs patients; an author means a man who needs readers; a teacher means a man who needs students – and so an examiner presumably means one who needs those who submit themselves to the examination. *XI²A 130*

Temptation

When I say that the explanation of suffering in relation to being a Christian as coming from the devil is not truly Christian, but that suffering comes from the relation to God, this must of course be understood with the addition that in a sense suffering also comes from the individual himself, through his subjectivity not being able at once, or entirely, to give itself to God.

In the older and more significant edifying writings one may read a great deal about tempting thoughts which the individual can suffer from, which are described as fiery arrows, and are ascribed to the devil. But this is not the true Christian explanation; one must say that such thoughts, which are innocent, come from the individual himself.

The fact is that when God loves a man, when a man is loved by God, this man, *qua* selfish will, must be entirely destroyed. This is what dying to the world means, the most intense of torments. But now, even if a religious man is ready for this with his better will, he can neither straightaway nor entirely place his will, his subjectivity, in the power of the better will; but his will, after making the most desperate resistance, continues to lie in wait for an opportunity to disrupt the whole revolution by which it was dethroned.

No religious man, not even the purest, is such sheer purified subjectivity and transparency that he can will only what God wills, so that there is not a residue of his original subjectivity, something which is not yet entirely penetrated, not yet conquered, perhaps not yet properly discovered in the depth of his soul; and it is from this that the reactions come.

But as the old edifying writings truly say, the individual is not in the least guilty. So far from being attributed to him as a fault, these temptations are a proof that he is thoroughly in earnest about the whole thing. The police are entirely innocent when, being thoroughly in earnest about some matter, they uncover more and more crimes; on the other hand the police are guilty, when in their ineffectiveness they give rise to the illusion that there is no crime. Thus material security and mediocrity know nothing at all of temptations of thought – this is precisely their offence and their guilt, a new crime and proof that they have no idea of what the task is from the Christian standpoint: for dying to the world and slaying one's will are in truth the kind of operation which cannot be carried off without being noticed, as though it were nothing.

XI² A 132

God – and the devil

. . . The absolute, that which exists in and for itself, is so fearfully demanding of a man, and that is why we should rather be rid of it, and saddle God with a purpose – and straightaway he is dependent upon finite things. He who has a purpose must also desire a means, and if he desires a means he must adapt himself – and so once more we reach the point that God cannot uphold ideality in relation to being a Christian, he must give way a little – for 'otherwise he wouldn't get anybody' – and if he has a definite purpose he desires to have Christians: ergo the demand is lowered.

That is why I repeatedly say that God is sheer subjectivity, that he has nothing of objective existence in himself, which could occasion his having purposes. That which is not sheer subjectivity, through and through, possesses in the objective existence, which it has at one point or another, a relation to the world around it, a relation to other things, and so it has, it must have, a purpose. Only that which in infinite subjectivity has its subjectivity infinitely in its power as subjectivity, only that has no purpose.

But the absolute, that which exists in and for itself, is so killing for a man. Think of the absolute demand, and then think that a man is nevertheless permitted to raise the question, 'Why, why should I have to give up absolutely everything like this?' Then think that the answer is, because God wishes to use you as an instrument to work upon other men; this is a relief, the absolute is something soothing, less killing, because this 'because' has been interposed, that is, a purpose has been introduced between the absolute and the man. But look closely, and you will see that it is no longer absolutely the absolute, that which exists in and for itself. And when you realize this, you will see that something is lying in wait here which little by little turns the whole situation upside-down, till the end of the matter is that God is a majesty who has a cause, humanly speaking, and so cannot hold absolutely to the absolute.

That is why I suspect the way in which the expression 'to serve God' is used. For God cannot be served as another majesty is served which has, humanly speaking, a cause, and purposes. No, the one expression which corresponds to God's majesty is 'to worship him'. In general a distinction is drawn between worshipping God, as referring rather to one's feelings and moods and their expression in words, and serving him, as referring to one's actions. But no, your action is true worship, and it is true worship when it is free of all busyness, as though God had a purpose. Worshipfully to forsake all things, and so not because God needs you as his instrument, no, not that at all, but to forsake all things as being absolutely superfluous luxuries – this is worship. . . .   *XI²A 133*

Christendom

The formula for being a Christian is to be related to, to turn to, God personally, as a single person, quite literally as a single person.

And then, in Christendom, we see these millions of men who, as I have said, say to one another, each one to the others: 'How splendid that everyone of us, absolutely every one, can turn personally, and at any time we wish, to heaven's majesty.' This is how they speak, this is what they preach. But when it comes to the bit, each one of them says, 'The cleverest thing is not to have to do as a single person literally with that infinite majesty,' and so the end of the matter is that no one at all does it.

But to all appearances this is something that everybody is doing: after all, we are all Christians, all these millions, and everyone can do it, and it is a blessing, we say, that everyone can do it, and at any time of day, and so on. To all appearances, then, man's turning personally, as a single person, to God is so continual, every blessed day, that it is almost as unimportant as looking in at the grocer's to buy four shillings' worth of goods.

The truth is very different. The truth in all the chatter about how blessed it is that everyone, etc., is that no one does it. And the truth about its being an unimportant event, continually happening, when a man turns personally as a single person to God, is that when it does happen it is an event without comparison, more important than a European war and a war between the five parts of the world; it is a catastrophe which moves existence to the very depths of its foundations.

Nothing is more certain. To come near to God brings catastrophe. Quite literally to turn as a single person to God brings the most intense catastrophe of existence. Even just to make a significant approach (and that means only a small number – large numbers subtract) brings a relative catastrophe. Nothing is more certain. It is as certain as a chemist knowing that a drop of this and this essence in a glass of water produces an effervescence, or that a drop from another bottle produces no effervescence – as certain as the chemist who says, 'Yes, that wasn't the essence', is the certainty that to come near to God brings catastrophe. . . .

In truth it is a fearful risk to have to turn to God as a single person, even just approximately as a single person, or as a single person to turn only approximately to God. What a risk this is, to do it literally as a single person, is seen in the life of the God-Man. For it was a life of sheer misery and distress, even (which is a part of it) to being forsaken by God, who is nevertheless love unchanging, and suffers in love. . . .

XI² A 135

'Man'

I suppose that all the extraordinary men who have ever lived, scattered, few in number, through the course of time, have given their judgement about 'man'. One has said that man is an animal, another that he is a hypocrite, another that he is a liar, and so on.

Perhaps my definition is not the most infelicitous, when I say that man is a chatterbox – and that he is this by means of speech.

By means of speech every man participates in what is most exalted – but by means of speech, to participate in what is most exalted, in the sense of chattering about it, is as ironical as being a spectator from the gallery of the king's banquet.

If I were a pagan I should say that an ironical deity had given men the gift of speech in order that he may be entertained by their self-deceit (+).

By means of speech man is distinguished from the animals, from the dumb creation – but perhaps the dumb creatures have the advantage, at least they are not fooled, or do not fool themselves, with what is most exalted. *XI² A 139*

[*In the margin*] (+) From the Christian standpoint it is of course out of love that God has given man speech, and thus made it possible for every man really to grasp what is most exalted – alas, God must look on the result with sorrow! *XI² A 140*

The relation to God (*silence*)
24 November 1854

Even in human relationships, if a girl who, as we cruelly say, is in other respects insignificant, should possess the quality, in relation to her beloved, of being absolutely reticent, not saying a thing to any other person about her relationship, then this gives her a real worth, it makes her pleasing in her lover's eyes.

So God loves silence (+). He does not wish that chattering with other men about one's relation to God. To do this is perhaps vanity – and that is not pleasing to God. Or it is from cowardice and lack of faith, for one is not really trusting, one is afraid of perhaps, if I may put it so, getting into trouble, and the like – all of which is displeasing to God. If it is objected that when one man is more advanced than another it is an encouragement to let the other participate in his relation to God, then again God is against this, for it is mere conceit. 'What conceit!' says God. 'For have I not let it be known that every man, absolutely every man, can turn to me – so that other man can also do it?'   *XI²A 142*

[*In the margin*] (+) Silence in the relation to God is a strengthening; absolute silence would be like a jack, or like the point outside the world of which Archimedes speaks. Speaking about one's relation to God is an evacuation which weakens.

XI²A 143

The popular

Anything that is to become popular must tend in the direction of the extensive and the manifold. The intensive is never popular. What is intensive is only for men of character, and they are even more rare than men of genius and talent, except that even the simplest man can be a man of character.

If I were to attack the present state of affairs in Christendom, and say that the Christianity we teach is a different kind of Christianity from that of the New Testament, then this attack could become popular. Why? Because there is a dose of nonsense concealed in it, as if there were talk of various kinds of Christianity. So this can become popular, people can get this kind of thing into their heads: there are various kinds of Christianity, just as there is extra-fine farm butter, and good butter, and simple butter, and cooking fat which is almost as good as butter. This is the law for what is popular – there must always be a certain dose of twaddle added to it.

On the other hand, a strict movement in the direction of Either-or will never be popular.

It is the manifold, the extensive, the outspreading, that can become popular. For example, if I had a reasonable number of adherents, in proportion to the size of the land, for me to be right could become popular, and I would then be considered right; for me as a single man to be right can never become popular. To this extent it would even be a wrong concession on my part to acquire a reasonable number of merely puppet adherents, so that it might appear as though I were one of many.   *XI²A 146*

Speech

is an ideality which every man has gratis. What an ideality, which God can use to express his thoughts in such a way that man by means of speech has fellowship with God!

But in the realm of the spirit there is never something which is simply a gift, as in the material world. No, in the realm of the spirit a gift is always at the same time something which passes judgement – and by means of speech, or what this ideality becomes in his mouth, man judges himself.

And in the realm of the spirit irony is also always present. How ironical that it is by means of speech that man can degrade himself below the level of the dumb creation – for a chatterbox is truly of a lower category than a dumb creature.   *XI²A 147*

Human existence

There are two poles in being a man – his determination as an animal and his determination as a spirit.

The determination as an animal has to do with propagating the species – and along this line everybody is willing to be human.

The consequence (and this is the misfortune for existence)

is that numbers increase out of all proportion to the number of single persons who are really related to spirit.

Yet this is not an exact description of the misfortune. No, the disproportion between numbers and the few single persons who ought to balance them is so great that between those few single persons and the mass of men there is interposed a whole intermediary authority, a medium – namely, the priests, the teachers of the people, and the like, who live by pandering to the mass, by transforming the true into the false.

If only those few single persons, who are really related to spirit, could manage to have an effect upon the common man, much would be gained. But it is the intermediary authority which is the misfortune of human existence. And it is a lie which cries to heaven, when this intermediary authority pretends to help men to get a little nearer to the truth. No, this authority is neither one thing nor the other, and all it does is help the mass of men to enter into the same indefiniteness. *XI² A 149*

The propagation of the species – Christianity
wants to bar the way

This is surely how Christianity should speak to a man who wants to get married: in which capacity do you wish to propagate the species – as one of the animal creation, or as a spiritual man? In the first capacity the matter is all too simple.

But if it is in the second capacity, then wait a moment. Does it not seem to you that to be a father demands that you are mature enough to possess a view of life which you are ready to answer for, and to pass on to your child when he asks you about the meaning of life? For he has a right to ask you, as a child who owes you his life. Or if, what nature attends to, it is the woman's special task to see to if that she has milk in her breast, and so on – would it not be abominable if she was ready to be a mother, to satisfy her lust, without having everything needful for the child? But a child has a right to ask for a view of life from its father, to ask that its father really have one.

But if a man should first have reached maturity, then a long time will pass before he marries, the years when his desires are strongest will go past. When he at last reaches maturity, and if his view of life is the Christian, then it could surely never occur to him to want to give life to a child. To give life to a child! A child is born in sin, having been conceived in transgression, and this existence is a vale of tears – is this what you will tell your child, will this give you openness towards the child which owes its existence to you?

O my God, the more I think of it, the more I see how Protestantism has fundamentally confused Christianity!

It is natural that man should centre human existence on the propagation of the species, this is where his entire egoism as part of the animal creation is to be found, or where it culminates. Christianity wishes to decentralize this relationship – and what a struggle it has been! In connexion with this alone, how terribly true are Christ's words to the apostles: 'I send you as sheep in the midst of wolves' [Matthew 10. 16] – yes, ravening wolves, that is what men become as soon as someone seriously touches on the point, seriously tries to wrest them away from what is everything in life to them.

And then Protestantism comes and presents Christianity – in its connexion with marriage. It is marriage that is well pleasing to God. . . .

The error in Catholicism is not that the priest is celibate; no, the error is that a qualitative difference between the layman and the priest has been introduced, which goes clean against the New Testament, and is a concession of weakness in relation to numbers. Certainly the error is not that the priest is celibate – a Christian should be celibate.

'But if you hold to this you will have no Christians at all!' If that is so, it is all one to me. 'And on the other hand, if you make Christianity consist of marriage, then you will get millions of Christians!' It is all one to me.   *XI² A 150*

The worst danger for Christianity

is not – this is what I claim – heresies, heterodoxies, not free-thinkers, nor profane worldliness; no, it is the kind of ortho-doxy which is hearty twaddle, mediocrity with a dash of sugar.

There is nothing which is so fearfully contrary to the being of Christianity as this, in which it does not so much perish as just pine away.

. . . This kind of orthodoxy is connected with the hearty twaddle of family life, and essentially finds its refuge in the heartiness of family life. This in turn constitutes the worst danger for Christianity, and not wild lusts, debauchery, terrible passions and the like. They are not so opposed to Christianity as this flat mediocrity, this stuffy reek, this nearness to one another, where it is certainly difficult for great crimes, wild excesses, and powerful errors to be produced – but where it is also even more difficult for the majesty to find what it requires, namely, the expression of submission. There is no greater distance from obedience to the either-or than this flat, hearty family twaddle.   *XI² A 152*

One reason more for marrying

Christianity says, Do not marry, this is well-pleasing to God, and is a matter of course if you are really a Christian.

Mankind answers. But if we all do this, the race will perish.

And that the race might perish is of course regarded by the race as the greatest misfortune.

So the consequence is not merely that men do not get married, no, they have obtained one reason more for marrying – that they may prevent the terrible thing (which is so near at hand!) – the terrible thing (which almost everyone is busy preventing!), that the race might perish.

This is one reason more for marrying!   *XI² A 153*

Celibacy

Creation is reserved for God, and this, if one may dare to speak of such a thing, is the supreme autopathic satisfaction.

To give life is a feeble analogy to this, which has been conceded to man – and human egoism culminates in this.

As the nerve filaments lie under the nail, so human egoism is concentrated in the sexual relation, the propagation of the species, the giving of life.

According to the teaching of Christianity God desires only one thing from us men – to be loved. But to love God a man must give up all egoism, and first and foremost the potentiated egoism of the propagation of the species, the giving of life.

Of course God knows only too well that the sexual is the centre of human egoism; thus it was here that he directed his aim. And only the slightest observation is necessary to assure us that it is here that human egoism is to be found *totaliter*.

So God demanded the abandonment of this egoism, and so indicated immortality. For as I have often said in these journals, the propagation of the species (as both Plato and Aristotle expressly say) was, both in paganism and Judaism, a substitute for immortality.

The sexual is the culmination of human egoism. Hence from a merely human standpoint, both the woman and the man regard their life as lost and a failure if they do not marry. Only the married man is a proper citizen in this world; the celibate is a stranger (and this is just what Christianity wants the Christian to be, and what God wants him to be, that he may love him). That is why the Jews (who certainly knew all about the propagation of the species) looked upon sterility as a dishonour for a woman. And that is why no misfortune touches a man so severely as that which concerns the propagation of the species. Everything else (being blind, or deaf, or lame, and the like) does not really trouble him, it does not touch the tender point of his egoism. Our self-esteem as part of the animal creation is connected with the propagation of the species, the giving of life. That is why the man who, through natural and unnatural excesses, has lost his procreative powers is so extraordinarily concerned to regain them, in order that he may recover his self-esteem, etc. etc.

So God wishes to have celibacy because he wishes to be loved.

But a man then says, 'I cannot bring you this sacrifice – but let me get married, and I will get you another ten to love you.' Splendid! But look more closely: these ten, if this progenitor and provider of people finally does produce ten – these ten will be celibates, who renounce this intensified egoism? No, these ten will behave just in the same way, and each one of them will perhaps produce another ten, always under the same formula – that instead of one, God will have another ten: whereas the truth is God does not get a single one, and is continually being fooled.

In Protestantism there is no beating about the bush in this regard; here it is simply taught that marriage is what is well-pleasing to God, and I see the day coming when it will be discovered by learned theology that the God of the Christians is not called Jehovah or Adonai, and is not even neuter gender, but is a woman called Maggie Matchmaker!

. . . In the Christianity of the New Testament God wishes to be loved, and therefore he wishes man to abandon the egoism of giving life.

The Fall is the satisfaction of this egoism – and this is where the history of temporality really begins, as the constant repetition of the same fault, constantly opposing or preventing what God has in view, which is to put a stop to this error – by means of celibacy. Every time we see celibacy from love of God we see an effort to comply with God's intention.

But I almost shudder when I think how far along this way I have been, and how wonderfully I have been halted and sent back to celibacy; how too I have certainly understood myself, but as an exception, and have known how to conceal what I knew from my contemporaries, till at long last I see how once more Providence has been with me, and wishes to have some quite definite result.

O infinite majesty, even if you were not love, even if you were cold in your infinite majesty I could not cease to love you, I need something majestic to love. What others have said, that they did not find love in this world, and therefore felt a need to love you, since you are love (to which I entirely assent) – this I should also say in regard to majesty. There was and there is a need of majesty in my soul, of a majesty I can never tire of worshipping. In the world I found nothing, no, I found no more majesty than there is beard on a young girl's cheek – even less than that, for I found it ridiculous.

XI²A 154

Father – son – the New Testament

In Christendom a father speaks thus to his son: 'Go out quite calmly into the world, there is a God, he will certainly care for you, just depend upon him, he will certainly help you, he always has resources, he gives help, he has all good gifts – and here is a book for you, the New Testament, where you can read further how blessed it is to have to do with God.'

As an exception – of course it is an exception, it happens perhaps once in a million times – it happens that there is a son who really does read the New Testament.

To tell the truth, my pen can scarcely express the change, the quite different situation which the son gets to know about.

Concerning himself he learns that he was conceived in sin, born in transgression – that his existence is therefore a crime, that therefore his father, in giving him life, has done something which is as far as possible from being well-pleasing to God. So he gets to know something that is not exactly favourable to his father, who presumably with the help of the New Testament has strengthened himself in the assurance that the begetting of children is not something one does for pleasure – no, it is the best deed one can do.

So the son learns that death awaits him – as a punishment, for his existence is crime and transgression. He learns that this life is to be a vale of tears, a prison, that the world lies in the grip of evil, that God wishes him to hate himself, and that if he does not wish what God wishes, eternal punishment awaits him.

And so on, and so on.

Is there anything more abominable, can anything more abominable be conceived than this, which is the quite simple consequence of all the lies in Christendom – when once it happens that a son really reads the New Testament?

I do not deny that the case is rare, and that it is possible for millions of Christians and thousands of priests and professors to live without its happening to them.   *XI²A 157*

The Wedding at Cana

The perpetual insistence in Christendom that Christ was present at a wedding and provided the wine is an indirect proof that men themselves have a suspicion that Christianity is against marriage. So this story is as important to them as the arguments they base on it are ridiculous.   *XI²A 160*

The martyr – asceticism

I have shown elsewhere[1] that Luther altered Christianity by changing the idea of the martyr, as though he did not have value in and for himself.

Thus I have elsewhere[2] described medieval asceticism as 'situationless'.

Here we may observe that it is quite true that medieval asceticism is situationless, and the Christian should go out into the world in order to be sacrificed.

But the idea of being sacrificed can, from another angle, easily become sophistical, as if it had to be left to a man's understanding to see where a sacrifice was required.

No, the Christian view is really that sacrifices are always necessary, and asceticism is really the view of life which

[1] *XI¹A 193.*
[2] *X⁵A 99.*

corresponds to God as the absolute, and to the world, for God, being in the grip of evil, not being a pleasance but a penitentiary – and this is God's view which asceticism strives voluntarily to express.

Medieval asceticism was 'situationless' basically as a result of the practice of direct recognizability: men wanted to be honoured, and were honoured, in relation to their asceticism. That is something quite different! So they were able to unite splendidly what otherwise seems impossible to think together, namely, an ascetic who was afraid of being killed, afraid of martyrdom. For his asceticism was not pessimistic, but a cunning invention to win a reputation among men, to *live* admired and almost worshipped. So the ascetic (for love of God) was so far from living in hostility to men that his relation to them was much more like that of a juggler to his public; and though he was an ascetic perhaps he clung to this life more than any juggler, and loved man's admiration with a passion greater than any actor. *XI² A 161*

Christianity transformed into optimism

In so far as the transformation of Christianity into optimism does not arise from the most utter thoughtlessness or a simple cheat, the idea is probably as follows.

For God this world certainly lies in the grip of evil – and that is what Christianity teaches – and we also admit that paganism and Judaism were in this state. But when we Christians behave well, and are decent people, then it could be a fine world, and we could rejoice in this life, for Christ in his suffering has made satisfaction for original sin . . .

This whole human existence, dating from the Fall, and which we men are so puffed up about as a devilish *tour de force*, is opposed to God, it is merely the consequence of a false step, which on account of the immensity of the consequences we should prefer to forget; but God does not forget.

This whole human existence is opposed to God, it is a fall

from him, a false step away from him, and all the time (for he is love) he pities man, but he also wants to pick a quarrel with him.

That is what Christianity is for – which straightway bars the way to procreation. This means: stop! I have put up long enough with this world-historical process, certainly I will have pity, but I do not want any more of the consequences of that false step.

So even if one became a Christian and died unmarried, he is still a transgressor, for his existence by means of procreation was a crime.

In this way the world can never become a splendid world in the eyes of God. For either there is a given generation – but in that case its existence has come about through procreation, or the question arises whether this is a splendid world or not. . . .   *XI²A 163*

Let the children come to me
[Matthew 19. 14]

Yes, quite right – Christ is indeed the Saviour of the world, and the little child by its existence belongs to the lost race.

But to interpret this passage by saying, as millions and trillions of people have said, 'Let us now just put children into the world – for Christ says, Let the children come to me': this is either bestial stupidity or effrontery.

Christendom has succeeded in turning Christ into a good fellow, one who provides wine for banquets, almost as though Christ had not come to the world to save a lost race, but to be godfather to all the children of the earth.

Yet the matter is quite simple: 'to save a race'. This means that the *race* is lost, we have had only too much of it, and we have to be saved out of the race, and consequently a beginning must be made by barring the way for our race.

Christ did not come in order to be the progenitor of a new race. Yet this is just how Christendom wants to re-edit Christianity, instead of letting stand as it is in the New

Testament. The race is lost, Christ will save – and not, Christ will be the starting-point for a new race. *XI²A 164*

God's majesty

As the effect of Draconian law is that no one at all is punished, so too one can exalt God in such a majesty that one is entirely quit of him.

This is the kind of majesty in which Christendom has got rid of God.

This is another reason why it must be emphasized that God is sheer subjectivity in one sense: if it pleases him something of the greatest unimportance can attract his attention. It is of course something different, as I have often mentioned, that in his majesty he punishes by ignoring men and all their efforts. But this is certainly not because he is so remote in his majesty that he cannot get it in his sight. And of course neither is he subjectivity in the sense, if I may dare to put it thus, that something should have the power to affect him: no, the greatest as well as the least is quite unable to do this. But, as I say, the most unimportant matter can attract his attention, when it pleases him. When it pleases him: that is the point. For he sees everything, he knows everything, what is greatest as well as the thing of greatest or of least unimportance. So let no one deceive himself. If a man piles transgression on transgression, and it goes unpunished, if indeed his whole life is sheer prosperity and triumph, let him not deceive himself, God sees it, God is very near, but he overlooks him: the man is punished by the most fearful of all punishments – he is ignored by God. If the religious man thinks that one or the other unimportant thing is so unimportant that God does not notice it, let him not be deceived, for God sees everything, and if it pleases him he can note it.

The text-book category that God is in heaven, and does all that is pleasing to him, is perfectly right, when it is understood as I have put it: God is sheer subjectivity. Everything is nothing to him, if it so pleases him, and nothing is everything to him if it so pleases him. But this mediating definition, 'if it so pleases him', is the infinite distance of God, of him who neverthe less in another sense is infinitely near. For everywhere, at every moment, he is the most near, but infinitely secure from all familiarity: for whether he lets it be noticed how near he is or not, whether he is subjectively near or not, depends solely on whether it pleases him.   *XI²A 166*

Numbers

How ironical that the law is this – that everything that needs numbers in order to be important is *eo ipso* unimportant, and the more numbers it needs, the less important it is. Everything that can be carried out, arranged, realized, only by means of great numbers, and that men then regard with stupefied admiration, as if it were really important – everything of this kind is unimportant. What is truly important is quite the reverse, it always needs less and less numbers in order to be realized. And the most important thing of all, which sets heaven and earth in movement, requires just one man; if more are required, this subtracts from the importance. European wars and revolutions and art exhibitions and immense headlines in the newspapers can certainly not be arranged by one man. So it is thought that such things are important, instead of which it is precisely their unimportance which requires many people, it is their lack of importance which requires numbers to be called in to give them importance. But the most important thing of all, which interests angels and demons, that a man really has to do with God – for this one man is enough.

So shudder when you think how we live – and that the truth is that every man can be that one man.   *XI²A 167*

Divine providence

Providence is omnipresent, and so in one sense the nearest of all. But in another sense he is infinitely far away. That is to say, he does not wish to intervene with power, but he omnipotently constrains his own omnipotence, for it pleases him to see what can become of the whole of existence.

In a certain sense he is like a scientist with his experiment: perhaps the scientist has it in his power to get his result in another way, but he wants to see if it can be produced by this particular experiment, he constrains himself to watch the experiment, he waits in patience, yet with infinite interest. Or God is like a teacher in a maieutic relation to his pupil. He has it in his power to tell the pupil the right answer straight-away, but instead he constrains himself, he holds out patiently, perhaps for years, for the pupil to exhaust himself, finding ever new nonsense.

But just as the experimenter and the maieutic teacher are anything but indifferent, so too God is infinitely concerned.

But what makes existence fearfully overwhelming for a poor man, seen from this standpoint, is that God possesses and makes use of such immense proportions, which is the very nature of majesty. (Just as, to use a weak analogy, the experimenter or the maieutic teacher may be graded according to how long he can hold out and according to the grandeur of the criterion for his experiment.) God makes use of centuries, he lets centuries be fooled away with nonsense and aberrations: proportions of this kind are so immense for a poor man.

In a certain sense one can therefore say that there is no providence, just as it is as though there were no experimenter, or the experimenter were nobody, since he does not intervene but just leaves it to the same steady powers to unfold. And yet the experimenter is utterly attentive, and in a flash he is there – which is only a weak image of God's presence, while in another sense he constrains himself from intervening with omnipotence.

Only once has providence intervened with omnipotence – in Christ.   *XI²A 170*

Christianity as doctrine

If it is really God's view that Christianity is only doctrine, a collection of doctrinal propositions, then the New Testament is a ridiculous book – to set everything in motion, to have Christ suffer thus, in order to produce a collection of propositions! Mankind would surely have to say, 'My heavens, if that is all you want, if that is what occupies you so much, we gladly accept whatever you want, we will do it as easily as if you asked us to wear a cocked hat instead of a round one.'

Truly, if Christianity in God's view is meant just to be a doctrine then the whole machinery of the New Testament, and the life of Christ, betray that – to put it plainly – God is in his knowledge of men just a simpleton.

But no: God who knows the scoundrel that man is aims at something else – at transforming character.

So God aims first and foremost at the cardinal point of celibacy.

Heterogeneity is what God desires, heterogeneity with this world; dying to the world instead of the lust of life; celibacy instead of marriage and births.

Once the only adornment in a Christian's home was a death's head. Now it is a Venus one sees in every house, now it is a mark of (Christian?) culture to introduce into everything a refined allusion to the sexual, and a woman's education consists of refined coquetry.

Yes – either a Venus as a symbol, or the Jewish view that the begetting of children is a blessing for this life: one or the other is the point in the life of Christendom or is the very life of Christendom.

This is the splendid result of turning Christianity into a doctrine: in Christendom the seriousness of life consists in the relation to the other sex – and this is supposed to be Christianity, the Christianity of the New Testament.   *XI² A 172*

'Christendom' a conspiracy

. . . 'Christendom' is a conspiracy against New Testament Christianity. I realize that Christendom wants to make us believe that they are splendid Christians, whereas free-thinkers and sectarians and so on are the conspirators. No, no, it is an old trick for a thief when he is being pursued to cry 'Stop thief!', in order to turn attention away from himself. Similarly 'Christendom' is busy defending orthodoxy against sects and free-thinkers and so on; but nobody is fooled by this, Christendom is itself the conspiracy against New Testament Christianity, and far more dangerous than any free-thinker or sect. . . . *XI² A 174*

A personal God

This is what professors and priests blether about: they try to prove that God is personal, and that this is what makes the faithful happy.

I will not speak of how ridiculous it is to wish to prove this, for it cannot be 'proved', but must be believed. But what I want to speak about is how men, here as everywhere, waste their time and their life in resolving difficulties which they themselves have created. Yes, God always makes fools of the wise.

Let us suppose that someone, a professor, spends his whole life in study and learning in order to demonstrate the person-ality of God – and let us suppose that in the end he succeeds. What then? Then at the end of his life he will have come to the beginning, or to the end of the introduction to the beginning. And this whole introduction is something the man has stupidly created himself, it consists of difficulties which he himself has thought up. But as I have said this is what you find in every-thing to do with religion, with Christianity. Men invent some kind of difficulty in advance, the introduction to the matter itself, and on this they waste their time and their strength and their life, and then they die, and so they never come to begin on the matter itself.

No, God is personal, the matter is certain.

But with this you are no farther forward. Here again there is a human aberration, it is imagined that when the professor has finally proved that God is personality, then he must be so without further ado for us all. Perhaps this is because we are so ready to transpose the matter out of the sphere of faith into that of proof, in order that with speed and certainty, and once for all, we may be quit of the matter, or have certainty.

No, God is certainly personal, but it does not follow from this that he is personal without further ado for you. Take a human relationship: a superior personality is certainly a personality, but he does not have it in his power, in face of his inferior, to be a personality in relation to him, or to be related objectively to him. Yet it is clear that the superior is and remains a personality.

So with God. He is certainly personality, but whether he wills to be this in relation to the single person depends on whether it pleases God. It is God's grace that in relation to you he desires to be personality; and if you squander his grace, he punishes you by relating himself objectively to you. And in this sense we can say that the world (despite all proofs!) does not have a personal God. For the world does not please God, and his punishment is to relate himself objectively to it, while he still certainly remains personality.

But while professors and priests drivel by the million about proofs of God's personality, the truth is that for a long time now men have been unable to bear the pressure and the weight of having a personal God. There is something frightening and touching in the truth with which a patriarch or an apostle speaks of dying weary of life. For in truth it can make a man weary to have had to do with a personal God. Imagine a plough-horse, even one which has worked hard at the plough – it has no idea of what it means to be as weary as a saddle-horse after it has been ridden. Alas, even if for the rest my life did not have torments and sufferings, this nausea would itself be enough which comes upon me every time I think of the nonsense men waste their time and their life over. It would surely be nauseating to imagine men not eating food but living on filth and vermin and the like: but it is just as nauseating to imagine men paying through the nose to priests and professors, and considering themselves happy to live off – drivel.

XI²A 175

Marriage

. . . Most men do not have enough self-esteem to be able to assert themselves in face of other men, so their self-esteem demands that they have some people who obey them absolutely, whom they have entirely in their power, so that they also feel that the man is the master. These people are children. God pity what takes place in family life! What brutality and what egoism are hidden there. It is unfortunately only too certain that the parents usually need more upbringing than the children. *XI²A 176*

Human culture

. . . Human culture is demoralizing, it is calculated to teach a man the *tour de force* of not betraying any expression or using any word or undertaking the least thing without having the guarantee that many others before him have behaved in the same manner. This is how men think they can succeed in avoiding all dangers, all conflicts, all the effort which is connected with singularity.

As in the world of opinion newspapers demoralize men, by disaccustoming them from having an opinion of their own, and from developing themselves by carrying it in the face of opposition to the opinion of others, and by accustoming them, on the other hand, to having the guarantee for any opinion they may have (a guarantee provided by the wide circulation of the paper) that a significant number of men have the same opinion – so human culture, so-called, has a demoralizing effect. . . . *XI²A 177*

Grace (paradox)

In order to prevent, if possible, the drivel about grace which has falsified Christianity in 'Christendom' and has demoralized men, let me describe the state of affairs in a few words.

The matter is very simple, if one only keeps in mind that 'grace', like everything Christian, is in the sphere of paradox. Therefore the falsification of grace, like the falsification of everything else in Christianity, consists in dragging it down into the sphere of directness.

Grace is a paradox – what does this mean? It means grace with the negative sign of suffering: so that grace is known, negatively, in that it brings suffering. So high is the Christian concept of grace, which springs from the fact that the divine majesty does not concern itself with this life, but only with the eternal; so that when it is introduced into this life, everything is turned round about.

So grace: grace means to be saved from eternal perdition – in God's view, this is infinite grace.

But at every weak moment things look very differently to man. What does 'a weak moment' mean? It means a moment when the eternal is not present to him. And when the eternal is not present to him, the temporal becomes important to him – and when it now appears in the temporal – as indeed the New Testament teaches – that to be a Christian means that suffering comes to this life, suffering one could be free of if one were not a Christian – then the whole thing is turned round about, and grace becomes that which brings suffering and torment – so far is it from being 'grace' in a direct way.

With God's idea of eternity, of man's guilt and of eternal perdition, Christianity is sheer grace, and suffering for a few years in this life is infinite, infinite grace. With your own idea of this life, grace is anything but grace, it is a torture, the greatest possible torture, since being a Christian is the most intense suffering of this life.

Blessed are those who are not offended! [Luke 7. 23.] Look, this is how it is: just because everything Christian is in the sphere of paradox, the possibility of offence is infinitely near.

This majesty of grace being in a lower sense suffering, torment, – how infinitely near offence now is, if one does not prefer the escape which Christendom offers, the escape of transforming everything Christian into sheer drivel: in a certain sense the offence is certainly avoided, even if in another sense I believe that it must be produced, when one thinks that such drivel is intended to be – the divine. I mean that in a deeper sense one must be said to miss the sign of 'the possibility of offence', so that one would have to say of this drivelling Christianity that it is impossible for it to be the divine, since there is nothing here to be offended at. *XI²A 182*

Christianity (irony)

If someone were to say, 'Christianity is surely an irony of God towards us men,' I should reply, 'No, my good man, but we men have it in our power to transform Christianity into irony, into biting irony.'

The matter is quite simple. God in his majesty takes so high a tone that if a man is unwilling to let go of his finite good sense, to give up his flat, self-indulgent mediocrity, then what God calls help, salvation, grace, and so on, is the most biting irony. So one cannot blame the finite understanding for saying, 'No thank you; I should prefer to have none of this help, and salvation, and grace.'

On the other hand, as soon as a man wills what God wills, is willing to let himself be taught by God concerning the relation between temporality and eternity, is willing to believe God, then of course God is sheer and utter love and pity.

But Christendom's escape is to turn God into a driveller snuffling something about salvation and grace and so on, in such a way that worldliness sees good sense in the words; and this is *lèse-majesté*.

As I have said elsewhere, no pagan people has worshipped such a ridiculous and nauseating deity as 'Christendom', which worships and adores – a driveller. Even the most primitive pagan took better care that his god stood out somewhat

above human life, was a little higher, whereas Christendom
has excelled in making God entirely human. . . .

XI²A 183

Children and women – man – Christianity as seriousness

Christianity is seriousness. Consequently its criterion is man;
the Christian demand is related to man, indeed, to God's idea
of what it means that human existence is found in adult man.

But everyone with the least experience of practical life, the
life of affairs, knows that when there is a question of sneaking
out of something then the regular tactics are to bring on
women and children.

And here we have a new explanation of the same thing, how
Christianity has been turned right round, into something that
men are pleased to call perfectibility, and has become exactly
the opposite of what it originally was.

Christianity, they say, is surely for men; a child is surely
a man, ergo the child is the criterion for what Christianity
is.

Now this is such a lie that it is plain unscrupulousness to
educate a child in Christianity. For a child is incapable of
assimilating what Christianity really is (could a child have
any idea of original sin, when it is brought up to see in its
father and mother its benefactors, and to thank them for the
great benefaction of existence, and so on?) Therefore one must
either turn Christianity into something other than it is in order
that a child can assimilate it (and has one the right to delude
a child about something under pretext of teaching it?); or
the child itself changes Christianity, for it cannot do otherwise
– but has one the right to cause a child to be established in
illusions, under pretext of instructing and teaching it?

No, the whole business of a child's relation to Christianity is
a cheat. Just as in business life, when, for example, the
superior comes and asks after a man, and he tries to sneak
away and produce women and children, in order that they may
make a touching and appeasing effect, so the recent history

of Christianity is a cheat in which man has sneaked away from it and has made it something for women and children. And when he has succeeded in this, and religion has become candy for children, then the man comes home again, the sneaking rascal, and shares in the sweetmeats, and speaks sentimentally of religion and Christianity being especially for women and children.

What effrontery and what a mean lie, that religion is something for women and children, presumably because its demand is too easy for that strong creature, man! Especially for such men as those of today!

No, religion, Christianity, is an ideality, a task, beneath which the highest ideality of human existence must almost sink. This is what Christianity was originally. It comes from the East. And what was the situation there? There the man was the human being, and women and children were almost like domestic animals. But just as the whole world-historical process is a *tour de force* of bungling of God's whole plan and turning it into its opposite, so it has been reserved for romantic Protestant Christendom to make women and children 'human beings' and to reduce man to zero. I anticipate that perfectibility approaches, when we shall have polyandry in place of the polygamy with which we began. But this change in which women and children have become 'human beings' has changed Christianity into the opposite of what it originally was: it has become a sheer gift, and it was once a sheer task. *XI²A 187*

Irony

3 December 1854

. . . In what did the irony of Socrates really consist? In expressions and turns of speech and the like? No, such trifles, even virtuosity in speaking ironically, did not make a Socrates. No, his whole existence is irony, and it was this: while the whole contemporary population of farm-workers, businessmen, and so on, in brief, all these thousands were all perfectly sure that they were men and that they knew what it means to be a man, Socrates was at a lower level (ironically) and occupied himself with the problem, what it means to be a man. And what he really says is that all the activity of these thousands is an illusion, mere juggling, tumult, noise and bustle, which from the standpoint of the idea are worth nothing, or less than nothing, in so far as these men could have used their life to ponder the ideal.

Irony in relation to Christendom has one moment more than Socratic irony, in so far, namely, as men in Christendom do not merely imagine that they are men (this is where Socrates stops) but also imagine that to be a Christian is to be something historically concrete. Socrates doubted whether we are men at birth; one does not so easily get the chance to become a man or to know what it is to be a man. For the ideality in being a man was what concerned Socrates, and what he sought. But what would Socrates think if he were told that now men have for a long time been so perfectible, that they have made such progress in nonsense, that there is now meaning in every child being practically born a Christian, and even 'in a definite denomination'?   *XI²A 189*

Benevolence (*Christianity*)

Paul says, 'Though I bestow all my goods upon the poor and have not charity, what does it profit me?' [I Corinthians 13. 3].

How characteristic this 'me' is for Christianity! We turn the matter differently, it is others who are to profit from our benevolence, so that what matters is benevolence itself.

Alas, no! Christianity is not so busy as that. It is not like the world, embarrassed for money, so that it is only a matter of making money and then making benevolence in and for itself into a virtue. No, Christianity has absolutely no such need of money. So the apostle says, 'what does it profit me?'

Here besides we have an example of how near irony always is to Christianity, so that it is really just the passion of our spirit which makes us deaf to the irony. The apostle speaks with a concern for eternity: what does it profit me? Socrates would have been able teasingly to say the same thing, what does it profit me? Would I be better, would I be wiser if I gave everything to the poor without love? *XI² A 190*

Man – woman – child – Christianity

. . . It is my testimony as a psychologist that no woman is able to endure a dialectical reduplication, and everything Christian has a dialectical element in it.

To be able to be related to the Christian task it is necessary to be a man, a man's hardness and strength are required to be able even to bear just the stress of the task.

A good which is recognized by the evil it brings; a salvation which is recognized by its making me unhappy; a grace which is recognizable by suffering, and so on – all such things (and all Christian things are such) can be borne by no woman, she would go out of her senses if she had to be stretched in such a tension.

As for children, it is of course sheer nonsense that they should be Christians.

A woman, and above all a child, are related to and breathe in directness. If something is a good, it must be recognizable through doing good; it is no use trying to constrain a woman (I say nothing of a child) to enter into a good which does evil, for it would break her.

Consider how it comes about that no woman can endure irony, that irony in relation to her passion slays her. Does this not arise from the fact that she cannot endure a dialectic?

In this respect I have certainly taken an honours degree. Just try it: make a girl unhappy, and say to her, 'Yes, but it is from love that I do it' – and you will break her, her reason will be shattered. Then adapt yourself to her and say, 'I am a wanton scoundrel', and she can bear it and will forgive you lovingly. But she will also have escaped dialectical reduplication.

And so with everything Christian. Only the man has such toughness from the hand of Providence that he can endure the dialectic. . . .

In the New Testament it is the man who is intended; religion is related to the man; the woman participates in religion in a secondary way, through the man. She herself cannot endure a dialectic, but by being a witness to how the man weighs the task she nevertheless receives an impression which is more than that of simple directness. The child makes shift for himself, till his time comes. To make a child swallow true Christianity (if it were possible at all, if the child's nature did not make it impossible for him to assimilate it) is just as beastly as to try (which is often enough done) to fill a child full of brandy, because the parents themselves drink brandy, and the sweet darling must be as well off as his parents. And to try to put something into a child, in the name of Christianity, which is not Christianity, is sheer irresponsibility. . . .   *XI²A 192*

Woman

To say that Christianity makes men and women equal, so that the woman must be related to Christianity in the same way as the man, is neither here nor there. Certainly, Christianity makes men and women equal, but it does not change their determination by nature. If it did one could on this way of thinking reach the result that Christianity must have the effect of making a woman as tall and as strong as a man; or even (if Christianity had any relation to it at all) that it would bring about the result that in Christendom children were born entirely without rule, and that now it was the woman and now the man who produced them.

To say that the woman is even more essentially related to Christianity than the man is a trick intended to return Christianity to the sphere of directness. No, in the scale of directness the woman certainly has the advantage in respect of fineness, depth and inwardness. But as soon as a dialectic is introduced the woman is in the same case as the southern

nations when they are asked to pronounce a word from a
Slavonic language which has five or six consonants before a
single vowel. *XI²A 193*

Morbidity

True religious ideality, which, just because it is constantly
before God, can take to heart as the greatest transgression
something that we men call quite insignificant, is readily
described as morbidity. Splendid, certainly it is morbidity; just
as the darning needle would also regard it as morbidity when
the finest English needle cannot stand what the darning needle
can stand before feeling something; or just as the table-knife
would regard it as morbidity that the finest honed and sharpest
surgical scalpel 'cannot endure the least thing' without feeling
the effects.

No, this morbidity is health, a higher health. It is only
morbidity when it ends up in chatter. It is surely not morbid
for the microscope, say, to be able to see the least insignificant
thing. No, it is morbidity to be able to see the insignificant
only when it means seeing imprecisely. But if the sight
remains sharply focused, then it is surely healthy and ad-
vantageous to be able to see even something quite insignificant.
It is surely not morbid of a watch to show both the minutes
and the seconds, what a clock would perhaps describe as a
kind of pusillanimity, a morbid unrest. No, when a watch
shows the minutes and the second with perfect precision,
then this is certainly an advantage. *XI²A 195*

Humanity

Christianity is God's thought. For God to be a man was an
ideality of which we have scarcely an inkling. The Fall was a
guilt which brought with it a degradation whose pain may be
properly felt only if one has an impression of the ideality that
preceded it.

All this is more and more lost in the course of generations. We have gradually got accustomed to the wretchedness in which we live as our natural state. Each generation began with the misery of the immediately preceding generation, and reached an even more miserable condition, from which the next generation began. . . .

Imagine a princely family degraded to servitude as punishment for some crime. Imagine the tenth generation, which has nine or eight generations preceding it as slaves, the son like the father. The result presumably will be that the tenth generation is very well pleased with its condition, it feels that it is in the station it was born to, what its father was before it, and the grandfather before that, and so on. And if someone should come and declare to this tenth generation that it was of princely blood, then he would be laughed to scorn, and he would discover that it was those who were most concerned who were most disturbed, even embittered, at someone wanting to spoil their ease, in which they had lived so long, son like father, father like grandfather, and so on.

And so with Christianity. With the firmness of eternity, immovable as the Pole Star, Christianity points to the Fall: that is what it is related to as its presupposition. But meanwhile with the consequences of repetition the Fall has swollen to such horrible proportions that it is like an immense parenthesis which no one can see fully, and see that it is a parenthesis. And within this parenthesis life goes merrily on, degeneration continues, in ever-increasing proportions from generation to generation, the next generation always less significant than the preceding, beginning with the previous insignificance and outstripping it, and so the two great powers unite, insignificance and numbers, to reduce man to such a bagatelle that New Testament Christianity, when it is brought into contact with it, is just sheer nonsense. . . .

But men (in contrast to God's memory) have long ago entirely forgotten that it is a parenthesis we have entered into, and that Christianity was introduced as the divine closure. No, we live merrily within the parenthesis, we propagate the race and arrange world history – and the whole thing is a parenthesis.

Question: is a parenthetic man immortal? *XI²A 201*

World history – a question

We men flatter ourselves that world history is something immensely important, something which must therefore attract God's attention to a high degree.

Question: I do not take it upon myself to answer it, I merely raise it, and I do so only because Christianity teaches that the propagation of the species is a mistake – but the personnel of history, these millions, are produced in this way. The question is whether the whole business of world history, the four monarchies – Hegel, Grundtvig, Geert Westphaler (he too establishes four monarchies!),[1] the railways and the telegraphs – whether all this concerns God, or pleases him more than all the uproar and hubbub which children make in their play-room, instead of sitting still and reading their books (as the parents would like)? Is this belief in the infinite importance of history not one of those human illusions which aims at maintaining and encouraging the pleasure in life, the pleasure of joining in the noise, inflamed by the tale of what all these various kings and emperors have managed to achieve of devilish uproar and noise during their life?

When his mother is cursing him, Richard III, in order not to hear her curses, turns to the drummers and says, 'Strike up the drum' – is it not so with us all? There is something in us we do not want to hear, and so we wish for noise, and world history too is just such a noise-maker. But is it more than a comfortable illusion that such stuff should interest God? Is this not just to attribute to him one of our own misunderstandings? . . . *XI²A 203*

[1] The reference is to Holberg's comedy *Mester Gert Westphaler* (translated as *The Talkative Barber*, Princeton Univ. Press 1950), scene 10. RGS

The Christian

Here is a definition, somewhat modernized.

Christians are the 'pages of absolute majesty'.

The only art they practise is also absolutely the only art – to worship absolutely, not with words and chit-chat, bombastic prose or sounding verses, but in the action of absolute obedience.

As the child of a tight-rope walker is from his earliest years made supple in his back and in every muscle so that, after daily practice, he is sheer suppleness and can carry out every movement, absolutely every movement, in the most excruciating positions, yet always easily and smiling: so with prayer to the absolute majesty, with praying to him absolutely, so that there is no thought of any reason or any wherefore, with praying to him absolutely in everything, always glad, grateful, smiling. Now one can understand what the ancient church meant when it said that the Christian after death is taken up among angels: this life is like a rehearsal for that.

But the concept of the absolute, and the view of absolute majesty have long disappeared from Christendom. God has been degraded, and dragged down into the wretchedness of relativity and finite teleology; it has been forced upon him, that he too should, humanly speaking, have a cause, should require men, and should be glad that someone wished to serve him; it has been forced upon him that the world's history was a thing of importance for him, so that he must have plenty to do in watching over it and managing it, and must see that he holds his thoughts together properly till the end, as one says.

No, heaven's majesty is not a majesty of this kind. Hence one single Christian existence, if there were such, concerns him more than all four monarchies of world history and all the business we men have invented and invented in order to bestow some importance on it. . . .   *XI² A 204*

Christendom (Protestantism) without God

. . . The human race has in the course of generations become ever more insignificant. This goes with the fact that in another sense it may be said to be progressing. For it has grown in understanding, in finite understanding. But this progress is in a deeper sense so ambiguous that it is a retrogression, a retrogression, that is, from the absolute, from the impression or view of the absolute, and it is progress in the direction of more and more understanding of the relative, the mediocre, of what is 'to a certain extent'. Thus it is also easy to see that this progress is a fall away from the eternal. For this world's life is 'to a certain extent', everything is 'to a certain extent'. When this point has been reached, that everything is just 'to a certain extent', then this world has reached the point of winning entirely free of all connexion with the eternal, which is its natural tendency, and which therefore takes place to the accompaniment of the jubilation of men, who admire themselves and the race for the incomparable progress which has been achieved.

The absolute, that which is in and for itself – yes, show me if it is so, but I doubt whether there is a single man who has the remotest conception of such a being, or could think of being related to such a being. For of course this is only possible through unconditioned obedience, through being willing to be annihilated, if one may put it thus, for the absolute is fatal for relative being, and only through such a death does it bring life.

But when the absolute does not exist for men, what does it help that they have something they call God – that is just a name, for God is surely absolute being.

So one of two things: either Christendom has no God, or it has a twaddler for its God.

The second is surely the truth. Take the New Testament: there is no definition of Christian that is not stamped with the absolute. Put beside this the usual preaching of Christendom, or rather the existential proclamation (for a little declamation is of no consequence, and for the rest the declamation itself is not precisely stamped by the absolute), and you will find that everything is 'to a certain extent', or what is the same thing, everywhere you will find reasons, a 'wherefore', to which one replies, in other words, there is no absolute. . . .

XI²A 205

The problem

Such is the distance of Christendom (of Protestantism, especially in Denmark) from New Testament Christianity that I must continually emphasize that I do not call myself a Christian. My task is to set the problem, the first condition for the possibility of speaking about Christianity.

It was a setting of fire on the earth (so Christ himself calls his mission [Luke 12. 49]), a setting of men on fire, by kindling a passion which made them heterogeneous with what is naturally understood by being a man: heterogeneous with the whole of this existence; a setting on fire which was to bring conflict between father and son, daughter and mother – in brief, in the most inward and dearest relationships; a setting on fire intended to tear 'kindred' apart in order to make single persons of them, which is God's will: hence the passion which was introduced was the love of God, with its negative expression of hatred of oneself.

It was a setting on fire. But it is not always water which is used to quench a fire. However, if it is so desired, I can stick to the metaphor and say that Christendom is the water which has quenched the fire. But as I say, one does not always use water; sometimes, for example, one uses bedclothes, mattresses and the like to – suffocate the fire. And so I will say that Christendom is the mass which has suffocated the fire once kindled, and now it has it so much under its power, under such an immense layer of numbers, that one safely and peacefully turns Christianity into precisely the opposite of what it is in the New Testament.

Whoever you are, if it is your intention and your plan to contribute to the stifling of the fire, then get busy, join in the spread of the masses, do it in the name of serving Christianity, and you will do the greatest damage which it is possible for you to do. But if on the other hand you want to have Christianity bursting forth again, as a fire, then do everything you can to get the feather-beds and the bedclothes and the mattresses and all that stuff removed – and the fire will surely be there.

By this token the word is, 'Away, away with abstractions – state churches, people's churches, Christian lands – these are feather-beds and bedclothes, every work of this kind is treachery to the fire, which contributes further to stifle it. But work towards dispersion into the 'single person' – that is the order of the day . . .' *XI²A 206*

The domestic goose – a stirring meditation

Imagine that geese could talk –
then that they had arranged things so that they too could have their church services and their worship.

Every Sunday they would assemble together, and a gander would preach.

The essential content of the sermon was the exalted destiny of geese, the exalted goal for which the creator has destined geese (and every time his name was named all the geese curtsied and the ganders bowed their heads). With the help of their wings they could fly away to far countries, blessed countries, where they were really at home: for here they were just like exiles.

And so every Sunday. Then the gathering broke up, and every goose waddled home. Then the next Sunday off they went to the service again, then home again. That was all. They throve and grew fat, they became plump and tender. Then they were eaten on Martinmas-eve, and that was all.

That was all. For while the sermon sounded so exalted on Sundays, on Mondays they would tell one another of the fate of the goose who wanted to take his high destiny seriously, with the help of the wings the creator had given it. And they spoke of the horrors it had to endure. But they prudently kept this knowledge among themselves. For of course to speak of it on Sundays was most unsuitable, for as they said, in that case it would be obvious that our services would be a mockery both of God and of ourselves.

There were also among the geese some that looked ill and thin. Of them the others said, 'You see, that's what comes of being serious about wanting to fly. It is because they are always thinking of flying that they get thin and do not thrive, and do not have God's grace as we do. That is why we get plump and fat and tender, for it is by God's grace that one gets plump and fat and tender.'

So the following Sunday they went again to the service, and the old gander preached about the high goal for which the creator (and at this point the geese curtsied and the ganders bowed their heads) had destined them, and the reason why he had given them wings.

So with the worship of God in Christendom. Man, too, has wings, he has imagination, which is intended to help him to raise himself up. But we just play with it, we let our imagination be diverted in a quiet hour in Sunday exaltation, and for the rest we stay where we are. And then on Mondays we consider that to get plump and fat and tender, and to be well larded, that is, to collect money and become something in the world, beget many children, be successful, and so on – we consider that all this is a proof of God's grace. And those who really have to do with God, and who therefore are bound to suffer (it cannot be otherwise and it is not otherwise, according to the New Testament) – of those we say that it is clear they do not have God's grace.

And if someone should read this, he will say, 'That's fine.' But that is all. Then he waddles home to his own affairs, and remains – or strives with all his might to become – plump and tender and fat. But the next Sunday the minister preaches and he listens – just like the geese. $XI^2 A$ *210*

The changing round of concepts is the sign of a new quality

Wherever a new quality appears, concepts are changed around.

Take the divine quality. Men occupy themselves with thoughts about the divine. But all such human thought leads no further than to the idea that the divine is the most superlative superlative of the human. This is easy to see: it is adding of quantity – the divine quality is not to be found here.

Christianity introduces the divine quality, and the sign of this is that every concept is turned around: the divine and the relation to it become just the opposite of what they are in the sphere of directness. Instead of having to do with God, and being his favourite, meaning sheer happiness, as the pagan thought, and as is indeed direct, straightforward thought, from the Christian standpoint it means sheer suffering. Instead of the direct idea of enjoying life it means dying, dying to the world. Instead of the direct idea that he who is loved by God becomes the man of power, it means, from the Christian standpoint, that he is abased, and so on. I have shown this in many different ways. Here we see that everything Christian is paradoxical, and that it is paradox which is the form of the divine quality.

Christendom's greatest service to Christianity (which according to what the professors say is perfectible) is to drive it back again by their drivel to directness, to relax the paradox in the hiatus of the most superlative superlative of directness, and at the same time to assure us that a qualitative change has appeared. *XI²A 212*

Beware of men
[Matthew 10. 17]

Men say, Seek help from men. Christianity says, Beware of men.

Christianity was a fire kindled by Christ, which should be kept burning. But materially it is a fact that water puts out fire, whereas spiritually it is a fact that the mass, the human crowd, puts out fire: beware of men.   *XI²A 220*

If only men could not talk!

Everything is so easy to understand and so simple in the animal world, because the animal has the advantage over man that it cannot talk. The only thing that talks in that existence is its life, its actions.

For example, when I see a stag in heat, then I see what it means, it is in the grip of a strong instinct, and there is nothing more to be said about it. If it could speak, then we should doubtless hear a flood of nonsense about its sense of duty urging it to propagate the species, duty to the community and to its kind, that it was bestowing the greatest benefit, and so on . . .

Make man dumb, and you will see that human existence is not so difficult to explain.

But what confuses everything is this advantage which man has over the animals, that he can speak. So it comes about that while our life expresses the lowest, our lips utter nonsense about the highest, and provide the assurance that this is what directs us.

Language, the gift of speech, surrounds mankind with such a cloud of nonsense and deceit that it is its ruin. God alone knows how many there are in each generation who are not ruined by speech, changed into fools and hypocrites. Only the most significant personalities can endure this advantage of being able to speak. . . .   *XI²A 222*

The half is more than the whole

These words of Hesiod are very near to what Asaph says 'Do not give me abundance' [Proverbs 30. 8]. To wish to have the whole is dangerous, the safest thing is to have the half.

In the realm of the spirit the opposite is true: to have the half is to lose the whole.

But in the world of sense the half is to be preferred, and all finite prudence has to do with halves.   *XI² A 225*

The blessedness of heaven

Once it was understood as a task, an exertion of which we can now scarcely have any conception.

Then things were given a turn, and we hear, No, it is sheer grace, no effort can grasp it, it is sheer grace. Then here too one's life becomes sheer gratitude to a measure of which can now scarcely have any conception.

But now the true and profound expression for grace has been achieved: it is grace to such an extent – that it is not worth thinking about.

Once upon a time men sold everything in order to buy heaven's blessedness from heaven's majesty. Nowadays we obtain it gratis like a pretty box or a poke of sweets when we buy something at the grocer's. And not just that, but it has been made *lèse-majesté* to do the least thing, even to think about one's blessedness is an affront to the divine majesty, when it is his will to give it gratis. Just as it is an affront to the grocer to try to pay for what he is giving away. God wishes grace to be gratis to such an extent that he does not even want thanks for it. No, as I have said, heaven's blessedness is not obtained like something just thrown in, but like the bag in which the sugar and the coffee are contained.   *XI² A 226*

The truth is naked

In order to swim one strips oneself naked – in order to aim at the truth one must undress in a much more inward sense, one must take off the inward clothing of thoughts, ideas, selfishness, and the like, before one is naked enough.

XI² A 227

The church – falsification

Christianity is so arranged that it is related to the individual. And it is in this that the immense ideality and effort of being a Christian consists, in being related to God as an individual, not protected by any abstraction, which, if you like, softens the blow, or, if you like, softens the burning rays of the sun like coloured glass.

But what everything human aims at is to be quit of God.

This is the common aim. The method is then twofold (as one speaks of a refined and a crude suicide). The first way is to rebel against God, or to deny that there is a God. I do not speak of this.

The second way is more refined: it is, under the pretext of zeal for God and the things of God to place an abstraction between God and oneself.

Such an abstraction is the 'church'. Men have struck on the idea of turning it into a person, and by first speaking spiritually about it as a person, about its birth and the course of its life, and so on, in the end grow accustomed to identifying the church with Christians – and there are no Christians in any other sense but this.

Then behind this abstraction the Christian makes holiday. There is solemn, profound and spiritual talk about the church – but as for single Christians, there are none, or, if you like, there are plenty of them, millions of them, so that a million Christians more or less does not mean more than a sausage when pigs are being slaughtered. . . .   *XI²A 229*

An experiment in thought

Imagine that Socrates had been appointed an apostle – and then imagine that one of the apostles came to him and said, 'Today in the course of an hour we have caught 3,000 souls': I wonder whether Socrates would not have doubted whether this could be right, that an ideal like being a Christian could catch 3,000 souls in an hour.   *XI²A 230*

Stupidity of enlightenment or artificial stupidity

As one speaks of artificially produced warmth and light, and of artificial nature (in contrast to natural warmth, daylight, natural flowers, natural beauty, and so on), so there is also a stupidity which is artificially produced.

There is no one so stupid about Christianity, not even the stupidest of all other men, as the 'professor'. His stupidity is produced artificially, and by means of much study.

In order to continue in this study he needs for one thing to read steadily in the works of other professors (+), and for another he needs a strong opiate, namely, the illusion that Christianity is perfectible. Everyone who is fortunate enough to have his eyes opened to this wisdom is well on the way to becoming a professor.

[*In the margin*] (+) I do not mean, in saying this, that the professor will have any essential benefit from reading other writings; he will simply change everything into his own stupidity.   *XI² A 233*

Christianity – Christendom

Christianity is the contact between the divine and the human.

And this is what has become history, and – note well – in such a way that every successive generation, continually increasing the distance, has become the history of the fact that the preceding generation was the history of the fact that the preceding generation . . . and so on backwards.

And this is the perfectibility of Christianity!

Christianity has been turned into – the history of Christianity, without its being noticed that this simply means to stand outside Christianity, and of course more and more with each generation.

When one receives a parcel, one loosens the wrappings in order to get at the content. Christianity was a gift from God; but instead of receiving the gift, Christendom has taken upon itself to wrap it up, each generation has delivered or provided a new wrapping round the others – and it is in this way that we are supposed to get nearer and nearer to Christianity.

Christianity has become history. Yes, unless the difficulty was that the first generations upheld celibacy, I am certain that in Christendom, whose religion is intended to be a religion of the spirit, it would long ago have been orthodox to hold that the main thing was not merely the apostolic succession but (the veterinary consideration) genuine succession by means of procreation.

The greatest difference between man and man is on the one hand to feel God to be so near that it is as though he stood beside one, near at every moment, and on the other hand to live happily in the view that God is removed from one by a distance of 1,800 years' history, and that God's nearness is a historical question. *XI²A 234*

Two wills in the world

cannot be tolerated. God is the one will.

Certainly, God has given man and the world of man power to have a will. But the world that wills its own will must then as a punishment put up with not existing for God, with his giving it up.

On the other hand, as soon as a will is willing to have to do with God, it must go. This is the meaning of dying to the world. When a will wills to do with God, it means just that; but it almost comes of itself, if God and the will are to agree together.

The god-forsaken world seems free in a quite different way from the Christian – for the god-forsaken world has been given up by God, it is free from God. *XI²A 239*

Original sin – Christianity

. . . To say that Christ has made satisfaction for original sin does not prove that Christianity desires the propagation of the species. For all reconciliation and atonement has surely always a retrospective and not a prospective reference. As in relation to actual sin, if one's sin was stealing, the atonement makes satisfaction for the past, but it does not mean that the man can now steal as much as he wants in the future. And similarly with satisfaction for original sin, which surely does not mean that now a man can enjoy himself as much as he wants with regard to the propagation of the species. No, Christianity blocks the way with celibacy. No, it says, your father's guilt, through which you exist – for that satisfaction has been made: but stop there: satisfaction does not mean that you now go off and do the same as he did; satisfaction does not mean that in this respect you can do as you please.   *XI²A 242*

Numbers – the proclamation of Christianity

. . . Every proclamation of Christianity which makes the least concession to numbers, forgets the majesty which the Christian has the honour of serving, it forgets the hatred which that majesty has – precisely of numbers.

And so, my good Luther, you were surely not quite sober but somewhat fuddled, or your brain was somewhat muddled by the spell of numbers, by the millions of Franz Cutlers,[1] when you altered Christianity and declared that it was impossible to live chastely outside marriage. Christianity is not in the least interested in such matters, it is too exalted to be imposed upon in this way, whether by one or a million Franz Cutlers. And in any case, dear Luther, you should have made it clear that what you had to say was not a matter of Christian progress, but of a reduction in the price.   *XI²A 243*

How far Christianity is from existing can best be seen from my own case.

For with such clarity as I have, I must say that I am not a

---

[1] *cf.* Holberg's comedy, *Der Politiske Kandestøber* (*The Political Tinker*), act 2, scene 3. RGS

Christian. For the situation as I see it is that in spite of the abyss of nonsense in which we are caught, we shall all alike be saved.

This is the consequence of having as a child acquired a so-called Christianity which is just the reverse.

But my position is certainly difficult enough. I am not like a pagan, to whom an apostle briefly and emphatically proclaims Christianity; no, I am the one who, so to say, himself must discover it, work it out, from the perverted state to which it has been reduced. *XI²A 244*

The witness of truth

And so when a witness to the truth dies, he says to God, 'Thank you, thank you for all my sufferings, o infinite love.' And then God replies, 'Thank you, my friend, thank you for the use I have made of you.' *XI²A 245*

Irony in relation to spirit – and what is of the spirit

There is no definition of spirit which does not carry a moment of irony with it.

A material view will hold that what is bound to determine a man in thinking about life is that the more he thinks about it the easier life is for him. But spirit means that the more a man thinks about life the more difficult and full of effort it becomes for him. 'He who increases knowledge increases grief' [Ecclesiastes 1. 18] – yes, and also effort in existing.

'But then spirit is just madness.' Yes, quite right. But this is the negative sign of spirit, that the lack of spirit is the way to make life easy – so noble is spirit.

Money, worldly power, and the like: material man understands that very well; he covets it, because he thinks – and to some extent rightly – that the possession of it may make his life easier. If amassing money meant without any doubt that with every thousand there was more suffering and vexation, then material man would certainly abstain – which he in fact does in relation to spirit, content with the way which in the course of centuries is more and more frequented and praised as the only true way, namely, the way of remaining more or less an animal creation, if one wants to have the most comfortable life.

Spirit joined with an existence as part of the animal creation gives suffering. . . .

XI²A 246

The true exceptions of the first class

do not feel so happy in this world as to wish to settle down in it. No, they are travellers, on a mission, they hurry away again, home, as soon as possible.

So when they feel that the end is drawing near, when they have practically fulfilled their mission, produced the most intense possible effect in the briefest possible time, they press upon a little spring they alone know of. So their life produces a catastrophe and in this way they are ejected from the world.

Here everything is heterogeneity from first to last, to leave this world in a catastrophe is the greatest heterogeneity over against an even and tranquil life and a peaceful death.

XI²A 247

For three things I thank God

1. that no living being owes existence to me;
2. that he prevented me from thoughtlessly becoming a priest in the sense that man nowadays become priests here, which is a mockery of Christianity;
3. that I voluntarily exposed myself to the abuse of *The Corsair*.

XI²A 248

The falsification of Christianity

What has been falsified is the concept of being a Christian.

It is not so much the teaching, as the proclamation of Christianity, the being a teacher in Christianity, which has been falsified. It is as if water, the supply of which was not itself tainted, was infected by being conducted through a pipe which was tainted – and one were to be taken to the supply and told, 'The water is all right.' 'Yes, but it is tainted by the medium through which it is brought to men.' In every situation in which something can be imparted only through a medium, it is practically as important what the medium is like as what that is which is mediated. From this we may see how dubious it is to talk about the proclamation of an objectively true Christianity. *XI²A 249*

My task – to make room

I am not an apostle bringing something from God with authority.

No, I am serving God, but without authority. My task is to make room for God to come (+).

So it is easy to see why I must be quite literally a single man, and so must be maintained in great weakness and fragility.

For if he who is to make room came at the head, for example, of several battalions – yes, humanly speaking that would seem to be a splendid way, and the surest way, of making room. But in that case he who was to make room could himself take up the room, he could take up so much room that there was no room for God to come.

My task is to make room: I am a policeman, if you like. But in this world the police come with power and arrest the others, whereas the higher police come suffering, and rather ask to be themselves arrested.

[*In the margin*] (+) My task is not to make room by giving orders, but by suffering. *XI²A 250*

Mynster and I

mean the conflict between the old and the new.

In general the new arrives with self-assurance, which picks a quarrel with the old, the sooner the better, and wants to overthrow it.

I came with resignation, even wanting to deal the new into Mynster's hand as his last round, concealing myself and all my suffering and sacrifices for the cause in the most profound incognito, even the incognito of the grotesque; and our whole generation, with myself at the head, bowed before Mynster as the man of our time.

Providence judged that Mynster never deserved this.

And I also saw this; but not to be recognized is my life, my element; to suffer, to bring sacrifices, and so on – I am ready enough for that – but not to be recognized is my passion.   *XI²A 251*

My contemporaneity with Bishop Mynster

The significance of this contemporaneity really lies in the question, whether it was not possible for me, in spite of my disposition for the catastrophic, instead of attacking to have become the last defence of the establishment?

I had to have time to think properly about that question. And that is why it was disposed by Providence that I should have as the head of the establishment the man for whose sake I was at the same time so infinitely ready to adapt myself in every way.

How I should have liked – for so many reasons – to have been that last defence! But in fact it was Mynster, through what I endured with him and through what I saw that his life led to, who changed me, or, more correctly, contributed to giving me clarity about myself.   *XI²A 253*

Mynster

was certainly an egoist, even in the following context: I am fairly convinced that he did not give Martensen any hint (in the eventuality of Martensen's becoming his successor) that I was really a man of a quite different significance than it appeared.

Martensen could well have used such a hint. But on the other hand Mynster could, it is true, not well give this hint without giving himself away just a little.

That is why I think that here too Mynster was egoist enough not to do it. But this is just an opinion.   *XI² A 256*

Providentia specialissima

To be a Christian means to believe in a special providence, not in the abstract but in the concrete. Only he who has this faith *in concreto* is individuality, every other is reduced to being like a copy of the species, he has neither courage not humility, he is neither tormented enough nor helped enough to be an individuality.   *XI² A 259*

Catastrophe

How is a catastrophe produced in the realm of the spirit? Quite simply by omitting some connecting links, by providing a conclusion without giving the premises, by drawing a consequence without first showing that of which it is the consequence, and the like: in this way the clash between the man who acts thus, and his contemporaries, can become a catastrophe . . .

This is the catastrophic conflict of genius.

It is quite a different matter when there is a conscious arranging of catastrophe, and such clarity that one can measure with one's eye that the distance is now so great that the clash must bring catastrophe – when there is a conscious planning of the whole thing. It is in this consciousness that the Christian element is to be found, the real Christian concept of being sacrificed, of a voluntary sacrifice.

But here I am once more tempted to ask whether a man is permitted to do this: is it not harshness to the others?

In Christendom one seeks in vain for enlightenment. And as for the New Testament, there it is the God-Man, and the God-Man is qualitatively different from every man.

On the other hand it is not possible to make an end of lack of character, of sophistry, of the chatter of reflection, without catastrophe. Catastrophe is the real $\mu\epsilon\tau\alpha\beta\alpha\sigma\iota\varsigma$ $\epsilon\iota\varsigma$ $\dot{\alpha}\lambda\lambda o$ $\gamma\epsilon\nu o\varsigma$; what the sign of the cross is for the devil, catastrophe is for reflection.

But to begin with the conclusion, omitting the premises, or the like – and then to say that one does this in order to produce catastrophe, is again to prevent catastrophe; for to give this explanation involves an approach which lessens the distance from the contemporaries, so that the clash does not become catastrophic. *XI² A 263*

To bring about a catastrophe

However afraid men would be of me if they got to know, however strange it would be to them, it is certain that what has occupied me in recent times is whether God wishes me to stake everything on bringing about a catastrophe – on getting arrested, condemned, and if possible executed. And there is a care in my soul lest, if I do not do this, I should eternally regret it, a care to which I can only oppose the thought in which I continually confide myself to God – that he will watch that I do not omit anything that I should eternally repent having left undone.

If I am to bring about a catastrophe, I had thought of giving the 'alarm', quite unexpectedly after the most complete silence, that public services are a mockery of God, that to take part in them is a crime.

But before I was entirely clear about this, I did something

else: I published the article on Mynster against Martensen.[1] This in itself was a weakening of the impetus to catastrophe. . . .

So I have great qualms about myself, whether I am fit to go to prison – if it were to come to that – and possibly to be executed, and whether this whole manner of fighting would not have such a disturbing effect on me that I could not control myself.

But in any case I must leave this in God's hands.

But in regard to bringing about a catastrophe there is a quite different doubt. It could not really be accomplished in the way I have considered. The establishment is so demoralized that one can spit in its face, and it prefers to sneak away. It takes good care not to bring any charge, or the like. I have some experience of this, in fact I have already acted in a way that leads to catastrophe. For if the establishment had the least thought of starting a legal action, then my last article against Martensen is as decisive as possible.

. . . To bring about a catastrophe I must do things quite differently from how I have understood them hitherto.

The method would have to be in the following style.

I should begin by showing that the matter is so serious that all learned polemic is childish. One would therefore have to demand of the establishment, in the name of Christianity, that it use the means in its possession to defend itself.

One should therefore have to ask for a case to be brought, ask to be arrested, and ask for the greatest possible severity in the procedure, as a matter of life and death.

The charge against the establishment would then have to be that the whole thing is a lie, that the worship of God is a mockery of God, and that to join in it is a crime. And at the same time the charge would have to be aggravated by proving that the establishment itself knew that it is a lie, and that this is the reason why no action is laid.

Yet even in this way I do not believe that it is possible to be arrested, let alone executed.

[1] In the newspaper *Fædrelandet*, 18 December 1854 (*Samlede Værker* XIV,[2] 11 *ff*). RGS

Oh, it is dreadful to think to what depths the establishment has sunk, to what a depth of wretchedness, philistinism, mediocrity and lies!

But for this very reason, how this incomparable epigram on the establishment will shine out in the course of time – that Bishop Mynster was buried as a witness to the truth, one of the real witnesses to the truth! *XI²A 265*

Luther – the Reformation

Luther is the very opposite of 'the apostle'.

'The apostle' expresses Christianity in God's interest, he comes with authority from God, in his interest.

Luther gives expression to Christianity in men's interest, as being essentially man's reaction against Christianity in God's interest. Hence also Luther's formula, 'I can no other', which is certainly not the apostle's.

From this alone one sees what confusion results from making Luther into an apostle.

In general what has always been lacking in Christendom is a diagnostician for sickness, and a dialectician. *XI²A 266*

The ideal

The ideal means hatred of man. What man naturally loves is finitude. To face him with the ideal is the most dreadful torture. Certainly, when the ideal is produced in the most exalted poetic fashion, like an enchanting vision of the imagination, he accepts this pleasure.

But when the ideal is produced as the ethico-religious demand, it is the most dreadful torture for man; it kills in him, in the most painful way, everything in which he really finds his life, in the most painful way it shows him his own wretchedness, it keeps him in sleepless unrest, whereas finitude lulls him into enjoyment.

That is why Christianity is called, and is, hatred of man.

This is man's relation to the ideal. The young girl blushes with enthusiasm, when she hears of it. The young man's heart beats violently. The unmarried man respects it. The married man does not completely turn away from it. But the greater distance from the ideal is that of the mother, madam. The real fury against the ideal comes from family life, from the lioness, or, to put it another way, which is also true from time to time, from a sow with young . . . (+) *XI² A 271*

[*In the margin*] (+) All who have truly learned about ideals have also praised celibacy. To marry means to make the relation to the ideal so difficult for oneself that it normally is equivalent to abandoning the ideal.

(To be married in the way Socrates was is something different from what one usually understands by marriage. Socrates regarded marriage as a hindrance, and that was why he married, and why he was *happy* with Xanthippe, or thought he was – namely, because of the difficulty.) *XI² A 272*

A particular relation to God in immediacy and in reflection

In Holy Scripture it is always in immediacy that God tells those who have a particular relation with him what they have to do.

I do not understand this; that is, it cannot be thought, for thought it is an inaccessible immediacy; which does not prevent it from being real all the same.

In any case this relation cannot arise in reflection. In reflection the relation remains dialectical. God must leave it to the man who is to have a particular relation with him to take the risk for himself of assuming the relation (+). God can provoke a man indirectly in many ways, so that he does take the risk; but there cannot be an immediate relation in reflection. So in the end everything depends on the man risking having to do with God particularly; and in this risk there is always included the possibility that he could have misunderstood all the indirect influences. But on the other hand all the indirect influences decide nothing by themselves: the risk must be taken. And when the risk is taken, there is an entire qualitative change.

The man who has a particular relation to God in immediacy therefore runs only the danger that is bound up with complying with what God has immediately commanded him to do. In reflection there is in addition a qualitative danger, the possibility of having failed to take the risk, and the possibility of having risked wrongly. *XI²A 273*

[*In the margin*] (+) Of a particular relation to God in reflection it is in one sense true that it is only known afterwards; it is not something that the man can immediately appeal to, for at every moment there is a risk, that is, at every moment there is the possibility of the danger of failing to risk or of risking wrongly. *XI²A 274*

My possible renown

Surely not even my bitterest enemy would deny that I shall acquire a certain renown. But I am beginning to wonder whether I will not become renowned in a quite different sphere than I have hitherto imagined – namely, as a naturalist. For I have discovered, or at least made a very significant contribution to the natural history of parasites, I mean priests and professors, those voracious and prolific parasites, who even have the effrontery (unlike other parasites) to try and pass themselves off as the friends and disciples of those whose sufferings they live on. *XI²A 277*

How did it come about that Christ was put to death?

I can answer this by showing at the same time what Christianity is.

What is 'spirit'? (And Christ is certainly spirit, his religion is that of the spirit.) Spirit means to live as though dead (to die to the world).

This mode of existence is so far from the natural man that it is quite literally worse for him than purely and simply to die.

When it is presented with great caution, at one remove in the imagination, in a 'still hour', then the natural man can endure the ideal, and even be pleased with it. But if it were to come nearer to him, so near that in all seriousness it was presented as a demand upon him, then the instinct of self-preservation of the natural man would rise up in him in such power that he would be seized by a veritable fury, as from drink, or as one says, a *furor uterinus*. And in this state, in which he is out of his senses, he demands the death of the man of spirit, or he rushes upon him to put him to death.

XI²A 279

LOOSE PAPERS

(1853–1855)

Hypocrisy

. . . In general the rule for all religious communication is
that it is true. Why is this so? Because the religious demand is
for action, for doing in accordance with what is said, and it is
precisely this movement which distinguishes the religious from
the aesthetic. The aesthetic leads into the blue; it comes like
a sneeze and goes like a sneeze. The aesthetic is the moment
and in the moment, whereas in the religious sphere it is the
next moment which is decisive, for it is then that I have to
act, and if I do not pay attention to this, then I will have
changed that moment, in church or at hymn-singing, into
an aesthetic enjoyment.

That is why it is so important that everything that is said
and sung in church should be true; not that it should be fine,
grand, splendid, charming, and so on – not that I should come
in order to weep, with beating heart: no, the point is that it
should be related as closely as possible to acting accordingly . . .

XI² A 280

Sewing without knotting the thread

As is well known, it was Til Eulenspiegel who summoned all
the tailors, to communicate to them some information of the
utmost importance. They came. Thereupon he got up into a
tree and said that they must not forget to put a knot in the
thread, otherwise they would miss the first stitch.

I do not wish to call the tailors and the seamstresses together. No! Nor am I entirely of Eulenspiegel's opinion that
by not making a knot one misses the first stitch; for if one
does not make a knot one also misses the second stitch and
so on – until the whole job is botched.

What I want to speak of is the proclaiming of Christianity without knotting the thread.

Imagine a speaker distinguished and gifted in every respect: he is preaching on the genuine Christian theme of self-denial, renunciation of the world. Splendid, incomparable! He is charming, fascinating, quite incomparable. In the gathering among others there is a rich man. He goes home very moved, deeply disturbed, and says to his wife, 'That was marvellous. I should like to thank the speaker by giving him a present of an expensive jardinière.' Similarly another rich man, deeply moved, dips deep into his pocket and gives the speaker a gold snuff-box, and so on, and so on – and the speaker returns hearty thanks.

The thread has not been knotted. In the Christian view the 'sermon' is on Monday, when the speaker returns the gifts and says, 'I teach self-denial, so I cannot accept such things, otherwise I would be in danger that what impelled me next time to speak about self-denial might be the prospect of getting a carriage and pair!' . . . $XI^2 A\ 281$

Bishop M.

If Bishop M. were an insignificant personality, if – yes, then it could quickly be shown that what he represents is not Christianity at all.

But – from the religious standpoint – the misfortune is that he replaces the decisive Christian element with something that – from the human standpoint – is so enchanting, so admirable. And again – from the religious standpoint – the misfortune so far as I am concerned is that there is in me so much of the aesthetic, the poetic, that I am only too much captivated by the enchantment and the admiration of this enchanting and admirable figure, not to mention the filial piety with which I feel myself to be drawn inwardly to this significant personality. . . .

Yet Bishop M. does not present Christianity in reality, but at one remove from reality (the poetic); instead of the decisive

Christian element he presents the artistic; instead of Christian dignity he presents the most charming and enchanting edition of human distinction, instead of Christian recklessness the most refined prudential consideration, instead of Christian heterogeneity over against the world the most tasteful worldly culture, instead of resignation and renunciation an exceptionally refined enjoyment of this world and this life.

XI²A 283

'Grace'

There was a noble family with great possessions.

The peasants were impoverished – and one of the ancestors of this noble family had not merely remitted all their debts but had also remitted their rents for all future time; he had even sent servants to them to put them at their ease by assuring them that their debts and rents were remitted.

At first the peasants themselves knew very well how much had been remitted. Later it was the servants of their noble master who reminded them.

But at last everything was quite brief, and they knew in a state of complete indolence that it had been remitted, but how much had been remitted, no one knew any more, and no one cared.

So it went on from generation to generation. Then one of that noble family said, 'No, this cannot be endured. Like my ancestors I will gladly remit everything – but what effrontery to accept one's goodness almost as though it were a right!'

XI²A 286

What qualities are necessary in one who in the realm of the spirit is to act as a 'stop'?

He must have *melancholy* in order to stir with the help of ideals. The thousands and thousands who are busy in the service of mediocrity can only be brought to a stop by means of ideals. Melancholy in order to charm and touch those who are susceptible and ready to yield – and come to a stop.

He must have *satire*, again with the help of ideals: satire in order to slay the incessant busyness of mediocrity – and bring it to a stop.

This is the power he must have, a twofold power which when it is seen more profoundly is one and the same.

But he himself must not be a power; for in that case he could perhaps, instead of acting as a stop, begin something new, or he could divide the two parts in half.

No, just as melancholy and satire, the two which are one and the same, are the power which brings about a stop, so he in whom this power resides, the one who brings about a stop, must not be a power but an impotence, a weakness – he must be a poet, and thus naturally without any bond not just with any party but also with any man at all.

And when such a poet is from the religious standpoint mere weakness, he is constrained whether he will or no. And when at the same time, from the religious standpoint, he is mere weakness in unconditioned obedience to the power that constrains him, then he is the one who brings about a stop. . . .

XI² A 294

Reality – not reaching reality

How is reality to be reached? Quite simply, by speaking in a definite way with the definite men you live with.

Take an example. In every age there are criminals whom the authorities punish. There are also criminals (and in proportion as the world becomes more corrupt, they seem to become predominant) whom the authorities do not punish. So in our time, and especially in every large city, there is a predominant vice which is called slander.

Imagine now a priest. If such a man is to do good, he has also to bear witness against the vices of the time. But most priests shirk this – and so do not reach reality.

But then there was one, the man of zeal, who did not seem

to have anything against being honoured in this way: he will bear witness against this vice.

But wait a moment. When slander has become so generally predominant, there must be some definite men who are the instigators. In order to reach reality it is then a matter of aiming at these particular men and attacking them without further ado. One is of course bound to be exposed by this in return to the whole weight of slander which these men direct against one: and in this way reality is reached.

But this is not how our honourable zealot conducted himself. Let me now show how an appearance of reality can be produced, which is nevertheless as far removed as possible from reality.

There was in the city – and this is a rare thing, which could have helped the honourable zealot, if he had truly wished to reach reality – one particular person of whom it was generally known that he was the instigator. Does this make the matter easy enough? Yes, if one really wishes to reach reality.

What does our honourable zealot do now? He flatters this particular person, pays him public compliments – and then preaches about 'slander'. That was clever, but it was at a fearful remove from 'reaching reality'. Our honourable man wins the reputation of being a zealot who bears witness against the vices of the time with great intrepidity, even against that which it is most dangerous to bear witness against, namely, 'slander'. At the same time he ensures the personal friendship of the slanderer, thus being fairly sure that the latter will not think of attacking him.

And this is what is called reaching reality! Consider this as another example of the objective proclamation of Christianity! *XI² A 296*

That the principle of works is simpler than the principle of faith

In speaking of 'works' one's thoughts turn to Catholicism. To avoid misunderstanding, I note (what perhaps is not necessary and in any case ought not to be necessary) that of course everything that Catholicism has invented concerning the merit of works is absolutely to be rejected.

But then I say that the principle of works is simpler than the principle of faith. And why?

Because the principle of works begins at the beginning: it begins with what is common to us men. Whereas the principle of faith begins so far ahead, that in every generation there are not many who get so far, so that it is bound to be quite meaningless to begin straightaway with it.

The principle of works begins at the beginning and with what in general is the truth, and that is why we should be treated, and why indeed it is most serviceable for us to be treated, in this way.

One treats a rascal, quite simply, by asking him, 'May I see your works?' If he comes along and assures you that he is ready to sacrifice everything in hidden inwardness, that in hidden inwardness he longs to sit and sing hymns and to fast in the silence of a monastery, while in his outward and visible life he is after profits and is a gay gallant in society, then you say to him – and this is the simplicity in the matter – 'No my dear friend, you must excuse me . . . we want to see your works. Alas, how very necessary that is for us men!'

O dear Luther, these are two entirely different things – a scholar who has used the twenty best years of his life (the years in which a man really studies) for the most intense study, and in his forty-eighth year, at the pinnacle of knowledge, has not found the satisfaction he sought, and finding himself suddenly at the end of his tether is brought to the opposite extreme, closes his books, and says, 'No, it is not knowledge that matters' – is this not a very different thing from an innkeeper, who was just passing and heard the scholar (for he lived there, the windows were open, and the scholar spoke in his passion in a loud voice), and this innkeeper could not even write his own name, and scarcely read it when someone else wrote it for him: is it not a very different thing when the innkeeper goes on his way, takes what he heard as a result, and says, 'It is not knowledge that matters'?

Precisely the discipline Luther had undergone, and which

was indeed pushed to an extreme of exaggeration, provides a guarantee that what he says about his inward life may be true. But it is infinitely exalted, not simple. For it is infinitely exalted to dare to be so certain about his inward life that to retain his earthly life does not mean that he desires to do so, but that he desires to do something even higher than giving it away. Yet where there are such guarantees it is a different matter: such a man knows what it means to renounce this world, he has made the attempt, he knows in himself and with God that he can do it; it is indeed a different matter.

But is it not quite a different matter when a man wishes to begin (not where Luther began, for Luther had many years previously begun quite simply at the beginning, with actions) but straightaway where Luther ended, so to speak, in order to make his new beginning, which, if it is to be in any way true, must always presuppose the simple beginning?

And just as I, if I were an innkeeper who could neither read nor write, because I knew I did not have the presuppositions of that scholar, which were his justification for saying that 'It is not knowledge that matters' – just as I could not dare to accept it as a result and repeat it after him, so I would even less (for the matter is much more important) accept the Lutheran position as a result, since I know in myself that I am not in the least experienced in what may be termed the presupposition which can produce the Lutheran truth in me.

When the gospel demands that we forsake this world (that there should be any merit in this is said nowhere in the gospel: it is a lying invention; but it is also a fraudulent invention to be so zealous to emphasize that merit is an irreligious human device that one forgets that the gospel quite literally demands that we forsake this world) – then we are faced with the simple demand that we do it. Next to this the simple thing, when one does not do it, is to confess that it is because we are too weak, and still cling too much to this world. But it is immensely exalted to retain this world, to acquire it, and then to dare to assert that one is like him who does not possess it, and that the man who fasts, and the ascetic, represent a lower standpoint. . . .   *XI² A 301*

Luther

As a man can get accustomed to doing something, for example, going for a walk the same way every blessed day – he is tired of it, he says to himself, 'You must go another way', he gets his hat and coat, and in no time there he is again on the same way: so too in the realm of the spirit. There is something one has thought about, at first incidentally, then it has been properly brought out and given the time it requires, then put aside again; but one cannot get rid of it, one says to oneself, 'You must really stop coming back always to this point' – but it is no use.

So it has been with me regarding Luther, in one definite thought.

Has Luther not really produced an immense confusion, however innocent he was in one sense, upright as he was?

Let us see what happened to Luther. After a score of years, filled with fear and trembling and temptation, which were so terrible that – note well! – scarcely one individual in each generation experiences it in this way, his human nature reacts, if one may put it so, and this fear and trembling are transfigured into the most blessed and happiest cheerfulness and joy. How remarkable!

But what happens now? This principle is then generalized in Protestantism, thus and only thus (for only this is true Christianity) is Christianity to be presented. The immensely powerful tranquillizing means which Luther discovered in the extremity of his *Angst*, in a fight to death in fear and trembling and temptation – this is what is to be proclaimed as the sole means for all. And yet there is not one individual in each generation with this experience. And yet if we take away the presupposition, the terrible fear and trembling and temptation which precede, then this principle only too easily becomes untruth, terrible untruth. For it is true that when the fear and trembling and temptation are there, then there is this remarkable cheerfulness and ability to rejoice in this life. But suppose that this fear and trembling and temptation are not present (and there is not one individual in each generation who experiences this as Luther did), is it such a remarkable thing to want to enjoy this life? And can it not easily become a terrible deceit when everyone who is pleased to enjoy this life is permitted (and we cannot control it) to ascribe this Lutheran inwardness to himself?

Can it be right that what is suitable for a particular state (which is that of fear and trembling and temptation, especially as Luther experienced them) should be made into a principle for everyone? . . . *XI² A 303*

At the end of the entry on *Luther,* or as a note to it, there should be added these words: it is not my intention in this to reintroduce the monastery, even if I could. My proposal is simply that we realize what truth can be in this, and that we take care to be related to the truth by this admission.

XI² A 304

Catholicism – Protestantism

Are Catholicism and Protestantism not related to one another (it could seem strange, but it is really so in the material world) as in the material world a building that cannot stand is related to a buttress that cannot stand alone, whereas the whole construction can stand even more securely and firmly when building and buttress are together? In other words, is Protestantism (or Lutheranism) not really a corrective, and has there not arisen great confusion through Protestantism having been turned into the norm?

So long as Luther lived this could not be clearly seen, for he was always in the tension of the fight, under the strain of polemics, and in the smoke of the battle. For it is true of spiritual battle too that as long as the battle continues there is something which corresponds to smoke, which brings it about that one cannot quite find the time, the peace or the clarity to see whether what one wants to set up can be realized. Luther fought, that is, he was in a constant polemic, against Catholicism. It cannot be done in this way, so it had to be shown how it had to be done; but there was never time to linger, for we must now go on to the next point, we are in the midst of a battle – it cannot be done in this way, and so on: and so it continued.

Finally, peace came. And now it had to be shown whether Protestantism can exist by itself. Whether this is possible or not cannot perhaps best be seen in a land where Catholicism exists alongside Protestantism, for although they do not fight, but each attends to itself, there will nevertheless in many ways be a mutual influence. In order to judge rightly whether and how far Protestantism can exist by itself, it would be desirable to see it in a land where there is no Catholicism. There it may be seen whether Protestantism (assuming that it has degenerated) does not lead to a corruption which Catholicism (assuming that it has degenerated) does not lead to, and so may indicate that Protestantism is not made to stand alone.

Let us look at it more closely. It was after a heavy yoke had lain on men's shoulders for a long long time, after men had from generation to generation been terrified by the thought of death and judgement and hell, and had been so terrified that they turned to starvation and flagellation, and so on – it was then that the bow broke. From a monastery cell the man Luther broke out. Now let us take care not to divide what really belong together, the background and the foreground, let us not make a landscape without a background, or reach absurdity.

What Luther risked, with his presuppositions, was truth; for the opposite had been brought to a false exaggeration.

So Luther broke out of the monastery. But there was not such a good opportunity to see with human sober-mindedness how much truth lay in the opposite when it was not exaggerated. Luther scarcely showed that he was very certain, and this also meant that he rather took advantage of the fact that he had broken out of the monastery in order to deal the opposition, if possible, a mortal blow.

Now take the state of things as it was when Luther broke out. There was falsehood. Entirely remove the presupposition as it was for Luther, and Lutheranism is entirely senseless. Imagine that what Luther in his extreme tension seized hold of as the extreme became a kind of result which eased the tension – in that case Lutheranism would be complete nonsense. Imagine a land far from all Catholicism, where the Lutheran result has been taken, and where the people live without ever having heard a single word about the side of the matter which is expressed by the monastery, asceticism, etc., and which the middle ages exaggerated. But from their childhood days they have been petted and spoiled with the Lutheran principle of soothing the anxious conscience. But note well, no one has ever, even in the remotest degree, made their consciences anxious. In that case what is Lutheranism? Is there any sense in the soothing of anxious consciences when the presupposition, anxious consciences, is not present? Does Lutheranism not become meaningless? What is worse, does it not become a refinement which points to the difference between a degenerate Protestantism and the corruption of a degenerate Catholicism?

And this is just what I wanted to show, that this too indicates that Protestantism is not made to stand alone.

When Catholicism degenerates, what form of corruption is likely to be seen? The answer is easy: it will be hypocrisy. When Protestantism degenerates, what form of corruption will be seen? The answer is not difficult: it will be spiritless worldliness.

Let the two be set against one another, hypocrisy against spiritless worldliness, and I maintain that there will appear one refinement more which cannot be produced in Catholicism, a refinement which is the consequence of Protestantism being intended for a specific presupposition. It is this refinement which I wish to indicate.

Let us do it quite simply. Think of a Catholic prelate who is entirely worldly, but not of course to such an extreme that the laws can punish it or nature itself take its revenge. No, he is too worldly to be so stupid. But everything is aimed with such human cleverness (and this is the greatest worldliness of all) at clever enjoyment, including the enjoyment of his

cleverness, and thus his whole life consists, more than that
of the most worldly worldly-wise Epicurean, of all possible
enjoyment: in such a case, what would a Catholic be likely to
judge of him? Now I assume (it is decent to do so) that he
says, 'It is not my business to judge a high cleric.' But for the
rest the Catholic will have no difficulty in seeing that it is
worldliness. And why will he have no difficulty in seeing this?
Because the Catholic at the same time sees a quite different
side of Christianity expressed – in virtue of which the high
prelate must also experience one alongside him who lives in
poverty; and because the Catholic has an idea which is full of
pathos, and truer than that of the prelate – for alas! the prelate's life is only worldliness.

Now think, on the other hand, of a Protestant country
where there is no thought of Catholicism, where Luther has
long ago been accepted – but without his presupposition;
where ascetics and fasting and monks and preachers vowed to
poverty have long ago been got rid of; and not merely that,
but they have been got rid of as something that is ridiculous
and foolish – so that if such a one should turn up men would
burst into laughter as at a strange animal. They have been
got rid of as something inferior and incomplete. Now imagine
that in this Protestant country there lives a Protestant prelate,
the exact counterpart of the Catholic prelate: what then?
The Protestant prelate has a refinement – and such a refinement! – which makes the Catholic prelate's mouth water.
For since in the whole of his surroundings there is not a soul
with the slightest conception of what forsaking the world
means (the kind of religiousness which all the same does have
its truth, even if it was exaggerated in the middle ages); since
the land's whole religiosity is built upon and rests upon
Luther's conclusion (but without his presupposition) that the
fear of God consists of cheerful readiness to enjoy life (which
is indeed wonderful if one has Luther's fear and trembling
and temptations): the consequence is that the Protestant
prelate enjoys a refinement – By Jove! perhaps the Catholic
prelate would say – the refinement, namely, of having his
worldliness and his worldly enjoyment of life understood by his

contemporaries as – true religion! 'Look,' said one of his contemporaries to another (while in Catholicism what happened with the prelate was that one said to the other, 'Let us not look at it or criticize it, it is just worldliness') – 'look at this Lutheran openness. See him at the turtle-soup banquet, there is no one who knows what's what as he does, see how he can suck enjoyment from every situation in life, see how cleverly he turns everything to his own advantage. So admire this Lutheran openness!' How high he soars, in Lutheran openness, high above the inferior and incomplete state of the monk, of fasting, of preaching Christianity in poverty, how high he soars above all this in spiritual freedom and Lutheran openness! The great thing is not to leave the world, to flee: no, authentic Lutheranism is to be like the prelate, for this is true religion. His contemporaries do not just put up with it, or take pains to look away from it, but they look at it with admiration as true religion.

Luther established the highest spiritual principle as sheer inwardness. This can become so dangerous that we can sink to the lowest paganism (for extremes meet), in which sensual debauchery is honoured as divine worship: so Protestantism can reach the point at which worldliness is honoured and esteemed as – true religion. And this, I maintain, cannot happen in Catholicism.

But why can it not happen in Catholicism? Because Catholicism has as a general presupposition that we men are scoundrels. And why can it happen in Protestantism? Because the Protestant principle is related to a particular presupposition – that of a man in *Angst* about death, in fear and trembling and great temptation; and there are not many such men in each generation.

It is not my intention with all this to reintroduce the monastery, if I could. I have simply tried to make a contribution to our understanding the truth by means of confessions.

XI² A 305

The true state of affairs with Bishop Mynster

As a character he was weak. At the same time he had a very powerful sense and taste for the enjoyment of life; not just the simpler enjoyments, but the finer, indeed, the finest of all – to be honoured, esteemed, and respected as a serious man, a man of character, of principles, who stands fast when everything is shaken, etc.

Now he possessed great intellectual capacities, as a speaker he was exceptional, and lastly he was eminently sagacious.

Such a combination was Bishop Mynster, and this combination brought about, from a Christian standpoint, the confusion of a whole generation. For the weakness of character never came to light, it was covered over by his eminent sagacity; his desire for enjoyment was never seen, it was regarded – a new refinement! – as a pious freedom of spirit in contrast to pietist anxiety.

What makes such eminent sagacity so dangerous (which again can be demonstrated from his sermons) is that there is perhaps not a single man in any generation with such a decided (and Christian) policeman's view that he can definitely see and point out the fraud. There is the pure doctrine, and yet it is so deceptive that there is perhaps not a single point of it where the – well-meaning – sagacity is not present in one way or the other, and has altered the Christian element, or the way of speaking of it, just a tiny bit, so that all in all it is not really Christian any more. It is well-meaning – I do not wish to doubt this – it means to win us men for Christianity. But on the other hand it also serves to conceal: one is more concealed behind this proclamation than behind a proclamation which is from the Christian standpoint correct: it is so immensely dangerous to have to do with it, both because it casts light – as though in hatred of him – upon the speaker himself, and because it so easily stirs up men against the speaker.

Thus what he had to say, so far as the words and speech are concerned, brought confusion to Christianity; but in regard to the other side of the proclamation, the speaker's life,

his eminent sagacity was again a help to him. Between the
'quiet hours' (where he was the speaker, the orator, and took
bold risks) and his personal life he established a deep chasm,
and then knew how to use all his eminent sagacity to ward off,
objectively, every contact, to keep at a distance if possible
everything – every situation or happening or the like – which
could lead to the revelation of just how truly he was the
serious man, the exalted character whom the 'quiet hours'
led one to respect him as. And in this respect he was a virtuoso.
I could write a whole book and perhaps not relate and describe
everything, all the forms and means he had at his disposal,
and all with such decided virtuosity.

Such was Bishop Mynster. I conceal nothing. I was infatuated with the man – alas! such is our human nature. On the
other hand, from the first moment my judgement was essentially the same as it is now. But over against this it has been
my lot, to an exceptional degree, to have been constrained to
notice, and with all my efforts to disclose, what I find in relation
to Bishop Mynster, whom I – for I conceal nothing – have
always been infatuated with, and basically am still.

XI²A 312

To hate oneself

. . . If you have a habit or the like of which you yourself
disapprove, but which you cannot properly resolve to give up
– well, this is what you must do. If hitherto you have concealed
it from others, change this, force yourself to let others know
about it – this will lead you to hate yourself. For a bad habit
is very ready to make itself one with a man to such a degree
that he wants to conceal it. When the man concerned, therefore, says to the bad habit, 'Well, if I cannot resist you, I am
too weak, one thing I can do, I can torment you and tease you
by bringing it into the open for others to see.' The bad habit also
knows very well that only when the man loves it so much that
he conceals it, does it have power over him.   *XI²A 313*

Have you seen men during a fire? How they behave? Is it not the case that everyone is full of the fear of death and thinks only of saving himself?

In the view of Christianity every moment that a man lives there is even greater danger than in the most violent fire, the danger of forfeiting eternity. Do men behave as if this were so? *XI²A 315*

The spirit is unrest. Christianity is the deepest unrest of existence – so in the New Testament.

In Christendom Christianity is to soothe us – 'so that we can enjoy life properly.' *XI²A 317*

The idea of Christianity is that these seventy years, or thirty years, in brief, that temporality is the critical time, is the crisis in which it is to be decided whether you are a Christian or not, and thus your fate for an eternity.

In 'Christendom' the matter is turned thus: as early as possible – if it could be said to the child in its mother's womb it would be done – one says, 'Be at peace, you are a Christian, and these seventy years are only the first tiny fragments of an eternity that lies before you, an infinite development, so that the seventy years are scarcely more than five minutes – so do not overstrain yourself, if you waste these seventy years – well, what are five minutes more or less?' *XI²A 318*

The method must be changed: for the truth is not that from a Christian standpoint there is progress (this supposition corresponds to the method hitherto used), but the truth is that from a Christian standpoint there is retrogression – *and that is why the method must be changed.*

Somewhere in a modern author (I think Böhringer) I have read something like the following observation. He is speaking of one of the critical points in the history of the church, and says that for the church only one of two things was to be done: either it had to admit plainly that the Christian church did not exist (but that would be suicide) or it had to put a bold face on it and maintain that it was the true Christian church.

So it would be suicide? Yes, truly, suicide, and yet an action well-pleasing to God. For that would mean that there is enough truth to kill oneself to make room for the truth, instead of stifling it with its beastly expansion which impudently claims to be Christianity.

But the church had neither the courage nor the truth to do this, to accomplish this heroic suicide – it preferred to kill Christianity with its lies.

But precisely what that author discards as preposterous, as something that the church could not think of doing, is what must be done.

The method must be changed: instead of the universal lie that Christianity is perfectible (which is to deny Christianity and to mock God), instead of this effrontery of thinking that we must 'go further', instead of the cunning and shrewdness which betrays no less effrontery in disdaining nothing in order to conceal the truth that Christianity is in fact in a state of retrogression, every generation must make its confession in order that with its help it may be related to Christianity.

XI² A 325

A measure of the distance

In the primitive church the most profound seriousness is joined to the most exalted pathos in the belief that with the fall of the angels the numbers were incomplete, and that it was therefore the infinitely exalted goal for Christians to strive for, to use this life properly and enter into the place of such a fallen angel. Alas, the number of these fallen angels was known by nobody – surely it was not a great number. And how much God was willing to raise the number in relation to the original design was a matter of dispute. But that it was possible to become an angel, and that this life, properly used, was commensurable with this decision for eternity – this constituted the Christian's most profound seriousness and his most exalted pathos. That is why he was ready to forsake all things and to suffer all things, to be sacrificed, and that is why every minute of precious time was infinitely important to him: he called himself to account constantly for every action, every word he said, every thought in his soul, every look on his face, lest he should be guilty of losing that which concerned him in the most exalted pathos. . . .

Normally this idea of becoming an angel seems ridiculous to us. If someone said in all seriousness that he was striving to become an angel, we should all laugh . . . we should scarcely consider it as ridiculous if someone were to assume that after death man became a camel. . . .   *XI²A 331*

. . . Fenger of Slotsbergbye has written an article in the northern *Kirketidende* maintaining the eternity of the punishment of hell, in which he mocks at the Christians who imagine they are Christians without having either heaven or hell. From the Christian standpoint he is right. But he is not in the least in character with what he says. To believe that there is a hell, that others go to hell – and then to marry and have children, live in a manse, think of obtaining a bigger charge, and so on, this is fearful egoism. The New Testament is not like this. Everyone who believes that there is a hell and that others go to hell is *eo ipso* a missionary, that is the least he can do.

Rudelbach (and similarly Grundtvig) cry out that it is the State Church which is destroying Christianity. And both of them retain their posts in the State Church. Grundtvig has the most comfortable living in the whole land, and Rudelbach has a large living.   *XI²A 334*

To point to the expansion of Christianity as the proof of its truth is, from the Christian standpoint, nonsense. The New Testament does not offer this proof, Christ and the apostles prove it on the contrary by being put to death for it. And this proof is, from the Christian standpoint, the only possible one. For Christianity is the polemic truth, so the sign of its truth and the proof must correspond to this, that is, they must be polemical.

But in 'Christendom' the sign has become directness (expansion) and this in turn is an indirect assertion that Christianity has been made into direct truth. *XI²A 338*

'Now miracles are no longer necessary, since Christianity is so widely spread': nonsense and hypocrisy! Miracles are more than ever necessary; but we are so cunning that we prefer to be dispensed from being able to perform miracles, we prefer what is plain and material and direct. We are clever enough to understand how much tension there would be in life if we had miracles as well, and so we are hypocritical enough to pretend that we are too modest to desire such things.

XI²A 339

With every word that Christ (and likewise the apostle) says, the situation must always be included, that Christ, namely, is persecuted, misunderstood, hated, brought low, and so on.

For example, Christ says, 'Believe in me, just believe in me and you will be saved' – but the one to whom this is said must carry it out in the contemporary situation, and then suffering is inevitable.

Here is the basic confusion in the use made of the New Testament, that the words are taken without the situation or even in the contrary situation, by which they come to mean something different, or lose their character. *XI²A 343*

How I understand the future

Certainly there must be a reformation; and it will be a fearful reformation, in comparison with which the Lutheran reformation will only be a joke (a fearful reformation, which will have as its battle-cry, 'shall he find faith on the earth?' [Luke 18. 8], and which will be recognized by millions of men falling away from Christianity). For the truth is that Christianity simply does not exist. It will be a terrible thing when a generation which is coddled in a childish Christianity, and captivated by the illusion that they are Christians, is struck once more with the mortal blow of what it means to become Christian, to be Christian.

Paganism understood rightly that Christianity is hatred of men – so terrible was it to become a Christian. But it is even more frightful, when one is coddled and softened with a little of the syrup which is called Christianity, when one is captive to the illusion that one is a Christian, to have to learn from the beginning again.

. . . Therefore, as I understand it, since God is patient, he looks at it and does not reject the whole race, he does not even set them a task which would be their destruction.

But this does not mean that everything will go on as before. No, a beginning has to be made:

We have to draw up a balance in all truth – and this is my task, so I understand it. . . .   *XI² A 346*

Christendom

To be a Christian in Christendom in direct agreement is as impossible as to vault in a strait-jacket.   *XI² A 349*

A teacher of Christianity

Only in one case can a teacher of Christianity, who is bound by an oath to the New Testament, defend himself for being maintained by the state – namely, when he has been arrested, and, let it be noted, arrested for the sake of Christianity.

XI² A 352

Rest

What man desires is rest, that he may enjoy (*nil beatum nisi quietum*, Epicurus).

What God (according to Christianity) does not wish man to have is rest – the spirit is unrest.

In this respect alone there is an ambiguity in Protestantism, so far as it tends exclusively towards setting at rest.

XI²A 353

When the priest is paid and has a steady income it seems well to him to do something for the money – and he gives himself to study, he transforms religion into a learned affair – that he might do something really good for the money. Alas, if Christianity possessed money it would surely give it to the priest gladly to stop what he is doing. For what he is doing is just the craziest thing he can do.

The meaning of Socratic ignorance was just to prevent the ethical becoming a learned knowledge – but to let it be practice. Nothing is more dangerous than that something which should be practised is transformed into learned knowledge. To neglect to practise it is not nearly so dangerous; but learned knowledge has the semblance of being something, and makes the carrying into practice almost impossible.

XI²A 362

Christ does not want what is objective

Hence his constant attack on the Sabbath; for on the Jewish view it was something objective; and so Christ wished to worship God – by breaking the Sabbath. *XI²A 366*

Shudder!

One of Grimm's fairy-tales tells of a man who went out into the world to learn to shudder.

He had to go who knows how far, and perhaps in the end he did not manage to shudder properly. Let me tell you of something which you do not need to go out into the world to seek: no, stay where you are, and yet it will make you shudder, unless you are so hardened and spiritless that you are not interested in mankind's most sacred concerns.

Think of all the learned nonsense, the mass of literature that
has been written by thousands and read by millions concerning
the learned question whether and to what extent the laity
should be forbidden to partake of Christ's blood in the
sacrament: think of this. 'Is that something to make me
shudder?' No, no, you interrupt me too soon. For certainly
this load of learned religious nonsense can always make one
shudder on man's account, it makes one shudder for the day
of judgement. But this is not what I meant. But think of this
mass of learning and nonsense, think of the thousands busy
writing and the millions busy reading – and then let me tell
what you perhaps do not know; or if you do know it, make it
really present.

In the primitive church, when martyrs still bled, when
being a Christian meant, if not becoming a martyr oneself,
at least like living next to the place where a fire was burning –
so near that one could, as they say, feel the heat on the wall –
in that primitive church that question once arose whether
the laity should be prohibited communion in the blood of
Christ. Whereupon a bishop, who himself became a martyr,
replied, 'When one asks the Christian to pour out his blood for
the Lord, how could one prohibit him the Lord's blood!'

Shudder! For see, when one is a Christian in this way, and
when being a Christian has this meaning, every question is
infinitely easy to answer. Then think of the drivel of professors, and of these thousands a-writing and these millions
a-reading! Do you believe that this is because the matter is
difficult? It has certainly become difficult, immensely difficult,
through the fearful drivel about being a Christian.

XI² A 368

A view of the matter

There is a pretence in 'Christendom' that Christianity is a
goal, which is perhaps away in the remote distance, to which
men aspire, and for which perhaps all these millions are
assembled.

There is a deceitful desire to avoid the truth that in fact Christianity lies behind us, that it once existed, and that what is taking place with all the increasing millions and this united aspiration is, from the Christian standpoint, a retrogression.

XI²A 371

State church – national church

Every effort to bring about a Christian state and a Christian nation is *eo ipso* unchristian, anti-christian; for every such effort is only possible in virtue of a reduction of the definition of a Christian, and is therefore against Christianity, and tending to establish the false claim that we are all Christians, and that it is therefore very easy to be Christian.

In the New Testament Christianity is the performance of 'duties towards God', and now it has long been decided that there are really no duties to God – yet we are Christians, and in fact this is precisely what constitutes Christendom. But all the conflicts which are to be found in the New Testament are impossible if there are no duties towards God.   *XI²A 374*

Try it! (*learning is of evil*)

Suppose that it was said in the New Testament – we can surely suppose it – that it is God's will that every man should have 100,000 dollars: do you think there would be any question of a commentary? Or would not everyone rather say, 'It's easy enough to understand, there's no need of a commentary, let us for heaven's sake keep clear of commentaries – they could perhaps make it doubtful whether it is really as it is written. (And with their help we even run the risk that it may become doubtful.) But we prefer it to be as it stands written there, so away with all commentaries!'

But what is found in the New Testament (about the narrow way, dying to the world, and so on) is not at all more difficult to understand than this matter of the 100,000 dollars. The difficulty lies elsewhere, in that it does not please us – and so we must have commentaries and professors and commentaries; for it is not a case of 'risking' that it may become doubtful to us, for we really wish it to be doubtful, and we have a tiny hope that the commentaries may make it so.

Then is learning not of evil? Is it not an invention of us men because we have no desire to understand, what is only too easy to understand – an invention by means of which we are strengthened in evil, in shirking and hypocritical evasion?

We have invented learning in order to escape from doing God's will. For we certainly understand this much, that in face of God and his clearly understood will no one dares to say 'I do not wish it'. We do not dare it in this way. So we defend ourselves by having recourse to the pretence that his will is so difficult to understand, and so (and he will surely be flattered and consider it praiseworthy on our part) we study and research and so on: that is to say, we defend ourselves by hiding behind folios.   *XI²A 376*

To become a Christian

according to the New Testament is to become 'spirit'.

To become spirit, according to the New Testament, is to die, to die to the world – for according to the New Testament no man is born as spirit, by natural birth to be a man is to be flesh and blood and soul. Therefore to die to the world is the crisis for becoming spirit.

To die is for the natural man the most terrible thing of all; to die to the world is even more terrible, more painful than all other human wretchedness and misery.

Yet it is of love that God wills it thus: you, o man, do not have God's conception either of the terribleness of sin or of the splendour of salvation. If you had, you would at least not complain at God's wishing to have such pity on you.

It is from love – blessed is he who is not offended! . . .
                                        XI²A 378

Faith

Faith in the New Testament is not a definition pointing to the intellectual, but it is an ethical definition, it indicates a relation of personality between God and man. Faith, therefore (as an expression for devotion), is demanded – believing against the understanding, believing though one cannot see (all this as a definition of personality, in the ethical sphere). The apostle speaks of the *obedience* of faith [Romans 1. 5]. Faith is put to the test, is tested, and so on.

The confusion in the concept of faith comes rather from the Alexandrians. Augustine has also confused the concept by taking his definition direct from Plato (in the *Republic*).

XI²A 380

Well meant

Imagine a medicine with the property that a full dose had a laxative effect, and a half dose a constipating effect.

Then comes a man suffering from constipation. But – no matter for what reason, whether there is not so great a quantity available, or whether there is some fear that such a large quantity might be too much – in any case, that something might be done, they give him, meaning very well, a half dose. 'It's always something.' 'Yes, true enough, it is something; for the full dose is a laxative, but the half dose is constipating – and he is suffering from constipation.'

So with Christianity. What is true of everything that is determined by an Either-or is true of Christianity, that the half has just the opposite effect of the whole. . . .

Cyprianus and other such writings are prohibited, by means of which superstition thinks that spirits can be conjured, for men are afraid of spirits. But the New Testament is broadcast on the widest possible scale, that it might, if possible, be in everyone's hands. Truly, if ever any book was able to conjure up spirits then it is this one – provided you are able to read it.

Yet perhaps there is once more an unconscious but highly refined cunning here, an instinctive cunning at play, namely, the idea that if this book is so widely diffused, if possible in everyone's hands, then one is best secured against it, best assured that it will be a complete cipher. Right! Just go on in this way, pave the streets with New Testaments, sell them as fuel cheaper than peat, use them as tiles for your houses, sell them so cheap that they can be used, cheaper than sand, as ballast for ships – and you will be completely secured, and at the same time you can meet for a great festival and a speaker will stand up and praise us and the labours of our time and our zeal in spreading Christianity! *XI²A 386*

Official Christianity (Christendom's Christianity) – New Testament Christianity

1. Official ('Christendom's') Christianity is quite simply a cheat, it is a cheating of God.

New Testament Christianity is a gift to man, but just as much an obligation laid upon man; and this obligation is so heavy that being a Christian is from the human standpoint the greatest misery and wretchedness.

Christendom's Christianity takes Christianity merely as a gift. That is why it makes so much ado about the sacraments (in the superstitious sense), and pretends not to know that the sacrament carries an obligation.

This is to cheat God, just as it is a cheat when a man is made an heir with a specific obligation, and accepts the inheritance – then turns his back on the obligation, and at most, instead of fulfilling it, utters compliments and empty thanks for the inheritance.

2. Official (Christendom's) Christianity is social, New Testament Christianity is anti-social.

This is easily seen, for the formula for New Testament Christianity is in hatred of oneself to love God. But hatred of oneself certainly includes slaying and hating the craving and hankering for sociality which is precisely one of the things most dear to the natural man. To hate oneself in union with others is not to hate oneself – for union is an expression of love for oneself.

It is therefore a swindle of official Christianity to make use of the fact that New Testament Christianity speaks of loving God and your neighbour, in order to transpose Christianity into the pagan or Jewish social principle, which turns Christianity into precisely the opposite of what it was in the New Testament. *XI²A 387*

... If there were no eternity, we should have to say that there has never been such an untrue word uttered as God's word, 'God is not mocked' [Galatians 6. 7]. *XI²A 390*

That 'Christendom's' Christianity does not just dilute and water down Christianity, but that it falsifies its principle, makes it from the Christian standpoint the most dangerous poison, so that Christianity slays instead of saving.

A

According to the New Testament, Christianity is *unrest*.

The New Testament holds that man, conceived in transgression and born in sin, is a cunning animal creation, bewitched and under a spell, infatuated with the world of sense, *loving rest.*

Then Christianity presents eternity as the most intense unrest, in order to save man from this bewitchment, this state of rest.

Christendom presents Christianity as restful.

The result is also that the condition of Christendom is a qualitatively profounder worldliness than anywhere in paganism. For in Christendom eternity is made use of to give rest, and the desire to enjoy life.

B

According to the New Testament God tries to catch men, for he desires to be loved by them.

338

So Christianity is unrest. Thus too the fisherman disturbs the water in order to frighten the fish up from the depths and the caves.

So Christianity is unrest in order to catch men.

And Christianity is unrest, because God wishes to be loved in a state of opposition (conflict with 'others').

In 'Christendom' Christianity is used in order to bring rest, as revenue to help the principle which is in fact opposed to it.

In Christendom there are Christian people, kingdoms, lands – a Christian world. That is to say, the state of opposition (to the others), through being a Christian and loving God, goes out, and paganism comes in.

C

According to the New Testament a man's eternal salvation is decided here in this life. (The decision of eternity is also related inversely to time, the shorter the time the better.)

In Christendom we play the game of regarding this life as merely a beginning, and the whole of eternity as an aspiration: we waste this life, wasting this life is supposed to be Christianity.   *XI²A 395*

Encounter (conflict) with others – the specifically Christian suffering

The suffering which New Testament Christianity aims at specifically is suffering at the hands of men.

God wishes to be loved – but on the other hand to love God must come to mean that you thereby enter into conflict with men.

The whole suffering of the middle ages is therefore not Christian suffering at all. All the fasting and the like, as something in and for itself, is neither here nor there. And when one has men's admiration for fasting, and is thus of one mind with them, then it is precisely not Christian.

No, the conflict man is most reluctant of all to enter into, the conflict with others – not being like the others, having to suffer because by loving God one is not like the others (and not the opposite, being honoured because one loves God like the others, which is a deception) – this conflict, which is the greatest suffering for our animal creation, is the very suffering which Christianity aims at.

Therefore there is nothing more opposed to Christianity than a Christian nation, a Christian world, where consequently the whole situation for being a Christian is changed, and the formula always becomes 'to be like the rest'.

Rest, animal indolence, being like the rest – this is what men love, and what Christianity hates.

If someone says that this idea of loving God in opposition to others cannot be carried through – when everyone is a Christian – I reply, Do you really imagine that you can fool God with this nonsense? He knows best what the world is like, and that even if he lets Christianity be proclaimed for all there is no fear that all will accept it.

Again, every man comes from the creator's hand so different from others that if he really loves God – even if everyone was Christian – he will all the same come into conflict with 'the rest'.

Finally, if you have doubts about whether the fact that all are Christians might hinder you from loving God in opposition to others, then become a missionary, which indeed every Christian is.   *XI² A 396*

The guilt of Danish Protestantism – the corresponding expiation

What Plato says of the supreme being is surely true of God, that he neither does nor suffers injustice, and that it is a matter of indifference to God what we men are like; it is a matter of indifference to the God of the Christians what Christians are like, he does not suffer from this.

Yet the apostle speaks as though God did suffer from it – he warns the Christians that they should not by their evil habits cause God to hear ill [Romans 2. 24, I Timothy 6. 1, Titus 2. 5].

From this point of view there have been times of which one must say that the Christian church, through its wild licentiousness, and the like, has directly dishonoured God.

But if one were to say what constitutes the guilt of Danish Protestantism, one could not truly say that it is wild excesses, impudent hypocrisy, and the like. No, its guilt consists in having dragged Christianity down to mediocrity and insignificance and hearty drivel – in having made God ridiculous.

The expiation will be corresponding, as the punishment always fits the sin. Danish Protestantism must submit to being seen for what it is, from the Christian standpoint, namely, ridiculous. This is the only honest course, and thus the only course which is well-pleasing to God. Any other course would be guilty of not grasping the sickness, the evil, in all truth, and therefore the expiation would not be to the point.

XI² A 398

The Christian state of Denmark – and I in it
12 May 1855

In the Christian state all are Christians; and Denmark is a Christian state.

That is the first thing. The second is: what is Christianity, New Testament Christianity? Now this can be described in many ways, but also as follows. Christianity is the preponderance of the viewpoint of eternity over everything temporal, it seizes a man so that for the sake of the eternal he forgets everything earthly, regards it as 'loss', and even exposes himself to suffer all possible persecution for the sake of the eternal.

Now let us look a little more closely at life in Denmark, in the Christian state where we are all Christians; and let me take as illustration my own life, what has happened to me in this Christian state.

In a state, then, where everyone is Christian, there lives a man of whom it would occur to no one to deny that he is in possession of significant talents and gifts, is extraordinarily industrious and extraordinarily disinterested. And this man must experience that for far the greater part of the populace his life appears as a kind of madness. And why? Because everyone knows that with my intense labours, year after year, I do not earn any money, but actually put my own money in, and with my intense labours, year after year, I achieve nothing, but become practically a nonentity, incurring all kinds of upset and trouble.

So such a life is a kind of madness.

And this in a society where everyone is Christian; where there are a thousand sworn pastors, of whom – yes, it is true that it is only for three-quarters of an hour on Sundays that the majority of the people learn from these men that Christianity is the renunciation of the earthly, and so on; for the rest of the Sunday, and for the whole of the week, they learn from these men, especially by their example (and example has, as is well known, a quite different effect from words), that Christianity and the seriousness of life mean to strive for the earthly, and that such a life as mine is a kind of madness.

And this is a Christian state – we are all Christians.

Furthermore, what have I experienced in this Christian state? After having held out for a long stretch of years with perhaps unexampled patience (also out of piety for my dead father), bowing before what was, from the Christian standpoint, that untruth in velvet which was the whole of Bishop Mynster's existence, after I then (when his successor knew well how false it was, yet dared to present Bishop Mynster from the pulpit as a witness to the truth, one of the sacred chain) at last make my protest against this, then it is regarded as Christian to declare that my action is a kind of knavery.

And this is a Christian state, where all are Christians.

This cannot disturb me, I do not write this for my own sake, but because I think it can serve as enlightenment for others. For as I say, it cannot disturb me. The New Testament comes wonderfully to my help. For it explains to me that this world in which I live is a world of lies and deceit. It is perfectly true.   *XI² A 399*

The personal – the official

17 May 1855

Christianity rests in this view of existence, that all salvation is related to becoming personality.

As the New Testament wishes it, so he who is to be a teacher of Christianity is prevented in every way from escaping into the objective, from evasion, from concealing his personality. But everything is done to ensure that his proclamation may become a pure personal transparence, that his life is his teaching. . . .

XI²A 402

This is the movement in the retrogression of Christianity

19 May 1855

To become what the New Testament understands by a Christian is something the natural man shrinks from more than from being put to death. And he is right to shrink from it, for to become a Christian, to become spirit, means to live so that the natural man in one is put to death, or to live by killing the natural man, and so the natural man has reason to shrink from becoming a Christian more than from death, for death is only a moment.

That the animal creation, natural man, should be so impressed as to wish seriously to be a Christian, to wish to die, requires divine authority.

Even 'the apostle' has reduced the price somewhat, and it seems as though the natural man were getting off a bit more lightly in becoming a Christian.

Gradually the masses stream in, until everything about the definition of being a Christian is changed, and with this stream the definition of a Christian is changed more and more.

Now there are entire lands and kingdoms which are called Christian.

Then there are just a few who still preserve a truer idea of what it means to be a Christian, that it means to die to the world – but they despair of giving expression to this in company with other men, for they understand that the natural man would be furious if dying were to be taken seriously, and in a state of fury he would have such a man put to death.

So the few flee from the world, in order to give expression, far from men and from their persecution, to something truer.

Then it strikes the world that to flee in this way is cowardly, that one should remain among men – for the world knows very well that nowadays men are not born with the courage and the nervous energy to be able to hold out and to express what Christianity is, when they are surrounded by millions of natural men disguised as Christians. *XI² A 403*

The 'moment' is when the person is there, the right person.
XI² A 405

The Church state and the state Church – the two forms of cheating

23 May 1855

God, the almighty lord of heaven and earth, majesty of majesty, wished in his rule to educate men by means of Christianity. Now it is understandable that he knows all about ruling. His intention was to rule with the help of the background of eternity: either eternal blessedness or eternal perdition.

How terrible – so terrible that mankind shook and trembled under the pressure of the majesty of this lord.

So some time passed. But soon that passion which is perhaps the strongest in man when he has learned to overcome the purely animal passion – the desire to dominate – turned its attention to Christianity, and wondered if through cunning it could not be mastered, and so in relation to other men it might play the part of our Lord, who reigns with the help of the background of eternity.

The really great effort of this kind is the Pope. His idea is to rule men with the help of eternity, for it is he, Peter of the keys, Peter of lies, who controls eternity. Wonderful!

The other effort of this kind is that of the state. This is less important, and in fact the state has entered into this remarkable situation *bona fide*. Nevertheless, the state can certainly not be acquitted of having had just the slight thought that it would not be a bad thing, that men might be better governed, to have eternity in the background. So the citizen and the Christian end by coinciding: being what the state calls a good citizen is the same as being a good Christian, who is therefore quite sure of eternal blessedness. And being what the state calls an unruly subject is the same as being a poor Christian, who will go to hell – unless the supine view had more and more penetrated that we are all saved.

Both these efforts lead, from the Christian standpoint, to a swindle. They are not efforts to fool God in himself, but they are efforts to fool other men by their pretence that they are God. *XI²A 410*

Tittle-tattle – or Kjøbenhavnsposten[1]

28 May 1855

There are different kinds of tattle: there is loose tattle, flippant tattle, stupid tattle, good tattle – and so on. There is also the kind of tattle which is indicated by saying tattle back and forth, and perhaps there is also a kind called tittle-tattle.

When a newspaper has, both in verse and in prose, declared a man to be mad, then the man might reasonably expect that the paper would not occupy itself further with speaking about him; and it would show contempt for its readers if, after declaring a man to be mad, it entertained them further by speaking of him as though he were not mad. To carry on like this is to tattle back and forth, it is tittle-tattle.

This is the way the Copenhagen *Post* has behaved to me.

[1] *Flyveposten* was a Copenhagen newspaper, in which an attack on K. appeared on 26 May. RGS

On the occasion of my first article against Martensen, the paper, both in verse and prose, called me mad. 'Good,' thought I, 'henceforth I am free of the *Post*, one detail less to be plagued by.'

Meanwhile the *Post* had other thoughts. Without recalling what it had said, it now wants to talk of me as though I were not mad. Perhaps what it said first was a trial it made to see whether it could be said, just like one makes at an auction to see if one may chance to buy what one bids a mere song for. . . .

It is for religious reasons – because it has so pleased the Almighty, who knows best how repugnant it is to me – that I get involved in the moment. They can get as furious with me as they will; but by occasionally speaking I shall ensure that I do not escape (but I shall not, by being silent, see that I escape) any hubbub, which it is my duty to expose myself to. So anyone who pays attention to me knows my judgement on what happens concerning the matter or concerning myself.

XI²A 411

The Christianity of Christendom

2 July 1855

This is how a child is brought up in Christendom: 'Go out into the world with complete calmness, there sits in heaven an almighty God, and however unhappily things turn out for you in life, just pray to him and you will see he will help you.'

It is an abominable lie that this is Christianity. No, Christianity is that in heaven there sits almighty Love, who loves and desires to be loved, and who for that purpose desires that you should die; he is your deadly enemy; he hates everything you directly love; and if it is possible and if you are clever, you should at least speak to him of what you wish and what you fear; for he only desires to help you – to die.

Yet it is clear that the turn which is given to Christianity must be of the first style, if the lying livelihood, the livelihood of the thousand carers of souls and of their families, is to prosper.

This is how a child is brought up in Christendom: 'Your father and your mother are two persons well-pleasing to God. But especially the story of how you were born, this achievement of theirs, is something that was well pleasing to God.'

Abominable lie! That achievement is from the Christian standpoint a crime, it is a crime in God's eyes, and the vileness of the crime is that those who were concerned do not themselves suffer for it, but that an innocent person, through being born, is drawn into this whole establishment of criminals which is this human existence.

Yet it is clear that the turn which is given to Christianity must be of the first style, if the lying livelihood, the livelihood of the thousand sworn masters of the stud, is to prosper. As masters of the stud they know their business – their sworn oaths are neither here nor there. If a religion is to prosper, if there is to be talk of making it a people's religion (and this is precisely the task, because when that is achieved the profit is highest), then it must be connected with the begetting of children, it must be made a religion of begetting children – in brief, the more one can have what men directly desire (eating and drinking, enjoying themselves, getting children, and so on) turned into religion, the sooner one has the religion turned into a people's religion.   *XI² A 420*

To be a Christian

2 July 1855

To be a Christian is the most terrible of all torments, it is – and it must be – to have one's hell here on earth.

What does a man most shudder back from? Surely, from dying, and most of all from the death-throes, which one therefore wishes to be as brief as possible.

But to be a Christian means to be in the state of dying (you must die to the world, hate yourself) – and then to live perhaps forty years in this state! [*In the margin:* One shudders to read what an animal must suffer which is used for vivisection; yet this is only a fugitive image of the suffering involved in being a Christian – in being kept alive in the state of death.]

And not just this, but there is even a further aggravation. For those who stand around a dying man's bed do not usually laugh at him, or hate him, or curse and abhor him, because he is lying in his death agony. But this suffering is a part of being a Christian, it comes of itself when true Christianity is expressed in this world.

And then comes the temptation, in which the possibility of offence is present every moment, and will make use of every moment, the offence that this is God's love, that this is the God of love of whom one has learned from one's childhood anything but this!

Nevertheless he is love, infinite love, but he can only love you when you are a dying man; and nevertheless he is grace, infinite grace, to turn eternal suffering into temporal suffering.

But woe to these hordes of sworn liars, woe upon them, for having taken the keys of heaven, and who not merely keep out themselves, but also keep others out.   *XI² A 422*

An image

3 July 1855

Imagine a large, well-trained hunting-dog. He goes with his master, who is visiting a family where, as unfortunately only too often in our time, there is a whole collection of badly brought-up youngsters. Scarcely have they seen the dog than they begin to maltreat it in every way. The dog, who has what these boys do not have, a decent education, straightway fixes his gaze upon his master, in order to know from his attitude what he commands him to do. And he understands his look to mean that he is to put up with the maltreatment, and indeed to accept it as though it were a positive benefit. Whereupon, needless to say, the boys get even more insolent,

and in the end they agree that it must be a frightfully stupid
dog that puts up with anything.

Meanwhile the dog is interested in only one thing – what his
master's look bids him do. Then suddenly that look is altered,
it means – and the dog understands at once – use your strength.
In the same instant, with a single bound, he has seized the
first lout and flung him to the ground. Now no one can stop
him, only his master's glance, and in the same instant he is as
he was a moment before.

So with myself. As the dog watched its master, concerned
only with his glance, so I like a dog watch the almighty majesty
of heaven and earth, the Lord, concerned only with his glance
in whose special service I was early engaged.

So I began as an author, for my part I was entirely committed, and my look was fixed on his alone, as the dog's on his
master's.

Very soon I realized that I was not in good company, and
that a petty, worldly-wise mediocrity, empty of ideas, was
seeking by every possible means to injure me.

My glance, which was fixed only on the glance of the divine
majesty, informed me that he understood the situation thus:
you must put up with this, and more, you must put up with it
with such ease that you seem to be one whom all men are
treating well.

Whereupon mediocrity became only the more impudent,
and finally got it into their heads that I was an entirely
unpractical man whom almost anyone can fool.

Then the glance of the divine majesty was changed, and it
meant, Use your strength.

And this is the point we have reached now. I have always
possessed powers; but I am like a dog who watches his master
– for whom everything depends on what his master's glance
commands.   *XI² A 423*

To love God – or to love ugliness

10 July 1855

In everything that concerns Christianity, if it is to be maintained as it is in the New Testament, there is a serious NB, whose effect, if it is maintained, is that practically everyone takes flight. The art of 'Christendom' has consisted, and consists, in getting rid of all the NB's, under the pretext that Christianity is perfectible. Thus Christianity has become sheer nonsense; and now it goes without any difficulty, now we get millions of Christians and the parson's trade flourishes.

To love ugliness – yes, quite right! For if I am (as indeed I am) flesh and blood, a being of senses, an animal creation, then 'spirit' is the most terrible thing for me, terrible as death, and to love spirit is the most terrible thing of all. So too Christianity understands it, it teaches that to love God means to die, to die to the world, the worst of all torments – blessed is he who is not offended.

That is why, in times when Christianity was taken seriously, those who took it seriously made use of a death's head for their constant contemplation. Of course one cannot say that the spirit is like a death's head, for the spirit is not like any object of the senses. But a death's head was the most significant symbol.

In 'Christendom' it is different. The death's head – heaven preserve us – there is nothing people flee from with more care, more even than in paganism from everything that called death to mind. No, the death's head, that remarkable ornament in a room, is no longer to be seen. On one pedestal one sees a naked Venus, on another the crucified Saviour, and a young lady and a speculative priest (both, of course, true Christians) discuss which is the more beautiful of the two figures.

In Christendom it is argued, in the name of Christianity, that to love God means to fill your life, your time, your thoughts, with the pursuit of earthly things, in thanking God if you succeed, and in praying to him that you may succeed.

That is to say, love of God means love of the beautiful. So there also flourishes in Christendom what one is proud to call Christianity's latest development and finest flower – Christian family life. Splendid! New Testament Christianity has a decided predilection for celibacy – and yet family life is now its culmination.

The whole thing is of course a lie; and in order to prevent, as far as possible, that it should occur to anyone that it is a lie, appropriate action has been taken to have the parson take an oath upon the New Testament.   *XI²A 426*

That from the Christian standpoint the mediocre, mediocrity, everything 'to a certain extent', the merely human, what we men call 'heartiness' – that all this from the Christian standpoint is the scandal and the insinuation of Satan

13 August 1855

It is of the utmost importance to hold fast to this, if you cannot then you will never reach the point of view where you see what Christianity really is, and what a swindle the whole of Christendom is.

But that it is really as I have said you can learn from Christ himself in his relation to Peter . . . Christ says that he must go to Jerusalem now, and suffer and be put to death [Matthew 16. 23]. Now think first of the apostle Peter: as an apostle he towers above what we call mediocrity, even if . . . in Christ's judgement he needs to be converted. For Christ says to him after he has been an apostle for some time, 'When you are converted' [Luke 23. 32]. Then Peter, when Christ seems to will deliberately to expose himself to death (which by ordinary human ideas is not permissible), and also because of the personal love he has for the Master, from whom he is so reluctant to be separated – Peter takes the opportunity to reproach him. And Christ says – take heed, you battalions of mediocrity, who in comparison with Peter are but ants, though the parsons persuade you that you are Christians and that by means of this kind of Christianity you will go to heaven – 'Get

351

thee behind me, Satan: thou art an offence unto me, for thou savorest not the things that be of God, but those that be of men' [Matthew 16. 23].

So high in Christ's judgement is Christianity and being a Christian that to try to dissuade his teacher and friend from voluntarily exposing himself to death is the scandal, it is a suggestion of Satan.

Nothing more is needed to see that the kind of levelling which is Christendom is neither more nor less than the scandal, the work of Satan, and that all these mediocre Christian teachers are the scandal and Satan's instruments. . . .

Hence there is only true relation to Christianity – in loving God to hate yourself. . . .   *XI²A 427*

The church – the public
30 August 1855

The basic corruption of our time consists of the abolition of personality.

No one in our time dares to be a personality, in cowardly fear of men everyone shrinks from being I over against, perhaps in opposition to, others.

So politicians make do with the public. The politician is not an I – heaven forfend! No, he speaks in the name of the public.

Quite the same, in the religious sphere, is the use made of 'the church'. What men desire is a protective abstraction, by means of which one may avoid being I, which in our time is certainly the most dangerous thing of all.

This abstraction, the church, is then embellished to be a person, one speaks of the course of the church's life, and so on – and at the same time one is spiritual, and personally uncommitted.   *XI²A 431*

That 'Christendom' is mankind's continued effort through the centuries, with increasing success – to defend itself against Christianity

22 September 1855

Christ desired to have 'followers'.

A true follower of Christ will soon be cast headlong out of this world. And if there comes another follower, the same will happen to him: briefly and decisively, everything is action.

But suppose that instead of followers there come people who just drivel on about how others have risked their life and blood. Now the expansion begins. Drivel is sociable, amazingly fruitful, fruitful of more drivel.

The generation which succeeds the drivellers is not a generation of followers, but likewise one of drivellers: the parsons and the professors, and the congregations who regard them as true teachers of Christianity. Besides what this next generation is itself able to supply in the way of drivel, it assimilates in the name of historical science the drivel the previous generation has provided.

And this is the rule: instead of action there is a continually increasing mass of drivel which is called science, and which, they say, must be studied if one is to understand Christianity.

For in truth this is just what men do not want – to understand Christianity, which is easy to understand. And in order to make sure that they do not come to understand it, they put forward as a means to understanding it this interminable mass of learned historical drivel.

There are insects which defend themselves against their enemies by raising dust. So 'man' instinctively defends himself against the idea and against spirit by raising numbers. Numbers are the enemy of the idea and of spirit. When men want to be secured from having anything to do with ideas and spirit, they raise whole battalions, legions, millions which strive, perhaps with united force – and the spirit vanishes, you have attained what you really wished, and what is left is the animal side of human nature.

Naturally there are always only very few who understand this. For to understand it requires the change in a man which Christianity aims at, namely, that he become spirit. Man as an animal is related directly to numbers, it is numbers he believes in.

If it is the view of Christianity that this world is an evil and sinful world, but that Christianity has come into the world to change it, is God's view, or aim, to make a splendid world out of it and then let it go on like that?

Or is Christianity not rather based upon the following consideration, that this world has come about through a fall away from God, that it exists against his will, and every day of its existence is against his will, and that he wishes to have it back? He does not wish to use his omnipotence to destroy it, because this is not how all things have been disposed: it is a world of freedom, which freely fell away from him, and which he wishes to have back again. For God this world is lost, and it is decided that everyone who is born merely augments the mass of perdition.

In order to get this world back again, and in his compassion, he has Christianity proclaimed. What it means to be a Christian is shown by the Model, that it is suffering from first to last, even to being forsaken by God. Compassion, grace, infinite grace, consists, through becoming a Christian, in enduring one's hell here on earth and so being eternally saved. To be a Christian means to accept thankfully this infinite grace of having to be a follower of Jesus Christ here in this life and thus being eternally saved by grace: a follower of Jesus Christ, cursed by man, hated, tormented, tortured in every way, and in the end also forsaken by God. And for every follower of Jesus Christ the situation is that if he can be said at all to have any other purpose in his life except in fear and trembling to work out his soul's salvation, then it must be to get rid of this world.

If it were not thus, if it were God's aim to make a splendid world out of this world, then mankind would be without a guide. For the New Testament, the message of Christ, is based upon the principle that this is an evil world, and all the characteristics of Christianity are in accordance with this. But if it were God's aim to change this world into a splendid place and let it go on like that, the characteristics of Christianity would be the very opposite.

But 'mankind' very conveniently forgets that for God there is neither time nor number, that a thousand years are like a day, and that a number so great that it would take a thousand years to say it simply does not exist for him. He remains with his own. In grace he has compassion on this lost world. He offers the conditions, it is infinite grace, but without pedantry. Whether there are many or only a few who wish to be saved does not change him or his conditions, it is not he but the others who are to be saved.

And mankind on its grand scale has the same bad habit as the single man: when they are invited they turn up straight-away with a wife and half a dozen children. So when God causes his grace to be made known for each single person, something else happens from what God had planned: mankind turns up in droves and wants to be saved in droves. But it is not like that. First the humiliation, which will drive most men to despair, of enduring to be a single person, of being drowned in this vast world, of disappearing in it – and then perhaps being saved. The other way is certainly more comfortable, and has something in common with visits to the Deer Park and other cheerful enjoyments, being eternally saved in droves.

For the Christian view of salvation must first get rid of every idea of numbers and any comfort to be derived from them. That is, the animal creature must be deprived of life. For as one deprives a bird of life by taking the air from it, so one deprives the human animal of life by taking numbers from it.

To be deprived of numbers, to have to stand alone, forsaken, scorned and ridiculed, is what animal man fears most of all, for as animal man he lives in the fear of man. So animal man has courage to do the most frightening things as soon as he has the support of numbers, when others are doing the same, or when others think that he is showing courage.

Numbers of men are the very life of animal man. So it is just
this conflict which Christ especially aims at, that we should
suffer at the hands of men. Christianity means precisely this,
to fear God in opposition to men, in opposition to what men
as animal creatures fear most of all, human numbers. And
that is why, to add this, it is easy to see from this standpoint
that in the many centuries of Christendom there is not a
single proclamation like Christ's. Human numbers were
introduced very early into Christianity – and from that
moment it was possible to be a Christian in the fear of men.
The whole of the rigid asceticism of the middle ages was in
the fear of men, it did not suffer at men's hands.

I know very well that what I write will in the course of time
be declared to be the highest wisdom. I also know that at that
time the form of the world will not be changed in the least,
for those who will be busy showing how profound and true
my words are will of course be – the professors, those animal
creatures. Yes, those animal creatures. I know it well, in this
sinful world, where everything is egoism, one is rather accustomed to call the common man the simple animal creature. But
I protest against this. In one sense it is true that we are all
animal creatures. But if there is one class of men who deserve,
in comparison with the rest of us, to be called animals, then
it is the parsons and the professors.

In the child one recognizes the animal when he wants to put
everything into his mouth: this is a wholly characteristic
expression for the animal. But to be so animal-like as to want
to put truth, spirit, into one's mouth, to live off the truth, to
live off the suffering of others for the truth, and to be bound
by an oath to the one thing those others have desired, namely,
to be followers – this is beastly. It is surely remarkable that
this bestiality is to be found combined with the most refined
culture and high-mindedness, which is so high-minded that it
simply does not see a dustman. And if a dustman dared to talk
to him he would high-mindedly let him know that he is only
an animal. It is surely remarkable, and yet the truth is quite
the reverse: the dustman is a man, but that fine cultured
figure, clothed in velvet and decorated with stars is just an

animal, an animal which puts truth into its mouth, believes that truth is something to be eaten, it is an animal more abhorrent than a beast of prey, for it lives off the sufferings of others, what no beast of prey does, which lives off its prey – and if it causes it to suffer by taking its life it still does not live off the sufferings of its prey. *XI²A 434*

LITTLE OBSERVATIONS

To be a Christian in the fear of men

23 September 1855

In the New Testament the formula for being a Christian is to fear God rather than men [Acts 5. 29], which implies all the specifically Christian conflicts. As soon as one can be a Christian in the fear of men, and indeed when one cannot refrain, out of fear of men, from calling oneself a Christian, then Christianity has *eo ipso* vanished.

From this one sees what nonsense it is to believe that true Christianity is found in 'the church', as the place where great numbers are to be found. Nothing is more opposed to the spirit of Christianity than this, which is human mediocrity, animal man's belief in numbers of men. No, what of true Christianity is to be found in the course of the centuries may be found in the sects and the like, without however the being in a sect or the being outside the church being in itself a proof of true Christianity. But what is to be found may be found in sects and the like. This is the only thing which resembles New Testament Christianity, a sect, as it is called in the New Testament.

Fear especially to lose your way
by describing as humility what is really shirking

Every man is a born hypocrite. And in every generation there is perhaps only a single man who in the course of his whole life has all the hypocrisy knocked out of him by Providence.

But this hypocritical creature, man, is to nothing more inclined than to avoiding effort under the guise of humility and modesty. When man sees what torments are bound up with being an apostle, he says, 'I am too humble to want to be an apostle.' The hypocrite! When he reads Christ's words about how difficult it is to enter the kingdom of heaven, he says, 'I am humbly content just to approach the threshold of the kingdom of heaven.' The hypocrite! And with such humility and modesty, by which he spares himself, and certainly also fools himself, he thinks he can cajole God into being pleased that he is so humble and modest. But this does not please God at all. It does not even please a teacher that his pupil, because he cannot be bothered to give the time and the application, says, 'I am too humble and modest to want a "Good", I am humbly and modestly content with a "Fair".' 'You rascal,' says the teacher, 'you dare to call this humility and modesty. Certainly, if instead of applying yourself properly you laze the time away, and so cannot do a better job than you have done, it would be sheer impudence to ask for a "Good". But I demand that you do your work so that your mark is "Good".'   *XI² A 435*

Only a man of will can become a Christian
23 September 1855

Only a man of will can become a Christian, because only a man of will has a will which can be broken. But a man of will whose will is broken by the unconditioned or by God is a Christian. The stronger the natural will the deeper can be the break, and the better the Christian. This is what has been described characteristically as 'the new obedience': a Christian is a man of will, who has received a new will. A Christian is a man of will who no longer wills his own will, but with the passion of his broken will – radically changed – wills the will of another.

A man of intellect can never become a Christian, at most he can use his imaginative powers to toy with the Christian problems. And it is this formation of Christians, if one may call them this, which introduces every possible confusion into Christianity. They become learned, scientific, they transform everything into long-winded discussions, in which they drown the real point of Christianity. But of course Providence in his compassion can do much for a man of intellect, to change him into a man of will, so that he may become a Christian. For the possibility of becoming a man of will is in every man. The most wanton, the most cowardly, the most phlegmatic man, a man who argues without beginning or end – bring such men into deadly peril, and perhaps they will become men of will. Certainly necessity cannot produce freedom; but it can bring the freedom in man as near as possible to becoming will.

Christianity, then, or becoming a Christian, has nothing to do with a change in the intellect – but in the will. But this change is the most painful of all operations, comparable to vivisection (which is indeed questioned as permissible, on ethical grounds). And because it is so terrible, becoming a Christian in Christendom has long since (so far as it has not been quite nullified, and turned into a matter of course) been transformed into a change of the intellect. Medieval asceticism of course saw things in a more proper light (compared with all this learned nonsense and rigmarole of demonstrations), that it was a matter of a change of will, and it attacked matters in this light. The defect in medieval asceticism was that it drew a line through specifically Christian suffering, that is, suffering at the hands of men. The ascetic permitted men to admire him for being extraordinary. Thus after all numbers entered into the matter, for it was numbers of men who represented ordinary Christianity. If the ascetic had said, what is the truth, 'There is no such thing as extraordinary Christians. What my life expresses is just an approximation to what is demanded of us all, an approximation to quite simply being a Christian' – then he would have been persecuted. One can avoid suffering at men's hands in two ways. Either by lowering the Christian requirement and oneself taking advantage of this, or by hold-ing to it more strictly, but egoistically calling it the extra-ordinary – in both ways the mass of men is included and one

escapes persecution. But in both ways the mass is transformed into the exact opposite of what it should be in relation
to true Christianity, either it becomes something one profits
by, quite simply in money or the like, or it becomes something
one profits by as an admiring chorus.   *XI²A 436*

Certainly Bishop Mynster was great!

24 September 1855

But from a Christian standpoint he was not great. Aesthetically he was great, as a falsifier.

Understood in this way he had, aesthetically, my whole
admiration. And personally he had my whole attachment –
'also out of piety for my dead father'. But from a Christian
standpoint Providence had in me brought alongside him the
person who was most dangerous for him.

Most men have simply no time for religion, in the same sense
as a child does not have time to collect his thoughts, so busy
is he with manifold sense-impressions. In this sense most men
have no time for religion; that they do have a religion, that
they are 'Christians' in 'Christendom' means for them merely
that they have a passport enabling them to enter into the
reality of this life. What occupies them is the manifoldness of
life, sense-impressions, busyness, curiosity, and so on, and so
on. As a child cannot stand still, but impatiently jumps around
in order to get permission to go out into the garden or the
playground, so these men are always impatient to get into the
whirl of the life of the senses. Since the 'Christian' state has
wisely arranged that no one can join the game without first
having a pastoral certificate that he is a Christian, of course,
oh of course, all these men are Christians. A pastoral certificate
that they are Christians means for them about the same as a
ticket for Tivoli or for a steamer or an omnibus – that they
may go too.

Those who have some time left for religion all wish to settle
it as early or as quickly as possible – that they too may get

busy enjoying this life. So perhaps they have a moment left over, now and then, for religion; but on condition that it becomes a kind of enjoyment, and that it is settled once for all that they have religion, so that they are sure of the blessedness of eternity.

Now if there is an ecclesiastic – and if he has great aesthetic gifts so much the better – who is ready to undertake in the name of Christianity to represent their kind of religion, then of course there is a great to-do, and enthusiasm, he is loved and adored, he is popular, etc. For these men know obscurely, as all men do, in their heart of hearts that religion is not to be had in this way, either by not having any time for it or by now and again having a moment to spare for it; they know that it is not in the least immodest of 'eternity' to demand practically a man's whole time. It is this demand that all men are above all afraid of; for they all love time, which is their element, and they fear eternity. Hence all the to-do about such a teacher.

Bishop Mynster was such a teacher. He was the bank for a whole generation. How all these many men have enjoyed life, who, when they hear with horror in eternity that this was not Christianity, will, if I may put it so, show a ticket signed 'Mynster'! For Mynster was the bank. In the deep and solitary silence in which I entertain myself – with myself and police knowledge – I have been in the habit of calling Mynster the State Bank. I was thinking of a particular incident which the Copenhagen police will understand; for they of course know very well that a number of years ago there lived in North Zealand a person (whether he is still alive, I do not know, though the police must know) who was well known to the police under the name of the State Bank. His business was the forging of notes, and he did it very well.

This was what they had in common, forging notes. For the rest there was of course no comparison, especially not in regard to the size of the business. On the whole, so far as extent and size are concerned, there is no analogy to the crimes which are committed in the religious sphere. Even the most experienced and intrepid police detective that has ever lived would shrink from setting to work on this matter, which involves drawing false notes on eternity and fooling a whole generation for a lifetime, and fooling them for eternity.

Nor can an analogy be found in the rest of the criminal world, or anything approaching an analogy to how these criminals pay themselves, or are paid – in gold, in goods, in all earthly things, and in adoration.

Perhaps it may be said that Mynster was all the same not rewarded sufficiently, and that his contemporaries were not grateful enough. Towards the end of his life an endowment was subscribed for, which was to bear his name. Mynster, always clever, found an opportunity to express his gratitude in public for the considerable sum of money, about 7,000 *Daler*. In truth, if it had been properly associated with Mynster's proclamation of Christianity, it seems to me that one of our millionaires should gladly have given 30,000 *Daler*. For it is the view of the New Testament that it is as infinitely difficult for millionaires to enter into the kingdom of heaven as is well-nigh possible; but Bishop Mynster made no difficulties for them; and when one is a millionaire this is surely well worth giving 30,000 *Daler* for. It would of course be rather different if the whole of Mynster's proclamation of Christianity were an optical illusion, and his notes on eternity were false; for in that case four shillings would be too much for the subscription for the endowment, and three shillings would be too much for the monument, if it is in his capacity as a Christian teacher that he is to be thanked. For as orator, rhetorician, artist in language, distinguished by a 'hitherto unparalleled style of speech', and as an actor distinguished by 'his plastic figure', it would be fitting enough.

XI² A 437

SMALL OBSERVATIONS

1. *An image of a Christian's suffering*

24 September 1855

There are men with such a fine and delicate nervous system that the weather exercises an almost terrifying influence upon them. They are aware of a storm long before it arrives, and they perhaps suffer most from fear and unrest and anguish when the approaching storm is announced by what is called 'brilliant weather', which is not really brilliant at all.

So this phenomenon of brilliant weather is regarded as splendid by all men of great animal strength, and they torment and tease the unfortunate man, feeling their superiority over him in animal strength; for they cannot understand what he means when he calls such brilliant weather bad weather.

But this lasts only a few days, and sometimes the man of fine nerves gets the benefit of their realization that he was right after all.

But imagine such weather lasting, and the unfortunate man having to endure a life-time in this state, surrounded by men of great animal strength.

So with a Christian's suffering. The phenomenon of this world looks splendid, a world that is bound to progress. It looks as though Christianity existed, everyone is a Christian, there are a thousand parsons – and now the poor Christian who is so finely constructed that he notices that the whole of this splendid world is a tissue of lies, that its progress is if anything a retrogression, and that everybody being Christian, with the thousand parsons, is an optical illusion – the poor Christian who is related in fear and trembling to the reckoning of eternity: let one try to imagine what he must suffer living among men whose whole nervous system is quite different from his. Unless he conceals the contents of his soul as carefully as possible, these men will use the opportunity to feel their animal superiority and to torment him. And if he is not patient (and indeed in another sense it is he who incites them) he will be declared mad, and if they cannot get the better of him in this way then they will put him to death.

2. *The chatter of men*

Men of ideas, bearer of ideas, achieve absolutely nothing, except that they attain to immortality, for everyone who sacrifices himself in patience, joy and gratitude in order to bear the idea is immortal.

But they achieve absolutely nothing. During their lifetime their words are drowned in the drivel of the time, and after their death they are drowned in the drivel of professors. Their significance lies merely in their giving men something to chatter about.

For as in a family, a society, a town there is the need for something to chatter about, so the whole of mankind feels this need. The difference is only that the chatter of a town is conducted by barbers and grocers and the like, whereas the chatter of mankind is conducted by professors and parsons and a great deal is made of it – it gets printed, and encyclopaedic sciences come into being in order to deal with this chatter.

That the chatter of mankind enjoys such great respect in comparison with the chatter of the town is certainly connected to a large extent with the fact that the parsons and the professors live by it. What a family man lives by is a serious matter. If barbers were to live off the chatter of the town, instead of another way, with chatter as a by-product, this too would share in the respect. This can be seen from the fact that chatter has really won respect since journalists took it up simply because they live by it. Men will have respect for what man has to live by. *XI²A 438*

1. *The free-thinker – and I*

The free-thinker wants to get rid of 'the priest'; for he thinks in his short-sightedness and prejudice that this also gets rid of Christianity.

I wish to get rid of 'the priest' – in order that Christianity may prosper. So long as there are 'priests' Christianity is impossible.

In his blind hatred of Christianity the free-thinker is polite enough to assume that from the Christian standpoint priests are in order. I see that 'the priest' and the free-thinker are allies, only that the priest is the most dangerous foe.

2. *'The priest' as the limit*

This is how these millions of Christians live in Christendom: 'the priest' is regarded as the exponent of the highest form of Christianity. So within this limit one is a Christian, so that it would perhaps even be regarded as blasphemy to wish to be a better Christian than the priest.

No; everyone who imagines that he is a Christian within the limit set by 'the priest', running with the flock, or the herd as limited by the priest, only deceives himself. A Christian of primitive times would therefore immediately understand (instead of playing at jumping inside the fence by jumping over a sheaf) that the task in the first place is to jump over the very low fence supplied by 'the priest'; and he will understand that this is the very weakest and easiest beginning.

3. *Where God builds a church, the devil builds a chapel*

If this were true, then it would almost be a fine world in which we live.

But it is not true; no, where truth has suffered, the devil builds both churches and chapels.

It is just one of the devil's arts to set the rumour going that churches are God's buildings, which is just as certain as that the priests are God's servants.

4. 'Christendom's' striving for the ideal

We laugh when we see a man looking for his spectacles when they are on his nose.

But the striving of 'Christendom' is in its way even more ridiculous.

The truth about the Christian ideal is that it has existed, Christ has lived, the Model has been given. And this ideal is related to the single person. Only as a single person can there be any talk of striving for it. And if the single person is to strive for it he must as a matter of course turn in the direction of the existence of the ideal, he must turn back to it, if he really is to strive for it.

Christendom has turned the matter thus: the ideal for being a Christian is a goal lying infinitely distant in the future, and this is what we must strive for. So Christendom turns its back on the true ideal, which has existed, and (in the name of striving for it) strives away from it. And that something may come of this striving for that ideal in the far future (so Christendom sees the matter) everyone must unite, with united strength everyone must strive, for this is how success will be achieved. Yes, success is to be achieved by striving with united strength with regard to an effort in which the truth is that only the single person, each single person, can strive. 'Take courage again,' Christendom cries out enthusiastically. 'Let us strive all together. We shall succeed. Only do not lose courage, but strengthen your hearts with the thought that Christianity is perfectible and that it is progressing. So onwards, ever onwards, to that goal which is lying ahead of us in the infinite distance – onwards to the ideal.' And from the Christian standpoint the ideal existed 1,800 years ago.

5. 'Does Christianity not exist?'

'It is surely the most absurd nonsense to maintain that Christianity does not exist. The one fact that there are 1,000 teachers of Christianity is enough to refute this nonsense. When there are 1,000 teachers of Christianity, then Christianity must also exist.'

Perhaps this could also prove that the 'Fussy Man' is a man who has plenty to do, for he has five secretaries; and when a man has five secretaries then he surely has a great deal of business.[1]

No; the existence of 1,000 teachers of Christianity proves that there are 1,000 livings for teachers of Christianity, which indeed I have never denied, as little as I doubt for a single moment that if there were 10,000 livings there would be 10,000 teachers of Christianity, which I doubt just as little as that Christianity simply does not exist, and that the Fussy Man does not have any business. *XI³B 197*

The Christian definition of this life

25 September 1855

The definition of this life is to be brought to the highest degree of disgust with life.

He who is brought to this point and can then hold fast, or he whom God helps to hold fast, that it is God who out of love has brought him to this point – he it is who from the Christian standpoint has passed the examination of life, and is ripe for eternity.

Through a crime I came into existence, I came into existence against God's will. The fault, which in one sense is not mine, even if it makes me a criminal in God's eyes, is to give life. The punishment fits the fault: it is to be deprived of all joy of life, to be brought to the supreme degree of disgust with life. Man desired to play the creator in his handiwork, if not

[1] The Fussy Man is the chief character in a comedy by Holberg, *Den Stundesløse*. RGS

in creating man at least in giving life. 'You shall surely suffer for it; for the definition of this life (always by my grace, for it is only to him who is saved that I show my grace) is to bring you to the supreme degree of disgust with life.'

Most men are so without spirit, so abandoned by grace, that the punishment simply does not apply to them. Lost in this life, they cling to this life which is nothing, they become nothing, their life is wasted.

The men in whom there is more spirit, and whom grace does not neglect, are brought to the point that life reaches the supreme degree of disgust with life. But they cannot be reconciled to this, they rebel against God, and so on.

Only the men who are brought to this point of disgust with life and are able to hold fast by the help of grace to the faith that God does this from love, so that not even in the inmost recesses of their soul is there any doubt concealed that God is love – only these men are ripe for eternity.

And it is these men whom God receives in eternity. For what does God want? He wants to have souls who are able to praise and adore and thank him – the occupation of angels. That is why God is surrounded by angels. For he is not pleased with the kind of being of which there are legions in 'Christendom' – who for ten shillings can roar and trumpet God's honour and praise: that kind of being does not please him. And what pleases him even more than the praise of angels is a man, who in the last lap of his this life, when God is transformed as though into sheer cruelty, and with the cruellest imaginable cruelty does everything to deprive him of all joy in life, a man who continues to believe that God is love and that it is from love that God does this. Such a man becomes an angel. And in heaven he can surely praise God. But the apprentice time, the school time is also always the strictest time. Like a man who thought of journeying through the whole world to hear a singer who had a perfect voice, so God sits in heaven and listens. And every time he hears praise from a man whom he brings to the uttermost point of disgust with life, God says to himself, This is the right note. He says, Here it is, as though he were making a discovery. But he was prepared, for he himself was present with that man, and helped him so far as God can help what only freedom can do. Only freedom can do it. But what a surprise for man to be able to express himself by thanking God, as though it were God who did it. And in his joy at being able to do this he is so happy that he will hear nothing about himself doing it, but he thankfully attributes everything to God. And he prays God that it may remain so, that it is God who does it. For he does not believe in himself, but he believes in God.   *XI²A 439*

INDEX

INDEX OF BIBLICAL TEXTS

Date Due
